"The ultimate guide to building a high-pe. world's leading experts: authoritative, data-driven, and extremely practical."

Tomas Chamorro-Premuzic, PhD
Chief Talent Scientist at Manpower Group &
Professor of Business Psychology at Columbia University & UCL

"The effectiveness (or ineffectiveness) of teams can make (or break) an organization. As the CEO of an organization, I live this every day. I also know that the material in this book is an excellent resource and guide for how to work the myriad challenges that teams face—literally a 'soup to nuts' tutorial on how to structure, steward, and evaluate. This is an invaluable resource for every leader as they shepherd their teams. Thanks to Gordy Curphy for his exemplar work!"

Dr Mike Thirtle
President and CEO, Bethesda Lutheran Communities

"It has been since the mid-1960s since the last major advancement in team effectiveness. Well, the wait is over. Finally, a new, simple and practical approach to building high-performance teams. Gordy, Dianne, and Bob have put together a how-to based on a team's current state, and loaded with easy-to-implement activities. This is the book that we have all been waiting for, and what I believe will quickly become the gold standard on how to drive real results through a common understanding of context and mission."

Michael Ehret
Head of Global Talent Management
Johnson & Johnson

"I've been through other team-building processes and workshops, but the Rocket Model truly sets the benchmark! Whether you're embarking to improve the operational performance of an already successful company or truly must transform the culture in a turnaround; this process will show you the underbelly few have the courage to face and fewer have the leadership fortitude to address."

David DeGraaf
President & CEO, Gill Industries

"The Rocket Model is a well-researched (based on work with 2,000 teams from across the globe) yet refreshingly practical approach to building high-performing teams. Top to bottom—the model, Team Assessment Survey, book chapters, and team improvement activities—this book and tools are all team leaders and facilitators need to supercharge team performance and organizational impact. One hallmark of these tools is the incredible flexibility in how they are deployed; they can be used to design and facilitate team off-sites, train leaders how to build high-performing teams, and identify high-potential candidates who can build teams. Few other team solutions can be applied to such a broad range of team issues. A must-have for anyone looking to build teams or enhance team performance."

Mike Benson
Vice President, Talent & Organizational Capabilities
General Mills

"There is no question that dysfunctional teams can make or break an organization, particularly if that team is the Top Team. As HR practitioners, it's often hard to know where to start to solve complex and messy team issues. The Rocket Model provides a framework, backed by science, for identifying your most critical team problems. It's a model that that allows you to get to the heart of team issues so that you can implement the most practical solutions. What I love most about the Rocket Model is the focus on addressing both the people and process elements of a team, given both are critical to any lasting organizational change. If you strive to unlock the full potential of your teams and the collective power of your organization, trust the Rocket Model to serve as your roadmap."

Karishma Patel Buford, PhD
Chief People Officer, Opploans

"*Ignition* sets fire to much of the non-evidenced-based practices around team development. Drawing from decades of research and experience, Dr Curphy gives teams a pragmatic approach that I have seen deliver better team performance again and again. This book is the distillation of what works, the assessment is clear, and the solutions are those that managers can own and run, allowing teams to boost their performance."

Adam Yearsley
Professor at Ashridge Hult University & Global Head of
Talent Management at Red Bull

"The simplicity and elegance of the Rocket Model is what makes it very practical and value added in today's constantly changing business environment.

I have deployed it within my global team and the results have been tremendous. Greater alignment, productivity and solution-driven activities that benefit the organization in how we support them. My team have been fully trained on the process and support the businesses to ensure they are developing healthy and engaged teams.

The authors knowledge, experience, and ability to speak in basic common sense business language allows the key concepts and ideas to be understood from the top to the floor level, thereby allowing it to be easily deployed with the appropriate level of buy-in and commitment.

A MUST-READ for those that want high-performing and aligned teams within their organization."

Paul Keane

EVP, Human Resources and HSE

CSA Testing and Certification Group

IGNITION

IGNITION

A GUIDE TO BUILDING HIGH-PERFORMING TEAMS

Gordon J. Curphy
Dianne L. Nilsen
Robert Hogan

HOGANPRESS

ISBN: 978-0-578-60316-2

For information, contact Hogan Press
11 S. Greenwood, Tulsa OK 74120
hoganassessments.com

HOGANPRESS

Interior Book Design by
Michelle M. White

Contents

PART I: Setting the Stage

PART II: Common Team Scenarios

PART III: Team Applications

PART IV: Team Improvement Activities

DIAGNOSTICS AND TEACHING AIDS

CONTEXT

MISSION

TALENT

NORMS

BUY-IN

RESOURCES

COURAGE

RESULTS

Preface

It has often been observed
that American culture is fundamentally individualistic. All our heroes are
cowboys or their modern counterparts (e.g., astronauts, entrepreneurs, bond
traders, movie stars, sports heroes). But the stubborn fact is that all great
human achievement is the result of team efforts (e.g., building the Panama
Canal, landing men on the moon, winning the Super Bowl). The degree to
which this fact is overlooked is alarming and is a consequence of the individualistic bias of our culture. On the one hand, many people believe that
when we join a team, we become susceptible to group think—i.e., we lose our
ability to think rationally and independently. On the other hand, many people
believe the only way to be authentic is to live off-the-grid in a state of extreme
self-reliance. The fact is, however, that a distinct evolutionary advantage of
humans is their ability to work in groups, and our survival as individuals and
as a species depends on the quality of the performance of the groups in which
we are embedded.

Academic psychologists have been studying teams for almost 100 years,
but the net result of that research is surprisingly meager. Much of the early
research focused on the determinants of morale—i.e., how much people enjoyed being part of various teams and the factors that impact their enjoyment.

The immensely popular t-group movement of the 1960s is an example of this orientation to team research—people participated in team activities for mental health purposes and as exercises in self-discovery. Gordon Curphy's first book on teams, **The Rocket Model**, essentially broke the mold for the psychology of teams in two ways. First, Curphy started with the observation that teams have jobs to do, and some teams are more effective at doing their jobs than others. People who follow sports have always known that certain teams outperform most other teams. People who have served in the military also know that teams can be ranked along a continuum of performance, and that the level of a team's performance can have life or death consequences.

The second way in which **The Rocket Model** broke the mold was in explicitly recognizing that the principal task of leadership is to build a high-performing team. This represents a break from the past because earlier team research ignored leadership—an astounding fact in retrospect. **The Rocket Model** was a guidebook, a systematic how to do it manual, for constructing a high-performing team. Since the publication of the original book, Gordon Curphy has conducted hundreds of team-building workshops with public and private sector organizations, and in the process, has refined and extended his original set of observations and guidelines.

Gordon Curphy is a co-author of the best-selling college leadership textbook in America; as a result, he has thoroughly mastered the academic literature on leadership. In addition, he has thousands of hours of experience helping leaders analyze their teams and shape their performance. His new book, **Ignition**, is an up-to-date summary of everything he has learned about leadership and team development. Teams vary widely in terms of their goals and their composition, and this variability matters in many ways. Nonetheless, there is one right way to build a team, and many wrong ways—when it comes to team building, how you do it doesn't depend on the circumstances as much as it depends on leadership. This book—**Ignition**—is the best single source available anywhere on how to carry out the fundamental task of leadership. It is a systematic, explicit, detailed, experience-based, and valid account of how to build a high-performing team.

Robert Hogan, Hogan Assessments

PART I

Setting the Stage

Chapter 1

Introduction

Billy was thrilled about his most recent promotion to airport station manager. Starting as a baggage handler, he had worked his way up the ladder and now would be responsible for a 300-person, 24/7 operation that handled 60 domestic and eight international flights daily.

The airline had big plans for the station, as it was located in a city enjoying double-digit population growth, a booming economy, and businesses that wanted more direct domestic and international flight options. Billy's marching orders were to prepare the station to handle 20% more domestic and 50% more international flights in the next 12 months. Billy's new station had an abysmal track record, so this was a big ask. Its on-time departure statistics were erratic, lost baggage claims were among the worst in the company, customer satisfaction survey ratings were poor, and union grievances were way up. Billy would need to bring about a major turnaround before the station would be ready to grow.

This role had been vacant for several months before Billy accepted it. The six members of the Station Leadership Team (SLT) had been running things in the interim, and Billy hired us to get an outside perspective on what he was walking into. We spent three days on location observing and talking to ticketing agents, gate agents, ground crews, club staff, and shared services personnel. We also interviewed each member of the SLT. What we learned about the SLT was appalling.

Saheeb, one of the two gate agent managers, had been furtively listening in to weekly regional station manager calls. The station was mentioned frequently during these calls, rarely for anything positive. To curry favor around the station, Saheeb leaked confidential information discussed during these calls with station employees.

Jacob, the ticketing agent manager, was a well-known gossip around the SLT. He viewed knowledge as power and loved keeping up on the latest buzz, sharing stories, starting rumors, and provoking SLT members to turn on each other.

Joanie, one of the station's ground crew managers, was a long-time airline employee with the responsibility of managing 75 ground crew personnel. By all accounts, she was an excellent manager, but she was also undergoing treatment for lung cancer. Because Joanie wasn't operating at 100%, she sometimes had to come in late or leave early.

Frank, the other ground crew manager, had no compassion for Joanie's situation and thought both ground crews should report to him. He had been overheard making statements like, "Ground operations are no place for a person with one lung," and "They need to put Joanie out to pasture." He didn't smoke, but would frequently leave open packs of cigarettes out on a table he shared with Joanie. Frank's crew hated him and would do anything they could to get him into trouble.

Zelda, the international manager, handled the ticket and gate agents for all international flights. She applied for the station manager role but was turned down because her customer satisfaction ratings were poor. She blamed the negative feedback on inadequate gate amenities and seating, but her staff said she was cold, curt, nitpicky, and demanding; no one wanted to work for Zelda.

Finally, Doug, the other gate agent manager, was well aware of what was going on at the station but did not feel empowered to do anything about it. He just stayed in his lane, kept his head down, and tried to distance himself and his staff from the rest of the station.

We also had the opportunity to sit in on one of the SLT's weekly meetings. Given the cast of characters, it's not hard to envision how this 90-minute debacle went. There was no discussion of station metrics, issues were raised but never resolved, individual employees and the entire company were thrown under the bus, people came and went throughout the meeting, and some spent more time browsing the internet than participating in team discussions. This total lack of leadership pervaded the station, and it was clear that Billy was inheriting a mess.

Most teams are not as dysfunctional as the SLT, but many have room for improvement. Take a moment to think about teams you've been on in the past. What percentage would you consider to be high performing? If you're like most people, the answer is less than 20%. Considering how much time we spend working in teams, and the extent to which organizations rely on teams to get work done, less than 20% is a frightening statistic.

Despite all the time and money invested in team-building efforts, research shows this statistic has not budged over the past 30 years. We're on a mission to change that. The purpose of this book is to equip team leaders, members, and facilitators with the tools they need to help teams become high performing.

Our approach to improving team performance is informed by both science and our consulting experience. Our research on teams began more than 20 years ago with a thorough review of the professional literature, and we continue to stay abreast of emerging research on topics such as teaming, psychological safety, virtual teams, and meeting effectiveness. We've also administered close to 20,000 team surveys, interviewed nearly 1,000 team members and leaders, and have consulted with hundreds of teams and leaders in a variety of settings. As consultants, we've advised teams around the globe in a variety of departments from marketing to legal, and in industries ranging from finance to engineering. In addition, we have conducted team-oriented leadership development programs for 5,000 leaders, whose stories and perspectives have shaped our thinking.

HOW OUR APPROACH TO IMPROVING TEAM EFFECTIVENESS IS DIFFERENT

You may have made various attempts at team building in the past which resulted in a temporary boost in morale but failed to translate into lasting results. Most team-building approaches get it wrong by focusing on feel-good activities that fail to raise the Team Effectiveness Quotient (TQ)—the capacity to operate as a high-performing team. TQ scores range from 0 to 100. Higher scores describe teams that are firing on all cylinders and achieving results better than the competition. Lower TQ scores denote underperforming or dysfunctional teams. Our research and experience show that a team can boost TQ only by doing real work, not by attending off-site activities which are often entertaining but ultimately lacking in substance.

Teams must do three things to boost their TQ score and establish a winning track record. First, they need to follow a proven *roadmap* that shows them how to get from where they are to where they want to go. Although that sounds obvious, our observation has been that many teams try a hodgepodge of best practice team-building exercises without a clear understanding of how these activities fit together or whether they're even the right activities. Second, successful teams get *feedback* about how they're doing compared to the roadmap. They understand how their strengths and weaknesses benchmark against other teams. And third, successful teams implement *proven methods* to address performance gaps.

A ROADMAP FOR TEAM EFFECTIVENESS

Roadmaps tell drivers how to get to a desired location. Likewise, team roadmaps tell leaders, teams, and organizations what they need to do to transform collections of people into high-performing teams. Based on our research, we've developed a roadmap for teams called the Rocket Model.

The Rocket Model consists of eight interrelated components: Context, Mission, Talent, Norms, Buy-In, Resources, Courage, and Results. Think about how your team is doing as you read through a description of the eight components. Are team members on the same page about the team's top challenges? Does the team have meaningful and measurable goals? Does it run efficient and effective meetings? How does it manage conflict?

Context. Team formation gets off to a good start when team members share a common view of the situation surrounding the team. For the SLT, the situation included key stakeholders such as customers, station employees, air crews, headquarters, the Federal Aviation Administration, elected public officials, and several important suppliers. Key influencers are also a part of Context, and for the SLT, this included the local economy, demographic trends, competitors (regional and international airlines), and the labor market. The SLT never discussed who these stakeholders and influencers were or what they were apt to do over the next 12 months. Nor did they agree on the top challenges facing the team. As a result, members were taking well-intentioned but misaligned actions that hurt team morale and effectiveness. Gaining agreement about the situation and the team's biggest challenges would be something Billy would need to tackle soon after starting his new job.

The Rocket Model

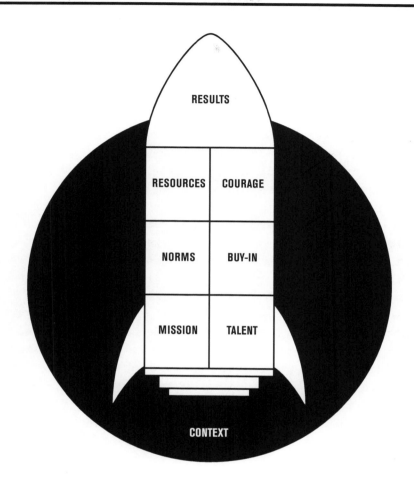

Mission. When team members agree on what success looks like, they set the stage for effectiveness. Why does this team exist and how should it measure success? What are the team's goals, when do they need to be accomplished, what strategies will the team use, and how will progress be measured? Teams need to translate goals into plans with actionable steps, role assignments, and regular progress reviews. Plans help ensure that day-to-day activities are connected to key priorities, real productivity, and tangible achievements. A clear understanding of the Mission is essential, as it affects all the other components of the Rocket Model.

Although the SLT had metrics to track performance, they did not use them to manage day-to-day activities at the station. Nor did they agree on the team's purpose; some felt that the SLT's primary reason for existence was to increase the number of ticketed passengers, others thought good labor relations or financial performance was what really mattered. There were no systematic plans to improve station performance, and progress reviews had largely devolved into finger-pointing instead of problem-solving. Billy would need to clarify the team's Mission soon after his arrival.

Talent. Although each SLT member had a well-defined role and the requisite technical skills needed to perform their job, the team suffered from serious Talent problems. Several members were team-killers who either lacked integrity or did not play nice with fellow team members. They were also largely incented based on department function rather than overall station performance, so they made decisions that optimized their individual department, but negatively impacted station metrics as a whole.

Talent may be the most challenging component of the Rocket Model. That's because most organizations assign staff members to a team based more on availability or politics than Talent. The team leader may believe that the skills, experience, and abilities of individual team members are all that matter, but as we see with the SLT, there are other equally important Talent considerations when it comes to building high-performing teams. High-performing teams are the right size, have reporting structures that support teamwork, and well-defined roles and responsibilities that optimize performance. Effective team leaders also show little tolerance for team-killers.

Talent was Billy's most pressing problem. He fired Saheeb and Frank in his first two weeks on the job and demoted Jacob and Zelda two weeks later. Billy filled the four open positions with high-performing managers, and six weeks into the job was leading a very different SLT. These personnel moves had an immediate, positive effect on both the SLT and employees across the station.

Norms. It is human nature for any group to develop Norms for greeting, meeting, seating, communicating, deciding, and executing. These unwritten rules usually solidify fast without any formal discussion. However, teams that take the time to talk through and consciously establish Norms leverage a powerful tool for achieving team cohesiveness and performance.

High-performing teams make efficient use of their meeting time and have clear rules and processes in place—some formal, some informal—for interacting with each other, maintaining productivity, managing communications, making decisions, delegating tasks, and ensuring accountability. The SLT had a set of Norms in place that hindered rather than fostered performance, and Billy set about establishing a new set of expectations and rules for SLT member behavior.

Buy-In. Team members have choices; they can choose to direct their energy and effort toward team goals, or they can spend their time engaged in other matters. Members of high-performing teams demonstrate a team-first, not me-first, attitude and are committed to accomplishing assigned tasks, abiding by team rules, and cultivating team success. They understand how their work contributes to the greater good and are optimistic about the team's potential.

The SLT had mixed levels of engagement, with some people working hard and others checked out. To counteract this, Billy painted a compelling vision of the future and got the new SLT involved in the creation of team goals, plans, roles, and rules. He ensured each member contributed equally and abided by team Norms. He avoided playing favorites, particularly with those he brought in from his previous job, as this would discourage overall commitment.

Resources. Early on, teams need to figure out what Resources are necessary for meeting their goals, and leaders may have to lobby key stakeholders to get those needs met. Tangible Resources include a realistic budget, office space, hardware and software systems, specialized equipment, access to data, and tech support. Intangibles may include political support and authority to make decisions.

High-performing teams have the necessary political clout and make efficient, effective use of their Resources. Even when there's a shortfall, the best teams maximize the Resources they have and find ways to succeed. Resources were an issue for the SLT, as the airline was located in a concourse that did not have enough gates and enough seats at the gates to accommodate customers. It also had old ground handling equipment and the airline club lacked decent amenities.

Courage. The best teams understand that managing conflict is not the same as minimizing conflict. Effective team leaders know that too little conflict with problems swept under the rug leads to artificial harmony and groupthink. Too much conflict, on the other hand, leads to chaos and backstabbing.

More often than not, the root cause of most team conflict can be tied back to misunderstandings or disagreements about the previous six components in the Rocket Model. Does team conflict occur because of disagreements about team goals and plans, unclear roles, poor decision-making rules, or disproportionate Buy-In? Diagnosing the root causes of conflict and dealing with them in a manner that promotes psychological safety is a challenge for team leaders. Another hurdle lies in ensuring there is enough tension on the team to promote creative thinking and effective problem-solving without alienating team members. Do team members feel safe challenging each other? Can they do this in a way that builds trust and morale rather than creating enemies?

Courage had been a big problem for the SLT. An overall environment of mistrust existed among team members, which stemmed from various disagreements about team challenges and purpose, the presence of team-killers, members not being held accountable for bad behavior, and mixed levels of Buy-In regarding team goals. Team trust and Courage greatly improved once Billy dealt with these issues.

Results. High-performing teams stay focused. They measure Results against goals, regularly track progress, learn from successes and failures, and devise ways to continually improve delivery. They understand that it is critical to align goals with important organizational outcomes and to measure progress in ways that lead to superior performance.

Achieving Results depends on how well the team handles the previous seven components in the framework. In other words, members must share assumptions about the situation, agree on the team's goals and plans, have clearly defined roles and skills, be willing to put forth the effort to complete assigned tasks, adhere to Norms, have access to necessary Resources, and manage conflict effectively. When the team falters at one of these steps, outcomes are affected. By making sure each component has been fulfilled along the way, the team will continue to improve over time, build confidence, and achieve even greater success.

Billy established weekly station performance reviews to improve the station's Results. During these two-hour meetings, the SLT relentlessly focused on key metrics, discussed how those metrics compared to other stations, and devised plans to improve performance. After six months, the station was meeting or exceeding airline averages for on-time departures, customer service ratings, and lost baggage claims, and by the end of the year was among the company's best on these statistics.

Using the Rocket Model. The model is diagnostic in that teams can use the model to determine which components are in relatively good shape and which ones need improvement. The model is prescriptive in that it recommends a sequence of components needed to ensure high levels of team performance. There is an intentional sequencing to the model. Components lower in the model should be addressed before those higher in the model because they build on each other. For example, Context affects Mission and Mission, in turn, affects Talent. If Context and Mission aren't sorted out, the team will probably have trouble managing conflict (Courage).

FEEDBACK ON TEAM EFFECTIVENESS

A useful feature of most GPS systems is that they indicate where you are on the route—not just where you're headed. Although the Rocket Model describes the route for high-performing teams, teams also need information about where they are on the journey.

In our work with teams, we have found the two most effective ways of measuring a team's progress against the Rocket Model are interviews and surveys. Team member interviews can be structured around the eight Rocket Model components and include questions like:

- Who are your biggest customers?
- What are your team goals?
- Are team members' roles clear?
- What feedback do you have about team meetings or decision-making?
- How does the team handle conflict?

Responses to these questions can then be used to spur conversations about team strengths and areas of improvement. Because team members tend to be more forthcoming when someone outside of the team conducts the interviews and consolidates the responses, this option is best managed by external facilitators. More information about conducting team interviews can be found later in this book.

The Team Assessment Survey (TAS) is a short, online survey based on our research with more than 2,000 teams from around the globe. One advantage of the TAS is that it provides teams with benchmarking information about each of the eight Rocket Model components. Scores on the TAS range from 0 to 100, with lower-performing teams scoring closer to zero, average teams receiving scores around 50, and high-performing teams scoring above 75.

We administered the TAS to the SLT as part of our station due diligence process. As shown in the graphic, the SLT received low scores across the board. They did not agree on the team Context or purpose, and Talent was lacking. Team Norms needed a considerable amount of work, and Buy-In, Resources, and Courage were also rated very low. Given the team's performance on key station metrics, the Results score was not surprising.

SLT TAS Results

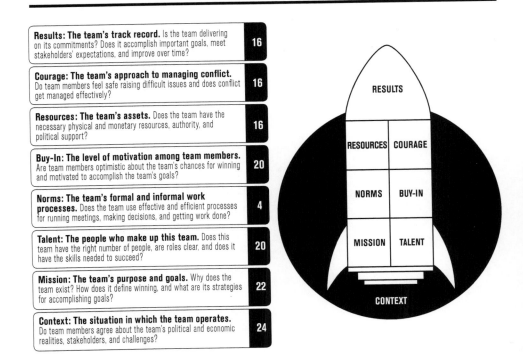

Results: The team's track record. Is the team delivering on its commitments? Does it accomplish important goals, meet stakeholders' expectations, and improve over time?	16
Courage: The team's approach to managing conflict. Do team members feel safe raising difficult issues and does conflict get managed effectively?	16
Resources: The team's assets. Does the team have the necessary physical and monetary resources, authority, and political support?	16
Buy-In: The level of motivation among team members. Are team members optimistic about the team's chances for winning and motivated to accomplish the team's goals?	20
Norms: The team's formal and informal work processes. Does the team use effective and efficient processes for running meetings, making decisions, and getting work done?	4
Talent: The people who make up this team. Does this team have the right number of people, are roles clear, and does it have the skills needed to succeed?	20
Mission: The team's purpose and goals. Why does the team exist? How does it define winning, and what are its strategies for accomplishing goals?	22
Context: The situation in which the team operates. Do team members agree about the team's political and economic realities, stakeholders, and challenges?	24

SLT TQ Score

TEAM EFFECTIVENESS QUOTIENT (TQ)

17%

The TAS also provides TQ scores. The SLT had a TQ score of 17%, which means more than 80% of teams in the global database had higher TQ scores. Given the description of the SLT gleaned from the station interviews, these results were not surprising. The TAS also provides item-level feedback for each of the eight Rocket Model components and team members' written comments about team strengths and areas of improvement. More information about ordering and interpreting the TAS can be found later in this book.

PROVEN METHODS TO IMPROVE TEAM EFFECTIVENESS

Feedback is a helpful step toward improving team performance, but feedback by itself doesn't get the job done. Once a team has an accurate understanding of its strengths and weaknesses, the team needs to create and implement a development plan. Just as there is no one-size-fits-all development plan for leaders, there is no one-size-fits-all development plan for teams. What's required to turn a team around depends on its history, the challenges it faces, and its specific performance gaps.

This book provides detailed directions for 13 common team challenges and 40 field-tested activities designed to improve team dynamics and performance. Unlike team-building interventions that solely promote interpersonal harmony, these activities build TQ by having teams do real work. We helped Billy and the new SLT work through some of these activities as they transformed from a low- to high-performing team.

Chapters 3-15 describe and provide case studies to address common challenges facing teams. The chapters also provide an overall team-building design, some of the rationale for the design, and a facilitator's guide with objectives, key questions to resolve, activities, and materials needed to engage teams in these situations. Topics include:

- Launching New Teams (Chapter 3)
- Helping Teams Get from Good to Great (Chapter 4)
- Fixing Broken Teams (Chapter 5)
- Combining Teams (Chapter 6)
- Virtual Teams (Chapter 7)
- Teams That Are Really Groups (Chapter 8)
- Matrixed Teams (Chapter 9)
- C-Suite Teams (Chapter 10)

- New Team Leaders: Getting off to a Fast Start (Chapter 11)
- Onboarding New Team Members (Chapter 12)
- Training Leaders to Build Teams (Chapter 13)
- High-Potentials and Teams (Chapter 14)
- Helping Organizations Foster Effective Teamwork (Chapter 15)

Chapters 3-15 make reference to 40 team improvement activities or exercises. This book describes each activity's purpose, key considerations, preparation, step-by-step facilitation instructions, and provides examples of completed forms or flip charts, support materials, and post-exercise activities. Having multiple teaching aids and activities gives team leaders and facilitators more flexibility when determining how to best resolve team issues.

Improvement Activity	Purpose	
1. Team Quiz	Clarifies myths and misunderstandings about groups and teams.	**Diagnostics and Teaching Aids**
2. Dream vs. Nightmare Teams	Clarifies differences between high- and low-performing teams.	
3. Groups vs. Teams Exercise	Determines whether people are working in groups or teams.	
4. The Rocket Model Slide Deck	Describes the eight components of the Rocket Model.	
5. The Rocket Model Puzzle	Improves understanding of the eight Rocket Model components.	
6. Team Assessment Survey (TAS)	Provides benchmarking feedback on TQ, team strengths, and areas of improvement.	
7. Team Interviews	Provides qualitative feedback on team Context and functioning.	
8. Team Feedback Sessions	Aligns teams on strengths, surprises, and areas of improvement.	
9. Organizational Teamwork Analysis	Evaluates the extent to which organizations foster effective teamwork.	
10. Context Assessment Exercise	Creates a common view of shareholders, influencers, and challenges.	**Context**
11. SWOT Analysis	Clarifies team strengths, weaknesses, opportunities, and threats.	
12. Vision Statements	Communicates the team's past, present, and future.	**Mission**
13. Team Purpose	Creates a common understanding of the team's why.	
14. Team Scorecard	Defines the team's goals, what it means to win, and how it can have an impact.	
15. Team Action Plans	Translates team goals into action steps with owners and dates.	

Improvement Activity	Purpose	
16. Roles and Responsibilities Matrix (P/S and RACI)	Clarifies team members' roles and responsibilities.	**Talent**
17. Followership Scatterplots	Evaluates team members' engagement and critical thinking skills.	
18. Feedforward Exercise	Provides team members with feedback to improve performance.	
19. Eavesdropping Exercise	Allows team members to share expectations for their peers.	
20. Wingfinder Assessment	Provides insights about team members' mental abilities and personality traits.	
21. Hogan Personality Inventory (HPI)	Provides insights about team members' bright-side personality traits.	
22. Hogan Development Survey (HDS)	Provides insights about team members' dark-side personality traits.	
23. New Team Member Onboarding Checklist	Helps new team members get integrated more quickly with teams.	
24. Team Norms	Establishes rules and expectations for team members' behavior.	**Norms**
25. Operating Rhythm	Improves the efficiency and effectiveness of team meetings.	
26. Operating Level	Determines whether teams are working on the right issues.	
27. Decision-Making	Clarifies who should be involved with and make team decisions.	
28. Communication	Establishes rules for team communication.	
29. Accountability Mechanisms	Establishes rules for ownership and expectations for deliverables.	
30. Self-Adjustment	Helps teams review and improve team functioning.	
31. Journey Lines	Shows how team members' past experiences shape current behavior.	**Buy-In**
32. Motives, Values, Preferences Inventory (MVPI)	Provides insights about team members' work values.	
33. Expectancy Theory	Clarifies links between team members' actions and rewards.	
34. Personal Commitments	Asks team members to commit to team goals, roles, and rules.	
35. Resource Analysis	Clarifies what the team already has and what it needs to be successful.	**Resources**
36. Stakeholder Mapping	Helps teams devise strategies to improve political support.	

Improvement Activity	Purpose	
37. After-Action Reviews	Fosters growth mindsets and productive dialogues in teams.	Courage
38. Team Journey Lines	Promotes team trust by systematically reviewing past experiences.	
39. Conflict Management Styles	Provides insight into how team members manage conflict.	
40. Personal and Team Learning	Helps team members and teams improve capacity.	Results

HOW TO GET THE MOST VALUE OUT OF THIS BOOK

This book is not intended to be read cover to cover. Instead, we recommend that everyone read Chapter 2, as it walks through some preliminary decisions that need to be made for any team engagement to be successful. After that, read the chapter or chapters that best fit your situation. For example, are you trying to help a new team get off to a good start? Then read Chapter 3 to understand the challenges facing new teams and become familiar with a design for effectively launching new teams. Follow up by reviewing the team improvement activities recommended in Chapter 3. Read Chapter 5 if you are trying to fix a broken team, or Chapter 13 if you want to build a leadership development program that teaches leaders the blocking and tackling skills needed to build high-performing teams.

Chapters 3-15 provide recommendations about which of the 40 team improvement activities best address specific team challenges. The chapters also describe a sequence for implementing these activities. These chapter recommendations are merely a starting point. Depending on the specific situation, the activities can also be done in a different sequence, left as stand-alone exercises, modified to better address existing problems, or replaced by other team improvement activities.

We understand that operational or delivery requirements can make it impossible for some teams to fully dedicate the time needed to properly resolve team challenges. Leaders and facilitators can still follow the sequence of team improvement activities outlined in the chapters, but do one activity every week or two. Most teams can find an hour or two every few weeks to improve performance.

The 40 team improvement activities make reference to handouts, articles, and PowerPoint slides. These materials can be downloaded from the Rocket Model website: www.therocketmodel.com.

Chapter 2

Getting Started

Chelsea had been a district
manager at a major coffee chain in an East Coast city for two years. Ten store
managers with stores located within a three-mile radius reported directly to
her. As the district manager, Chelsea was largely held accountable for aggregated results across all 10 stores. For example, her annual revenue goal for the
year was $18.5M USD, which was the summation of revenue goals across her
10 stores. Some goals, like the district's overall customer satisfaction ratings
and employee turnover rates, were shared by all store managers.

The 10 stores operated mostly independently and varied in size, clien-
tele, and operating hours. Annual store revenues ranged from $1-3M USD and
store staffing varied from eight employees to 30. Several stores were in down-
town office buildings, some were stand-alone stores on pedestrian malls, and
two stores had drive-through lanes. Stores in office buildings operated from
5 a.m. to 6 p.m. Monday through Friday, while stand-alone stores were open
from 5 a.m. to 10 p.m. seven days a week. Store managers were responsible for
financial and operational results, hiring and training staff, and managing labor
schedules. Annual store turnover averaged 60%, so personnel issues took up
a considerable amount of store managers' time.

Chelsea had recently promoted Haley to store manager. Hardworking, ambitious, and bright, Haley displayed a mastery of the store metrics and frequently earned first place in district store rankings. Customers adored the bubbly Haley, as did Chelsea, who secured her a spot in a district manager training program for high-potentials. But all was not well at Haley's store. As good as Haley was with customers, she was hard on her staff. Turnover at her store was much higher than the average, and employee morale was very low. Quarterly employee engagement scores were problematic too, but Haley was always able to explain them away, saying that one or two disgruntled employees were dragging down her results. Because of her chronic turnover problems, other stores were constantly asked to provide labor to support Haley's store. This put a strain on other managers, as they had to send fully trained staff to provide coverage. Not surprisingly, the on-loan employees did not like working in Haley's store, and some even refused to do it. Haley's peers tried to raise their concerns to Chelsea but she would hear none of it.

In addition to having to cover for Haley, store managers had other things to worry about. Because of an incident that put the company in the national spotlight, all employees were required to attend two hours of diversity training led by the store managers. Managers didn't receive the training materials until an hour before the national rollout, and the training raised sensitive topics that many were ill-equipped to handle. Store managers also struggled with a complex new staffing software system that was difficult to use and caused them to lose good applicants.

Between store managers' animosity toward Haley and their complaints about the diversity training and new applicant tracking system, Chelsea felt her team was falling apart. Store managers weren't collaborating, and there was a lack of trust on her team. She knew she had to do something, so she set up weekly team-building sessions with all 10 store managers. In the first session, she gave them a long pep talk about teamwork and had them share their personality types. During the second session, they participated in several trust-building activities involving blindfolds. The third week, Chelsea arranged a scavenger hunt in the district. The fourth week, two store managers had to leave early because of previous commitments. The fifth week, three had family commitments that prevented them from attending. Meanwhile, dynamics on the team were as bad as ever and two months later, Chelsea was looking for four new store managers.

Like Chelsea's efforts, most team-building engagements are planned with good intentions but fail to yield intended results. This chapter provides guidance that can prevent this from happening. Leaders and facilitators need to understand some key elements before planning team engagement activities, such as the difference between groups and teams, how to properly prepare for and facilitate team-building sessions, and the roles team leaders, members, and facilitators play in team improvement efforts. Mastering these topics will increase the likelihood that team engagements have a tangible impact on team performance.

TEAM OR GROUP?

Many people use the terms *group* and *team* interchangeably, but they actually describe two different methods of getting work done. Groups are collections of people who have individual rather than common goals, whose actions have little impact on the others in the group, and who are rewarded based on individual efforts. Teams are collections of people who have collective rather than individual goals, whose actions significantly impact other team members, and who ultimately win or lose together. Most collections of individuals are hybrids that fall somewhere in the middle of the Group Versus Team Continuum, with members having some combination of individual and collective goals, some work activities that impact others and some that do not, and rewards earned based on a combination of individual and team contributions.

Group vs. Team Continuum

Dimension	Group	Hybrid	Team
Goals	Individual. Members are focused on achieving individual performance goals. Team goals are merely a roundup of individual goals.	There is a mix of individual and collective goals.	Collective. There are only common goals everyone on the team is striving to achieve together.
Effort	Independent. What one member does has little bearing or impact on other members of the group.	Some activities have little impact on team members, others have considerable impact.	Interdependent. What one member does greatly affects others on the team.
Rewards	Based on individual performance. Overall group performance has little bearing on members' rewards.	Some rewards are based on individual achievements, others are based on overall results.	Based on team performance. Members are rewarded based on the team's collective accomplishments; individual accomplishments are downplayed.

Chelsea's store managers were more like a group than a team; they had their own store metrics, operated largely independently of each other, and were rewarded based on their own store's performance. Spending time on activities to improve collaboration was not going to help them manage their stores better; in fact, it took away from the time they had to do their work, which only added to their stress levels. Chelsea's district had problems, but a lack of teamwork wasn't one of them.

Leaders and consultants get into trouble when they treat groups like teams and teams like groups. The former drives group members crazy, as spending time on team-building activities takes away from time that could be spent achieving goals. Treating teams like groups can be equally frustrating, with leaders controlling all communication, work coordination, and problem-solving through one-on-one meetings rather than having people work through issues collectively. Chapter 8 provides more information about the differences between groups and teams, guidance about appropriate improvement activities for groups, and how to promote better groupwork.

PREPARING FOR TEAM ENGAGEMENTS

Leaders get paid to solve problems, and Chelsea's solution is typical for managers facing team morale problems. Unfortunately, her solution was the wrong one and better planning might have led to a better outcome. There are a number of things leaders need to consider *before* organizing a team event.

Who should attend? This question is not as straightforward as it seems. Teams are only as effective as their least-productive team members, so if leaders are serious about improving team performance, they need to address ineffective or disengaged members prior to a session. It's extremely frustrating to participate in team engagements where one or more people are completely checked out. It's better to resolve this problem before an off-site event rather than allow a few members to poison the well for the entire team. Chelsea should have met one-on-one with all store managers, listened to their concerns, and took action as needed before attempting a team-building event.

On a related note, some teams can be too big to participate in impactful team engagements. Robust discussions become impossible when teams exceed 10 members. In these situations, the team leader should identify a smaller core, or tiger, team made up of key team members. The core team does the initial work on various team improvement activities, and then the broader group is solicited for input and feedback.

Engagement planning. There are a number of questions that need to be answered when planning a team engagement, such as:

Engagement Objectives	Why is the team getting together? What does success look like?
Stand-Alone or Part of an Off-Site?	Is the team engagement a stand-alone session or part of a larger off-site? How does team engagement tie into the off-site?
Attendees	Who is attending the event? Is attendance mandatory?
Dates and Times	How much time has the team set aside for the engagement? What are the dates and start and stop times? Can people leave early?
Location	Where is the engagement taking place? Is the room conducive to breakout conversations and coaching the leader?
Team Assessment Survey (TAS) Logistics	Will the team complete a TAS as part of the engagement? What are the logistical details for the TAS administration?
Team Interviews	Will team members participate in interviews as part of the engagement? What are the logistical details for the interviews?
Prework	Is there any engagement prework that needs to be sent out? When does it need to go out? Who will make this happen?
Communication	What communication needs to go out to team members about the prework and engagement?
Materials	What materials need to be created for the engagement? Who will ensure they get to the engagement?
Engagement Roles	Who will be doing what before, during, and after the engagement?

These questions seem obvious, but as we saw with Chelsea, team engagements can easily go sideways if these issues have not been sorted out beforehand. A major disconnect occurs when dysfunctional teams assume fun, experiential events are going to help them surface and resolve real issues. Another problem occurs when these teams set aside one hour in a three-day off-site to improve team dynamics and performance. Because leaders tend to overestimate team performance, this happens more often than one might think. If team leaders are serious about team performance, they will need to adjust the objectives and agenda for an engagement once TAS and team interview results are reviewed.

When team facilitators are involved, they need to meet with the team leader to work through these issues prior to the engagement. This usually happens over the course of two meetings. The first meeting consists of working through the first nine items listed in the table above, such as defining the engagement objectives, determining whether team members will complete a TAS or take part in an interview prior to the engagement, and sorting out the communication plan for the engagement. A second meeting is required if TAS results or interviews were used to gather information about the team. This meeting is used to review the results, design the engagement, and work out the team leader and facilitator roles during and after the engagement.

Leaders opting not to use an outside facilitator have two options when it comes to setting up and running team engagements. They can either work through the planning details themselves or delegate responsibility for planning and running team engagements to team members. The latter can be a tremendous developmental opportunity because staff can learn new skills that they can apply to other teams. If team engagements are delegated, then team leaders will need to work closely with team members to ensure all the planning questions have been addressed and that they are prepared to facilitate the team improvement activities selected for the engagement.

FACILITATING TEAM ENGAGEMENTS

Over the years, we have learned a few lessons—often the hard way—about facilitating team engagements. In this section, we will walk you through 10 considerations about what to do before, during, and after a session that will increase the odds of a successful outcome.

Be earnest in preparation and flexible in facilitation. Team leaders and facilitators need to do their homework before any team engagement. They need to know the history of the team, its key stakeholders and influencers, its challenges and goals, and its members and who they report to. They also need to review any data pertaining to team dynamics and performance (team interviews, TAS results, team scorecard, or track record), know how to facilitate selected team improvement activities, and bring copies of materials to engagements. If they are external facilitators, they also need to clarify the objectives, agenda, and roles and agree on how to do in-the-moment coaching with the team leader prior to an engagement.

Effective team leaders and facilitators have a well-designed plan for any engagement, but also recognize that even the best plan can go awry. Topics will emerge that had not been considered and other topics will generate more or less interest and discussion than planned. Team leaders and facilitators need to adjust as needed to ensure the team is working through the right issues. In a practical sense, this means that team leaders and facilitators should resist the temptation to over-engineer team engagements. Have a well-defined plan, but don't try to complete too many team improvement activities all at once.

Go where the energy is. Related to the previous point, teams usually see the most improvement when they take the time to identify and work through their biggest challenges. Usually team interviews and TAS results identify these issues, but sometimes problems will crop up that leaders and facilitators knew nothing about. Papering over these issues as Chelsea did will only make them worse; it is better to deal with them in a straightforward and timely manner. If these issues cannot be dealt with immediately, they still need to be acknowledged. Sometimes it is better to pause, collect additional information, then re-engage to address the new issues that surface in the session.

LESSONS LEARNED

- Be earnest in preparation and flexible in facilitation.
- Go where the energy is.
- Use small group activities to promote psychological safety.
- Leaders need a dose of reality.
- People are infinitely interested in themselves.
- Conversations matter more than numbers.
- Make the implicit explicit.
- Teams get built by doing real work.
- Intentions are good. Accountability is better.
- Facilitators don't fix teams. Teams fix teams.

Use small group activities to promote psychological safety. We recommend processing issues in small groups and then reporting them to the large group. This approach helps promote productive dialogues, as people tend to be more comfortable speaking up in groups of three to five than in larger groups. People in small groups are also more likely to point out the elephant in the room. Small group activities increase the energy level in meeting rooms and make it safer for individuals to share their perspectives.

Leaders need a dose of reality. Our research shows that team leaders rate team performance between 1.0-1.5 points higher than team members using the TAS 5-point rating scale. There are several reasons for this: team members may only share good news with team leaders; some team leaders don't care about team performance; some leaders only hear what they want to hear or don't listen very well at all; and some are preoccupied with other tasks and spend little time with their teams. The leader's overestimation is a key reason why so many teams underperform. How can team leaders fix problems they don't see? Or if they see the problem, what if they intervene too late or not at all? Chelsea is a good example of this, as she dismissed many warning signs concerning Haley and underestimated the toll the diversity training and new hiring system would have on the district. Team leaders are often shocked when they see TAS scores, but team members are rarely surprised.

Because of potential discrepancies in perception, team leaders should see how their own TAS ratings compare with the rest of the team prior to any team engagement. This can give them an insight into how well they are reading their team and where they may be over- or underestimating team performance. It will also tell them where they need to gain a deeper understanding of the team's perspective.

People are infinitely interested in themselves. People are naturally curious about themselves and like feedback whether it is from personality or 360-degree assessments, employee engagement surveys, or TAS feedback reports. Most also want to know how they compare to others, which is why we added percentile scores to the TAS. These scores tell teams where they are worse than, on par with, or better than other teams on the eight Rocket Model components.

This natural curiosity can be leveraged to improve team performance. Most teams are motivated to improve when they see what they are lacking in comparison to other teams. Sharing TAS results should generate enthusiasm for doing the team improvement activities described later in this book.

Conversations matter more than numbers. "Frankly my dear, I don't give a damn" perfectly describes our perspective on the specific scores that are reported on the TAS. Although the TAS is one of the best assessments out there for accurately measuring team dynamics and performance, the primary purpose of the TAS is to drive conversations, not represent the truth. Teams determine their own realities and they do this by talking through their TAS results. Through these conversations, teams will agree on which results are valid, which scores are too high or too low, and what areas warrant further discussion.

Make the implicit explicit. Team members have ideas about customers, workload balances, the rules governing team decisions, and how conflict gets managed. Whether they share the same ideas about these topics is an entirely different matter. Many leaders assume team members see the world the same way they do, yet far too often this is simply not the case. This is particularly true with new teams, virtual teams, or when restructuring results in new teams. An important aspect of any team engagement is to get team members' thoughts out on the table, work through any differences, and agree on next steps. This process would have produced better results for Chelsea and her store managers than the golf and dinner outing.

Teams get built by doing real work. One big obstacle to improving teamwork is that team building is often associated with ropes courses, scavenger hunts, or sharing scores on dubious self-assessments. These activities can be fun and engaging, but they usually do not help teams tee up the right issues or do real work. Teams build trust, capacity, and commitment by pinpointing the issues interfering with effective teamwork, working out solutions to overcome obstacles, following through with commitments, and being held accountable to agreed-upon actions.

This is not to say that traditional team-building activities have no place in building high-performing teams. However, they should be used sparingly and must always tie in with a particular problem a team is trying to resolve. They should never be done when team morale is poor or because team facilitators happen to like them.

Intentions are good. Accountability is better. Like individuals, teams tend to fall off the wagon. Teams get all fired up during engagements only to fall back into old habits six weeks later. To avoid post-engagement disillusionment, teams need to build in accountability mechanisms for any agreements made during team engagements. These might include team scorecard reviews, team action plans with dates and owners, informal evaluations of team norms, a second TAS to measure progress, or peer feedback.

All teams need a sheriff, and team leaders play a critical role when it comes to enforcing team accountability. It's the leader's job to ensure all team commitments are being met. Asking team members to hold each other accountable is nice in theory, but rarely works. The first time or two an agreement is violated, the offending party is to blame, but repeated offenses fall on the leader's shoulders. Enforcers do not win popularity contests, but they do help teams perform at higher levels.

Facilitators don't fix teams. Teams fix teams. Team facilitators should use a light touch when working with teams and generally avoid teamwork delegation attempts, such as doing TAS interpretations for teams, making electronic copies of team improvement activity results, completing team action plans, or holding teams accountable for agreed-upon actions. This is the work of the team, not the facilitator. The more teams take responsibility for their actions, the more likely they will follow through with their commitments. However, facilitators may write up their observations and recommendations for follow-up actions and share them with team leaders.

ROLES DURING TEAM ENGAGEMENTS

Team leaders. These individuals play pivotal roles in team engagements. Team leaders decide whether a team engagement is going to take place, control how time will be structured, set the overall tone for the event, and determine whether post-engagement obligations and deliverables have been fulfilled. Effective leaders also know the fundamentals of building high-performing teams and when to lead from the front versus from behind. They lead from the front when painting a vision for the team, teaching how to win, setting expectations for team member behavior, encouraging team members to put forth effort toward team goals, selecting and running activities to improve team performance, and selecting or deselecting team members. They lead from behind by asking questions, encouraging all team members to participate in discussions, and having team members take the lead on different team improvement activities. Both types of leadership are important during team-building sessions.

LEADING FROM THE FRONT VERSUS FROM BEHIND DURING TEAM-BUILDING SESSIONS

Lead from behind by asking more questions than offering opinions, minimizing airtime, speaking last, and deliberately creating opportunities for team members to take the lead. Leaders should avoid grabbing the marker and flip chart and being the spokesperson during report-outs.

Lead from the front by introducing the session, clarifying expectations, and taking a stand when the group doesn't reach consensus.

Striking the right balance between leading from the front versus from behind can be tricky. Leaders who over-index on leading from the front spend more time talking than the rest of the team put together. This significantly diminishes team members' input, engagement, and buy-in over time, and eventually learned helplessness creeps into the team. When leaders complain about having to make all the decisions, rest assured they are spending too much time leading from the front. Over-indexing on leading from behind can be equally problematic. Leaders who fail to spell out expectations, take a stand, and want the team to come to a consensus on every topic will waste inordinate amounts of time. Team members will become frustrated with leaders who can't make lonely decisions. Below are three rules of thumb for leaders during team engagements:

1. Participate in but never be a scribe for small group activities.
2. Never speak on behalf of your small group during report-outs to the larger group.
3. Never take up more than 20% of the airtime. Use your time to ask questions and summarize decisions and deliverables. Let team members take 80% of the time sharing perspectives, identifying problems, and generating solutions.

Team leaders also need to be comfortable in the sheriff role, as they are ultimately responsible for holding team members accountable for completing assigned tasks and adhering to team rules. This means they must ensure the right people are on the team and cull underperformers or chronic malcontents when appropriate. Team leaders carry a big stick and they need to be willing to use it. Effective leaders leave teams in better shape than they inherited, and the root cause of much team dysfunction can be attributed to leaders spending too much or too little time leading from the front, leading from behind, or being the sheriff. Chelsea failed as the team's sheriff because of her unwillingness to hold Haley accountable for store morale.

A fourth role for team leaders is developing team members to be effective team leaders. They do this by delegating responsibility for team engagements to team members and coaching them on how to prepare and run effective team improvement sessions.

Team members. Team members need to be willing to share their perspectives, lean in when identifying issues and solving problems, dedicate time and energy toward accomplishing assigned tasks, follow through with commitments, and abide by team rules and agreements. Because many have a history of working for ineffective leaders or being on dysfunctional teams, these requirements can be difficult to meet.

Facilitators. If teams opt to use an external facilitator, there are several things these individuals must do to ensure team engagements are successful. First, team facilitators need to conduct due diligence prior to any team engagement. Meeting with the team leader to understand his or her perspective on the team, the rationale for hiring a facilitator, and goals for the engagement is a must. Facilitators also need to gather information about the team's history, customers, competitors, key deliverables and challenges, members, cliques and coalitions, and norms. They can gain this knowledge by reading the organization's annual reports, web pages, and pertinent articles, and by interviewing team members.

Second, facilitators need to prepare and coach team leaders prior to team engagements. This entails reviewing the engagement objectives, design/agenda, and flow of the team improvement activities; helping leaders with their opening and closing remarks; and clarifying roles during engagements.

Third, facilitators need to be comfortable going with the energy of an engagement, and keeping the agenda flexible, as sometimes teams need more time than planned to work through issues. Facilitators should also be comfortable asking questions, minimizing their airtime, and avoiding playing the expert role. Teams will be more engaged by working through answers to well-placed questions than being told what to do. Experienced facilitators select and modify activities to better fit team needs.

Fourth, facilitators should also coach team leaders during engagements. This typically happens offline and centers around things team leaders can do more of, less of, or differently when it comes to leading from the front, leading from behind, or being the sheriff. Facilitators also provide teams with lots of coaching during team off-sites, and this usually entails feeding back observations about the team. For example, a team may commit to equal participation and be willing to challenge each other and subsequently let one team member completely dominate a conversation. Team facilitators can help team leaders reflect by asking how well the team is living up to these two norms and what it needs to do in the future to improve.

Fifth, facilitators need to understand that even the best engagement will not fix a team. Team coaching also takes place after the team engagement. Good team facilitators write up and review team observations and recommendations after team off-sites with team leaders. These write-ups may contain sensitive information about team members, however, so team facilitators need to clarify who has access to this information before it is sent to clients. Facilitators can also conduct engagement debriefings with intact teams. This often involves asking team members what worked and what did not, key lessons learned, and what needs to happen next to improve team performance.

SHOULD TEAMS WORK WITH AN EXTERNAL FACILITATOR?

Team leaders and members can follow the guidance provided in this book without relying on external facilitators, but in certain situations, such as with new teams, senior leadership teams, or broken teams, facilitators can prove invaluable. Because facilitators are not part of a team, they have an easier time raising difficult issues and speaking truth to power. Good team facilitators can help teams have the right conversations, develop effective solutions to their problems, reach decisions, build plans, and adopt accountability mechanisms to ensure team decisions and plans are successfully implemented.

CONCLUDING COMMENTS

This chapter summarized the key considerations for running effective team engagements. Team leaders and facilitators need to understand the differences between groups and teams, what to consider when preparing for and facilitating team engagements, and the roles of team leaders, team members, and facilitators in team engagements. Teams also greatly benefit when leaders properly demonstrate when they need to lead from the front, lead from behind, and take on the role of sheriff. These lessons apply equally to Chapters 3-15.

PART II

Common Team Scenarios

Chapter 3

Launching New Teams

We recently worked with a team tasked with a highly visible, mission-critical project for a midsized company specializing in product safety testing. The company had a well-deserved reputation for technical excellence; its engineers were world-class experts in product safety and customers appreciated their recommendations for product improvement. Unfortunately, the company also had a reputation for lousy service. Customer prototypes would sit on shelves for months before going through safety testing, engineers often failed to return phone calls, and customers never knew if their products would pass safety testing on time for scheduled marketing and sales launches.

Although annual revenues had grown about 5% a year over the previous four years, much of that growth came from acquisitions and price increases. A deeper analysis revealed that the company was losing customers faster than it was gaining new ones. The CEO tasked a high-potential leader, Andy, with improving customer service.

Because this project had the CEO's backing, Andy was able to recruit some of the best and brightest people from across the company to work on the project. The 10-member task force included leaders from Marketing, Sales, IT, Finance, the call center, and Product Safety. The CEO gave the task force four months to develop a workable solution, and Andy felt a face-to-face meeting was needed to get the team properly launched. However, he was unsure what to do in this initial meeting.

WHERE DO NEWLY FORMED TEAMS GET STUCK?

Head and Shoulders shampoo once had a tagline that said, "You never get a second chance to make a first impression." The same applies to new teams. A proper launch goes a long way toward sustained team success, but there are several challenges team leaders and facilitators need to overcome if they want to transform a collection of strangers into a high-performing team. Teams that get off to a good start quickly clarify why the team exists, how it defines success, how team members contribute to team success, and how people will work together to succeed. The sooner this happens, the sooner new teams will be on the path to high performance.

We used the Rocket Model framework to identify how new teams tend to struggle in each area:

- *Context:* Because people are coming from different backgrounds and business units, team members will not have a common view of the situation or challenges facing the team.
- *Mission:* Often the team's purpose, goals, and plans haven't been de-fined. In the absence of a common purpose or unifying goals, team members will row the boat in different directions.
- *Talent:* If roles, responsibilities, and boundaries are not clear to every-one on the team, conflict is likely. The team may also have some talent gaps.
- *Norms:* Team members often have different expectations about com-munication, decision-making, and accountability, so it's important that everyone agrees to and abides by the same rules.
- *Buy-In:* New teams need to spend time ensuring all members are com-mitted to the team's Mission and are optimistic about the chances of success. In addition, it's often worth discussing where team members' loyalties lie—with this team or another.
- *Resources:* Once the Mission is clarified, the team should take inven-tory of available resources. Does the team have the data, budget, au-thority, and equipment needed to accomplish its goals?

- *Courage:* New teams need to set explicit expectations about raising difficult issues, expressing disagreement, and creating a safe zone for constructive conflict.
- *Results:* New teams need to clarify how they will measure success and create feedback loops for ongoing improvement.

COMMON CHALLENGES FOR NEW TEAMS

- Unfamiliarity
- Different views of team context
- Unclear purpose and goals
- Role ambiguity
- No team norms
- Lack of buy-in
- Absence of trust

SOLUTION

We worked with Andy on the overall design of the team engagement. The task force was to meet four days over a period of several months; we facilitated Session 1 and Andy ran the last two sessions. Task force members worked on assigned tasks between sessions, and the team had a solution ready to present to the Executive Leadership Team (ELT) four months after the initial session.

THREE MONTHS			
Session 1: Day 1	**Session 1: Day 2**	**Session 2**	**Session 3**
• Opening Remarks • Dream vs. Nightmare Teams • Rocket Model Overview • Context Assessment Exercise • Team Purpose • Project Deliverables • Journey Lines	• Reviewing Day 1 Work • Roles and Responsibilities Matrix • Team Action Planning • Team Norms • Operating Rhythm • Next Session Deliverables	• Project Deliverables and Action Plan Review • Team Problem-Solving • Stakeholder Mapping • Team Action Planning and Next Session Deliverables	• Project Deliverables and Action Plan Review • TAS Feedback Session • Team Problem-Solving • Team Action Planning and Final Deliverables

Session 1. After opening remarks and familiarizing the team with the Rocket Model, we led them through a Context Assessment exercise. The team also spent time defining its purpose, clarifying project deliverables, and participating in the Journey Lines exercise at the end of the first day. The Journey Lines activity accelerated trust-building and was fodder for discussion over dinner. The task force spent the second day of Session 1 finalizing the Context and Mission components of the model, sorting out who was responsible for what, and establishing rules for how the team would work together, communicate with each other, and run meetings. Session 1 ended with the creation of a four-month Team Action Plan that spelled out key actions, owners, and due dates. The team left the first session with a clear understanding of the situation, team goals, task assignments, meeting times, proper methods of communication, and deliverables that needed to be met before the next meeting.

Session 2. Prior to this session, team members gathered information about current customer service practices, customer complaints, call center data, and customer financial and satisfaction metrics. Time was spent during the session reviewing this data, updating deliverables, discussing progress on the Team Action Plan, sharing key learnings, and working through ongoing issues. This included problems with how customer satisfaction was being defined and measured by the company. As the team started to formulate tentative solutions, Andy facilitated a Stakeholder Mapping exercise to identify key players and their attitudes towards possible solutions, and determine how to build support.

Session 3. Prior to this session, team members worked on their action items and prepared report-outs. They also completed a Team Assessment Survey (TAS) and Andy helped the team interpret the results, review Team Action Plan progress, and work on recommendations to the ELT. By the end of Session 3, the task force was well on its way to operating as a high-performing team and delivering an effective solution to the company's customer service problem.

ACCOUNTABILITY MECHANISMS

Andy started Sessions 2 and 3 with Team Scorecard and Action Plan reviews, and both sessions ended with a review of the deliverables for the next session.

OUTCOMES

The team presented their recommendations to the ELT. The company opted to go with many, but not all, of the task force recommendations.

CONCLUDING COMMENTS

In our experience, it takes about two days to work through the Context, Mission, Talent, Norms, and Resources issues needed to successfully launch a new team. Although this may seem like a large amount of time, it is better to allocate the necessary time up front than to spend more time turning around a failed team later. In addition, the two days are usually spread out over a two- to six-month period, with time split between taskwork (e.g., solving problems and working on projects) and teamwork (e.g., implementing different activities to improve team functioning and dynamics). If new teams do not have this much time, then they should work through as much of the Context, Mission, Talent, and Norms content as possible.

This design is just one approach to launching new teams. Given the urgency and visibility of the project being delivered, this team required more handholding than most to properly launch. We've seen other team leaders conduct a series of two-hour sessions, change the order of the activities, and use different activities altogether when launching new teams. For success with any design, there needs to be a common framework for building high-performing teams, agreement on how to operate effectively, and accountability mechanisms to ensure commitments become reality.

Facilitator's Agenda for Session 1, Day 1

Time	Objectives	Key Questions	Activities and Materials
8:00-8:15 Opening remarks by team leader	• Outline objectives • Set expectations for participation • Review the day's agenda • Set meeting ground rules	• What do we need to accomplish at the off-site?	• Flip Chart
8:15-8:30 Facilitator leads Dream vs. Nightmare Teams exercise	• Engage participants in discussion about effective vs. ineffective teams • Ask participants about the prevalence of effective teams	• What are the characteristics of nightmare teams? Dream teams? • How common are dream teams? • How do you make dream teams happen?	• Dream vs. Nightmare Teams (p. 201)
8:30-9:15 Facilitator reviews Rocket Model	• Familiarize participants with the eight components of effective team performance	• What does the team need to do to operate effectively?	• Rocket Model Slide Deck (p. 209)
9:15-9:30 Break			
9:30-11:00 Facilitator leads discussion of Team Context	• Help team members understand the diversity of perspectives on the team • Get everyone on the same page about stakeholder expectations and contextual issues facing the team	• What do stakeholders expect from the team? • What external factors affect the team? • What are the team's biggest challenges?	• Context Assessment Exercise (p. 237)
11:00-12:00 Facilitator leads discussion about Team Purpose	• Create shared understanding of why the team exists	• Why does this team exist?	• Team Purpose (p. 253)
12:00-12:45 Lunch			
12:45-3:00 Facilitator leads group through exercise to draft Team Scorecard	• Translate high-level goals into specific deliverables • Establish benchmarks for measuring the team's performance	• What are the meaningful and measurable goals for this team? • How does this team define winning?	• Team Scorecard (p. 257)
3:00-3:15 Break			
3:15-5:00 Facilitator leads group through Journey Lines	• Help team members learn about each other • Begin building trust and camaraderie	• What life experiences have shaped team members?	• Journey Lines (p. 333)
5:00-5:15 Closing remarks by team leader	• Review what the team accomplished during the day • Remind the team what they will be doing on Day 2	• What progress did we make today? • What do we need to get done tomorrow?	
6:00-8:00 Team dinner	• Provide informal time for socializing		

Facilitator's Agenda for Session 1, Day 2

Time	Objectives	Key Questions	Activities and Materials
8:00-8:30 Opening remarks by team leader and reflection	• Outline objectives of the session • Understand key learnings and reactions from Day 1	• What do we need to accomplish at the off-site? • What were participants' reactions and learnings from Day 1?	• Flip Chart
8:30-10:00 Facilitator helps the team finalize Context and Mission	• Finalize assumptions about key stakeholders and influencers • Finalize Team Purpose and goals	• What is the situation facing the team? • What are the team's challenges? • What does the team need to accomplish?	• Context Flip Charts • Purpose Flip Charts • Team Scorecard Flip Charts
10:00-10:15 Break			
10:15-12:00 Facilitator helps the team create a Team Action Plan	• Create a plan that translates team goals into action steps, owners, and due dates	• What do we need to do to achieve our goals?	• Team Action Plans (p. 261)
12:00-12:45 Lunch			
12:45-2:00 Facilitator helps the team create a Roles and Responsibilities Matrix	• Clarify owners, task assignments, and workload balances for team members	• Who owns each of the action steps in the Team Action Plan? • What other team activities need owners (e.g., setting up and running team meetings, etc.)?	• Roles and Responsibilities Matrix (p. 265)
2:00-2:15 Break			
2:15-3:30 Facilitator helps the team set Norms	• Clarify the rules by which team members will interact, communicate, and treat each other	• What are the team's rules? • What are the expectations around communication, assignments, and how team members treat each other?	• Team Norms (p. 303)
3:30-4:30 Facilitator helps the team set up an Operating Rhythm and master calendar	• Determine the frequency, timing, and rules for team meetings	• When should the team meet? • What should it talk about? • Who runs the meetings? • What are the rules during meetings?	• Operating Rhythm (p. 307)
4:30-5:00 Closing remarks by team leader	• Review the session deliverables • Review details for the next team meeting • Provide encouragement to participants • Session pluses and minuses	• What does the team need to get done before the next session? • Who owns these deliverables? • When is the next team meeting? • Who is running the meeting? • What needs to get done before the next team meeting? • What worked well during the session? • What does the team need to do differently at the next session?	

Team Leader's Agenda for Session 2

Time	Objectives	Key Questions	Activities and Materials
8:00-8:15 Opening remarks by team leader	• Outline objectives of the session • Set expectations for participation • Review the session agenda • Review session ground rules	• What do we need to accomplish at the off-site?	
8:15-9:30 Team leader runs a review of the Team Scorecard and Team Action Plan	• Review progress made on the Team Scorecard • Review progress made on the Team Action Plan • Identify problem areas	• Is the team on track with its goals and Team Action Plan? • Where is the team falling short? • What areas need more discussion?	• Team Scorecard (p. 257) • Team Action Plan (p. 261)
9:30-9:45 Break			
9:45-12:00 Team leader runs a team problem identification and solving discussion	• Review and discuss data collected between sessions • Identify the biggest problems facing the team • Develop solutions for biggest problems facing the team	• What are the Team Scorecard, Team Action Plan, and data telling us? • What are the biggest problems facing the team right now? • How should the team solve these problems?	• Flip Chart
12:00-12:45 Lunch			
12:45-2:00 (cont.) Team leader runs a team problem identification and solving discussion	• Review and discuss data collected between sessions • Identify the biggest problems facing the team • Develop solutions for biggest problems facing the team	• What are the Team Scorecard, Team Action Plan, and data telling us? • What are the biggest problems facing the team right now? • How should the team solve these problems?	• Flip Chart
2:00-2:15 Break			
2:15-3:30 Team leader runs a Stakeholder Mapping exercise	• Determine the key stakeholders affected by different solutions • Devise strategies and tactics to manage stakeholders	• Who might support the team's solutions? • Who might resist the team's solutions? • How should the team manage key stakeholders? • How can the team gain critical support for its solutions?	• Stakeholder Mapping (p. 355)
3:30-4:45 The team updates the Team Action Plan and reviews Session 3 deliverables	• Revise the Team Action Plan • Set deliverables for the next team meeting and Session 3	• How does our Team Scorecard and Team Action Plan need to change based on what was learned in Session 2?	• Team Scorecard (p. 257) • Team Action Plan (p. 261)

Time	Objectives	Key Questions	Activities and Materials
4:45-5:00 Closing remarks by the team leader	• Review the session deliverables • Review details for the next team meeting • Provide encouragement to participants • Session pluses and minuses	• What does the team need to get done before the next session? • Who owns these deliverables? • When is the next team meeting? • Who is running the meeting? • What needs to get done before the next team meeting? • What worked well during the session? • What does the team need to do differently at the next session?	

Team Leader's Agenda for Session 3

Time	Objectives	Key Questions	Activities and Materials
8:00-8:15 Opening remarks by team leader	• Outline objectives of the session • Set expectations for participation • Review the session agenda • Review session ground rules	• What do we need to accomplish at the off-site?	• Flip Chart
8:15-9:30 Team leader runs a review of the Team Scorecard and Team Action Plan	• Review progress made on the Team Scorecard • Review progress made on the Team Action Plan • Identify problem areas	• Is the team on track with its goals and Team Action Plan? • Where is the team falling short? • What areas need more discussion?	• Team Scorecard (p. 257) • Team Action Plan (p. 261)
9:30-9:45 Break			
9:45-11:00 Team leader conducts a TAS Feedback Session	• Review TAS results • Identify team strengths, surprises, and areas of improvement	• What are the team's strengths? • What does the team need to work on? • How does the team compare to other teams?	• TAS Feedback Report • Team Feedback Session (p. 227)
11:00-3:00 Team leader runs a team problem identification and solving discussion Working lunch	• Review and discuss data collected between sessions • Identify the biggest problems facing the team • Develop solutions for biggest problems facing the team	• What are the Team Scorecard, Team Action Plan, and data telling us? • What are the biggest problems facing the team right now? • How should the team solve these problems?	• Flip Chart
3:00-3:15 Break			

Time	Objectives	Key Questions	Activities and Materials
3:15-4:45 The team updates the Team Action Plan and final deliverables	• Revise the Team Action Plan • Set deliverables for the next team meeting and final presentation to the CEO	• How does our Team Scorecard and Team Action Plan need to change based on what was learned in Session 3?	• Team Scorecard (p. 257) • Team Action Plan (p. 261)
4:45-5:00 Closing remarks by the team leader	• Review the session deliverables • Provide encouragement to participants	• What does the team need to get done before the final presentation? • Who owns these deliverables?	

Chapter 4

Helping Teams Get from Good to Great

Several years ago, we got a call from the chief creative officer (CCO) of an advertising agency who wanted our help running a team-building session for her team. She was looking for a fun-and-games event: boating, followed by storytelling around a campfire, and perhaps having everyone share their scores on a color-coded personality test. We listened politely to her ideas and then told her that this wasn't how we worked. Surprised at our response, she asked what we *did* do. We said we were in the business of helping teams become high performing, and that we believed teams got stronger by doing real work together.

We then asked what was behind her desire to have a team-building event. She explained that while the company was growing and making money, it was starting to miss deadlines and go over budget on creative projects. Although the team got along well and meetings were amiable, directors seemed to be operating in their own lanes rather than actively working together to address the problems underlying the company's lackluster project performance. It sounded like she had a problem worth solving, and one that wasn't going to be solved by boating, storytelling, and color-coding.

We walked the CCO through the eight Rocket Model components fundamental to team effectiveness and suggested that perhaps one of the team's problems was that it wasn't engaging in *enough* conflict. We asked her whether she was interested in seeing how the creative team's effectiveness compared to other teams, and in pinpointing and addressing a few areas that could take her team to the next level. Despite a less than promising start to the meeting, she decided to hire us.

DIAGNOSIS

The project began with a thorough diagnosis. We interviewed all 10 of the directors on the creative team, asking about what the team was doing well, where it was struggling, and what they needed from the CEO. We also administered the Team Assessment Survey (TAS) and observed a creative team meeting. One issue identified during the interviews, and confirmed by the TAS, was that the team was not aligned on its Context. The directors held different views about what customers wanted, where the industry was headed, and the need to invest in technology. This, in turn, fueled disagreement about the team's Mission.

Another factor feeding into the low Mission score was that the cofounders were considering selling the business, so the team disagreed about whether to focus on short- or long-term strategies. Furthermore, we discovered that the team did not have a team scorecard in place to track their performance on customer service, marketing, sales, creative, operations, and financial metrics.

TAS Results

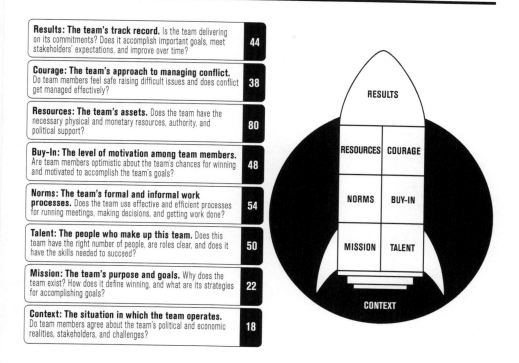

Results: The team's track record. Is the team delivering on its commitments? Does it accomplish important goals, meet stakeholders' expectations, and improve over time?	44
Courage: The team's approach to managing conflict. Do team members feel safe raising difficult issues and does conflict get managed effectively?	38
Resources: The team's assets. Does the team have the necessary physical and monetary resources, authority, and political support?	80
Buy-In: The level of motivation among team members. Are team members optimistic about the team's chances for winning and motivated to accomplish the team's goals?	48
Norms: The team's formal and informal work processes. Does the team use effective and efficient processes for running meetings, making decisions, and getting work done?	54
Talent: The people who make up this team. Does this team have the right number of people, are roles clear, and does it have the skills needed to succeed?	50
Mission: The team's purpose and goals. Why does the team exist? How does it define winning, and what are its strategies for accomplishing goals?	22
Context: The situation in which the team operates. Do team members agree about the team's political and economic realities, stakeholders, and challenges?	18

The low score on Courage was plainly illustrated during the team meeting we observed. The CCO was the only person asking tough questions and, like many teams, members seemed more concerned about getting along than getting to the bottom of issues. Issues were raised but quickly tamped down without resolution.

Although the TAS indicated average scores on Norms, interviews indicated there was an appetite to run meetings more effectively and some key decisions were getting bogged down because people were not aligned about who owned client relationships. From our observations of the team in action, we saw that discussions wandered without coming to conclusions.

Overall, the team scored in the average range on Buy-In, but a closer examination of the item-level results and feedback collected during the interview indicated that half of the team members were committed to the team's success, while the other members were largely going through the motions.

SOLUTION

This ended up being a four-session engagement. We ran Session 1 and focused on reviewing the Team Interview Summary (TIS) and TAS results and working on the team's Context and Mission. Between Sessions 1 and 2, the CCO assigned team members to create and circulate electronic copies of the team's Context Assessment exercise and Scorecard. Team members provided feedback on drafts of these documents prior to Session 2.

Sessions 2-4 took place after the creative team's regular monthly meetings. The CCO facilitated Session 2, where the creative team finalized the Scorecard and Action Plan and developed a set of team Norms. The CCO asked one of the directors to run Session 3 and another to run Session 4, as this would allow her to lead from behind and further develop the two directors. The team spent three hours in Session 3 clarifying roles using the Roles and Responsibilities Matrix and establishing Accountability Mechanisms, and another two hours in Session 4 establishing a new Operating Rhythm.

FOUR MONTHS			
Session 1	**Session 2**	**Session 3**	**Session 4**
• Opening Remarks • Dream vs. Nightmare Teams • Rocket Model Overview • Team Feedback Session— TAS and TIS • Context Assessment Exercise • Team Scorecard • Team Action Planning • Team Dinner	• Finalize Team Scorecard • Finalize Team Action Plan • Team Norms	• Roles and Responsibilities Matrix • Accountability Mechanisms	• Operating Rhythm

ACCOUNTABILITY MECHANISMS

The team discussed different Accountability Mechanisms and opted to complete deliverables report-outs and Scorecard reviews as part of every monthly meeting. In addition, the team evaluated the extent to which it had lived up to its agreed-upon Norms at the end of each monthly meeting. The team also opted to complete a second TAS nine months later to measure progress.

OUTCOME

As a result of these actions, the creative team became laser-focused on performance, had lively debates during monthly meetings, and left meetings with a clear understanding of how the team was doing, what everyone needed to accomplish over the next month to meet team goals, and how to work better as a team. Nine months later, they were on track to hit annual revenue and margin targets and realized noticeable improvements in TAS scores.

CONCLUDING COMMENTS

Sometimes team leaders want to do some team building just because it seems like a positive thing to do, even though nothing is obviously wrong with the team. Most often, these team-building sessions involve fun outings that don't result in stronger teams. There's nothing wrong with teams having fun together, in fact we encourage it, but please don't consider it team building.

In situations where a team is serious about taking performance to the next level to become one of the 20% of teams that are considered high performing, we strongly recommend these three steps: First, start with a diagnostic to determine the team's current level of functioning on the eight components of the Rocket Model. Second, use the analysis to implement a solution that targets areas of improvement and strengthens the team's performance. Last, build in Accountability Mechanisms to ensure the team is getting tasks completed, abiding by agreed-upon rules, and making progress. That's team building.

There is no best way to help a solid team become a high-performing team. It depends on where they're getting stuck, which is why a thorough diagnosis is so important on the front end of these engagements. Success with any design depends upon the team establishing a common framework, accurately identifying strengths and areas of improvement, reaching an agreement on what the team will do to improve, and adopting Accountability Mechanisms to make sure commitments become reality. Fun team-building activities are poor substitutes for these actions and rarely yield the performance benefits associated with doing real work.

Facilitator's Agenda for Session 1

Time	Objectives	Key Questions	Activities and Materials
8:00-8:15 Opening remarks by team leader	• Outline objectives of the session • Set expectations for participation • Review the day's agenda • Set meeting ground rules	• What do we need to accomplish at the off-site?	• Flip Chart
8:15-8:30 Facilitator leads Dream vs. Nightmare Teams exercise	• Engage participants in discussion about effective vs. ineffective teams • Ask participants about the prevalence of effective teams	• What are the characteristics of nightmare teams? Dream teams? • How common are dream teams? • How do you make dream teams happen?	• Dream vs. Nightmare Teams (p. 201)
8:30-9:15 Facilitator reviews Rocket Model	• Familiarize participants with the eight components of effective team performance	• What does the team need to do to operate effectively?	• Rocket Model Slide Deck (p. 209)
9:15-9:30 Break			
9:30-9:50 Rocket Model Puzzle	• Familiarize participants with the eight components of effective team performance	• What activities are associated with each component of the Rocket Model?	• Rocket Model Puzzle (p. 211)
9:50-11:30 Team Feedback Session—TAS and TIS	• Provide teams with benchmarking information about team functioning and performance	• How does our team compare to other teams? • What are our team's strengths, surprises, and areas of improvement?	• Team Feedback Session (p. 227) • TAS Feedback Report • TIS
11:30-12:15 Lunch			
12:15-1:30 Facilitator leads discussion of team Context	• Help team members understand the diversity of perspectives on the team • Get everyone on the same page about stakeholder expectations and contextual issues facing the team	• What do stakeholders expect from the team? • What external factors affect the team? • What are the team's biggest challenges?	• Context Assessment Exercise (p. 237)
1:30-3:30 Facilitator leads group exercise to draft Team Scorecard	• Translate high-level goals into specific deliverables • Establish benchmarks for measuring the team's performance	• What are the meaningful and measurable goals for this team? • How does this team define winning?	• Team Scorecard (p. 257)
3:30-3:45 Break			

Time	Objectives	Key Questions	Activities and Materials
3:45-5:30 Team Action Plan	• Build plans with action steps, owners, and dates to achieve team goals	• What does the team need to do to achieve its goals? • Who is responsible for what, and when do tasks need to be completed?	• Team Action Plans (p. 261)
5:30-5:45 Closing remarks by team leader	• Review what the team accomplished during the day • Remind the team what they will be doing on Day 2	• What progress did we make today? • What do we need to get done tomorrow?	
6:00-8:00 Team dinner	• Provide informal time for socializing		

CCO's Agenda for Session 2

Time	Objectives	Key Questions	Activities and Materials
1:00-1:05 Opening remarks by CCO	• Outline objectives	• What do we need to accomplish at the session?	
1:05-2:30 CCO helps the team finalize Mission	• Finalize team goals, metrics, and Team Action Plan	• What are the team's challenges? • What does the team need to accomplish? • How will it track progress? • What are its plans?	• Context Flip Charts • Team Scorecard Flip Charts • Team Action Plan Flip Charts
2:30-2:45 Break			
2:45-4:15 CCO helps the team set Norms	• Clarify the rules by which team members will interact, communicate, and treat each other	• What are the team's rules? • What are the expectations around communication, assignments, and how team members treat each other?	• Team Norms (p. 303)
4:15-4:30 Closing remarks by CCO	• Review session deliverables • Provide observations and reactions to the off-site • Provide encouragement to participants • Session pluses and minuses	• What does the team need to get done before the next session? • Who owns these deliverables? • When is the next team meeting? • Who is running the meeting? • How did the session go? • What would make the next session even better?	

Director's Agenda for Session 3

Time	Objectives	Key Questions	Activities and Materials
1:00-1:05 Opening remarks by director	• Outline objectives of the session • Set expectations for participation • Review session ground rules	• What do we need to accomplish at the session?	
1:05-2:30 Director leads group through Roles and Responsibilities Matrix	• Clarify owners, task assignments, and workload balances for team members	• Who owns each of the action steps in the Team Action Plan? • What other team activities need owners (e.g., setting up and running team meetings, etc.)?	• Roles and Responsibilities Matrix (p. 265)
2:30-2:45 Break			
2:45-3:45 Director facilitates discussion on Team Accountability Mechanisms	• Explain why Team Accountability Mechanisms are important • Share different types of Accountability Mechanisms • Select Team Accountability Mechanisms	• What team improvement activities will the team use to drive team accountability?	• Deliverables Report-Outs • Team Scorecard and Action Plan Reviews • After-Action Reviews (p. 361) • Team Norms (p. 303) • Feedforward Exercise (p. 275) • Self-Adjustment (p. 329) • TAS (p. 215)
3:45-4:00 Closing remarks by director	• Review the session deliverables • Review details for the next team meeting • Provide encouragement to participants • Session pluses and minuses	• When is the next team meeting? • Who is running the meeting? • What worked well during the session? • What does the team need to do differently at the next meeting?	

Director's Agenda for Session 4

Time	Objectives	Key Questions	Activities and Materials
1:00–1:05 Opening remarks by director	• Outline objectives of the session • Set expectations for participation • Review session ground rules	• What do we need to accomplish at the session?	
1:05–2:30 Director helps team set up new Operating Rhythm	• Determine the frequency, timing, and rules for team meetings	• When should the team meet? • What should it talk about? • Who runs the meetings? • What are the rules during meetings?	• Operating Rhythm (p. 307)
2:30–2:45 Closing remarks by director	• Review session deliverables • Review details for the next team meeting • Provide encouragement to participants • Session pluses and minuses	• When is the next team meeting? • Who is running the meeting? • What worked well during the session? • What does the team need to do differently at the next meeting?	

Chapter 5

Fixing Broken Teams

The chief human resources officer (CHRO) of a global manufacturing business asked us if we could help the leadership team of one of its business units. Their financial performance was dragging down results for the entire company, and a well-respected, high-potential leader had recently quit in frustration after being on the team for only a year. On his way out, he was brutally honest about the problems he saw on the team which got the attention of the company's senior leadership.

The business unit leadership team consisted of the unit vice president and directors of marketing, sales, engineering, operations, distribution, finance, and HR. The team was matrixed with members reporting to the chief operations officer, chief commercial officer, other functional heads at headquarters, and the unit vice president himself. Team members were geographically dispersed and because their financial results were poor, there had been little money for face-to-face meetings. We asked how long the business unit leadership team had been struggling and heard the dysfunction had outlasted multiple changes in team membership. The problems were so longstanding that no one could remember exactly when or how it all started.

DIAGNOSIS

In trying to untangle this proverbial Gordian knot, we approached the diagnostic phase with extra curiosity. We looked at internal and external factors that were having a negative impact on the team's ability to function effectively. In addition to conducting a Team Assessment Survey (TAS) and interviewing everyone on the team, we interviewed some of the leaders to whom team members reported, as well as some direct reports and even indirect reports in key positions. In all, we talked to more than 25 people about the team's history and current challenges. We also sat in on the team's monthly teleconference to gain firsthand observations of the team in action. Finally, we visited plant sites to better understand the team's resource constraints.

The business was in a negative spiral. Revenues remained flat and margins had dropped from 12% to less than 2% over the past three years. Because financial results were poor, there was little money to invest in much-needed infrastructure improvements. The lack of investment in equipment and people made it next to impossible to improve performance. Given the poor condition of the plants, it was difficult to attract experienced manufacturing talent and turnover exceeded 100%. New employees left before they were fully trained and productive, leading to production and quality problems. Members of the team went to work every day expecting to fail.

TAS Results

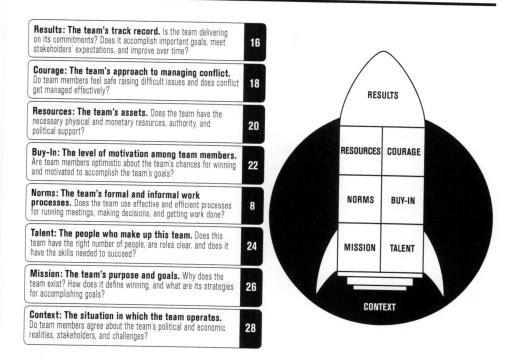

Results: The team's track record. Is the team delivering on its commitments? Does it accomplish important goals, meet stakeholders' expectations, and improve over time? **16**

Courage: The team's approach to managing conflict. Do team members feel safe raising difficult issues and does conflict get managed effectively? **18**

Resources: The team's assets. Does the team have the necessary physical and monetary resources, authority, and political support? **20**

Buy-In: The level of motivation among team members. Are team members optimistic about the team's chances for winning and motivated to accomplish the team's goals? **22**

Norms: The team's formal and informal work processes. Does the team use effective and efficient processes for running meetings, making decisions, and getting work done? **8**

Talent: The people who make up this team. Does this team have the right number of people, are roles clear, and does it have the skills needed to succeed? **24**

Mission: The team's purpose and goals. Why does the team exist? How does it define winning, and what are its strategies for accomplishing goals? **26**

Context: The situation in which the team operates. Do team members agree about the team's political and economic realities, stakeholders, and challenges? **28**

Team members believed in the Mission, but no one stood back to take a look at the big picture. Sales focused on hitting monthly revenue goals, regardless of whether the business was profitable, promised timelines were realistic, or operations had the capacity to meet last-minute production changes. Operations was held accountable for production and quality goals, which were impossible to meet given the facilities' aging equipment and staffing problems. Maintenance did a laudable job fighting fires but did not have enough staff to do preventative maintenance. Production lines were often down and equipment was in a constant state of disrepair. New product development was stalled because there was no capacity on the production lines to do test runs. Products were being released without being fully vetted, causing excess amounts of scrap and negatively impacting production numbers.

Talent was a problem, in part due to excessive turnover on the team. (Few people want to stay on a team with a losing track record, dismal prospects for future success, and low to nonexistent annual bonuses.) In addition, several long-term members of the team were ill-suited for their roles. Decision-making rights were a mess. Meetings were ineffective because problems were never addressed. Buy-In was meager due to pervasive pessimism. The team lacked the resources they needed to succeed and, due to widespread quality problems, scrap piles had so overrun the facilities that they were causing safety problems.

Trust was also a major issue with the business unit leadership team. Leaders focused on their own goals and only gave lip service to helping others. They were likely to avoid things agreed upon in meetings, to point out problems in other parts of the organization, and to blame others when they failed to deliver on assigned goals. Many felt other team members were setting them up for failure but never raised their concerns in team meetings. Courageous conversations on the team were stifled and conflict played out on the manufacturing floor every day.

In a nutshell, our diagnosis found no good news except for a strong desire to make things better. And although every member of the team was personally willing to do their part, none of them believed their colleagues would do the same. Trust was lacking and team members were pessimistic about their chances for success.

SOLUTION

Given this situation, we needed to find the delicate balance of providing the team with optimism that things would get better, while also tamping down any expectations that the fix would happen quickly. Our design included establishing some early wins and a long-term plan with milestones to show steady progress over time.

After we shared our diagnostic report with the chief operations and chief commercial officers, the team gained advocates who were visibly committed to turning things around. The company set the team up for success by making investments in the plants, lowering their short-term expectations of the business, and setting goals that were within reach.

As a result of our diagnostic work, two members of the team were replaced, which had an immediate positive impact. In addition, some reporting relationships were changed and two team members began coaching engagements. Dealing with talent issues is a primary consideration when working with broken teams because an ineffective team leader, ineffective reporting structure, or a couple of bad followers will get in the way of meaningful improvements.

With these changes underway, the team was ready for their first off-site. Demonstrating corporate's commitment to the business unit, the chief operations and chief commercial officers attended the first morning. They expressed optimism about the long-term prospects for the business and shared the news about the upcoming investments and relief on goals. This set a positive tenor for the remainder of the session.

In addition to reviewing the TAS and interview results, the team worked on creating an integrated business plan. The first step was having the directors of marketing, operations, and engineering present their plans for the year, which made it apparent to everyone that resources were being double-counted. For example, Operations devoted the same people to a cost reduction project that Engineering devoted to new product development. Barring the miracle of cloning, the groups were setting themselves up for conflict. This led to fruitful discussions about priorities and the creation of an *integrated* plan. We also worked on building an integrated Team Scorecard.

Two issues we did not directly address in Session 1 were team Context and trust. Interview results largely indicated that the team was on the same page about its stakeholders and influencers, and we felt getting an integrated Team Scorecard and Team Action Plan took higher priority. Several business unit team members, including the unit vice president, asked when we were going to deal with team trust. We told the team that trust is not built by doing some sort of soul-bearing exercise involving colors, personality types, or a ropes course. Trust builds over time by having the team discuss real issues, do real work, and stick to its commitments. All of the team improvement activities employed during and between the sessions built trust, but did so indirectly rather than dealing with the issue head on. Our experience is that dealing directly with team trust rarely yields intended results.

SIX MONTHS				
Session 1 (2 Days)	**Session 2**	**Session 3**	**Session 4**	**Session 5 (2 Days)**
• COO and CCO Pep Talk • Dream vs. Nightmare Teams • Rocket Model Overview • TAS and Team Interview Summary Feedback • Functional Plans • Integrated Action Plan • Team Scorecard • Team Deliverables • Team Dinner	• Deliverables Update • Finalize Team Scorecard • Update Action Plans • Team Problem-Solving • Team Norms • Personal Commitments • Team Deliverables	• Deliverables Update • Team Scorecard Review • Team Problem-Solving and Action Planning • Decision-Making • Team Norm Evaluation • Team Deliverables	• Deliverables Update • Team Scorecard Review • Team Problem-Solving and Action Planning • Journey Lines • Team Deliverables • Team Dinner	• Deliverables Update • Team Scorecard Review • Team Problem-Solving & Action Plans • Time 2 TAS Results • Context Assessment Exercise • Strategic Planning and Budgeting Process • Team and Personal Learning • Team Deliverables • Team Dinner

Session 2 was spent updating the integrated Team Scorecard and Action Plan, resolving high-priority business issues, establishing team Norms, and making Personal Commitments to the team's success.

Session 3 focused on reviewing progress against team goals and Team Action Plans, resolving high-priority team issues, establishing decision-making rights, and evaluating progress against team Norms.

During Session 4, the team revisited progress against team goals and plans, resolved high-priority team issues, and shared Journey Lines. The team leader and select members started running some of these activities, with the facilitator only providing guidance and support when necessary. We met with these individuals prior to the session to ensure they were fully prepared. The discussions generated by the Journey Lines exercise continued over dinner. At this point, the team had established enough trust and goodwill that members looked forward to the dinner rather than seeing it as a mandatory fun event.

Prior to Session 5, we re-administered the TAS to evaluate team progress and identify what the team needed to do to further improve. The session focused on both taskwork and teamwork, with the former involving the Team Scorecard and Action Plan reviews and the creation of an initial strategic plan and budget for the next year. A Context Assessment exercise was completed as part of Session 5 as a lead-in to the strategic planning and budgeting process. The session ended by having team members reflect on what they learned about themselves and the team over the past six months.

In addition to working hard during the sessions, the team was active *between* sessions. They made progress together by refining and using the Scorecard, Action Plan, Norms, Operating Rhythm, and master calendar and applying what they learned to jointly solve problems.

ACCOUNTABILITY MECHANISMS

It's all too easy for nightmare teams to backslide, so putting Accountability Mechanisms in place is critical. We began Sessions 2, 3, 4, and 5 by reviewing deliverables from the previous session. Next, the team evaluated progress against team goals, Team Action Plans, and the extent to which it had consistently lived up to its agreed-upon Norms. Finally, the team completed a second TAS to measure their progress.

OUTCOME

The second administration of the TAS showed significant improvements with the average score rising from 20 to 47. Business revenues went from being flat to increasing by 6% with the release of two new products. Productivity improvements and cost reduction projects propelled margins from less than 2% to over 7% in about a year. Although the team has yet to achieve the level of financial performance expected out of this business, they are optimistic about their future and have the tools in place to continue improving.

CONCLUDING COMMENTS

Paraphrasing Tolstoy: every functional family is alike, but every dysfunctional family is dysfunctional in its own way. We think this sentiment applies to teams too: every dysfunctional team is dysfunctional in its own way. But the *worst* teams appear to be dysfunctional in every way. The worst teams lack a common view of Context, aligned goals and rewards, the necessary skills, clear roles and responsibilities, Buy-In, loyalty, and trust. They also exhibit unhealthy conflict, poor followership, low morale, ineffective Norms, poor communication, and little accountability. And of course, their Results are nothing to cheer about.

Poor teamwork is often allowed to fester for years. Individual team members and overall performance suffer greatly when this happens, and help is finally sought when one of three things occurs: the team's results are so awful that the problem can no longer be ignored, the level of dysfunction leads to high-visibility departures, or the team gets a new leader with the skills and gumption to get the team on track. Turning around nightmare teams is possible, but just as the dysfunction didn't happen overnight, fixing the dysfunction will not happen overnight either.

Depending on the diagnosis, the solution for fixing a broken team may look very different from the one featured in the case presented here. Team leaders and facilitators will be on the right path if their designs help teams identify the right issues, come to an agreement on how to address these issues, and put mechanisms in place to track progress on team goals. It is important to remember that fixing broken teams is not likely to happen overnight or by using gimmicky team-building activities.

In most cases, team leaders are in a good position to do all the work necessary to launch new teams, combine teams, lead virtual teams, etc. Broken teams and C-suite teams may be the exceptions to this rule. In these scenarios, external facilitators can be extremely helpful in transforming these entities into high-performing teams. With no dog in the hunt when it comes to raising contentious issues, speaking truth to power, or providing feedback, external facilitators can provide an outsider's perspective, select assessments and activities to direct teams toward the right conversations, and hold a mirror up to the team.

Facilitator's Agenda for Session 1, Day 1

Time	Objectives	Key Questions	Activities and Materials
8:00-8:15 Opening remarks by team leader	• Outline objectives of the session • Set expectations for participation • Review the day's agenda • Set meeting ground rules	• What do we need to accomplish at the off-site?	• Flip Chart
8:15-9:00 COO and CCO pep talk	• Set new objectives for the business • Express confidence in the team • Provide support	• What does corporate think about this business? • What support will corporate provide to turn the business around?	• COO and CCO Slide Deck
9:00-9:15 Facilitator leads Dream vs. Nightmare Teams exercise	• Engage participants in discussion about effective vs. ineffective teams • Ask participants about the prevalence of effective teams	• What are the characteristics of nightmare teams? Dream teams? • How common are dream teams? • How do you make dream teams happen?	• Dream vs. Nightmare Teams (p. 201)
9:15-10:00 Facilitator reviews Rocket Model	• Familiarize participants with the eight components of effective team performance	• What does the team need to do to operate effectively?	• Rocket Model Slide Deck (p. 209)
10:00-10:15 Break			
10:15-11:45 Facilitator leads Team Feedback Session	• Teach team members how to interpret their TAS and TIS results • Gain consensus on the team's strengths and areas of improvement	• How does this team compare to other teams? • What are this team's strengths? • What are the team's biggest challenges?	• TAS Feedback Report • TIS • Team Feedback Session (p. 227)
11:45-12:30 Lunch			
12:45-2:45 Functional plan presentations	• Marketing and Sales plans • Engineering plans	• What are Marketing and Sales planning to do in the next year? • What is Engineering planning to do in the next year?	• Function Slide Decks
2:45-3:00 Break			
3:00-5:00 Functional plan presentations	• Operations and Maintenance plans • Finance and HR plans	• What are Operations and Maintenance planning to do in the next year? • What are Finance and HR planning to do in the next year?	• Function Slide Decks
5:00-5:15 Closing remarks by team leader	• Review what the team accomplished during the day • Remind the team what they will be doing on Day 2	• What progress did we make today? • What do we need to get done tomorrow?	
6:00-8:00 Team dinner	• Provide informal time for socializing		

Facilitator's Agenda for Session 1, Day 2

Time	Objectives	Key Questions	Activities and Materials
8:00-8:30 Opening remarks by team leader and reflection	• Outline objectives of the session • Understand key learnings and reactions from Day 1	• What do we need to accomplish at the off-site? • What were participants' reactions and learnings from Day 1?	• Flip Chart
8:30-10:00 Facilitator helps team create Integrated Action Plan	• Create a monthly plan that combines key initiatives for Marketing, Sales, Operations, Maintenance, Finance, and HR	• What do we need to accomplish each month? • Where are our bottlenecks to getting work done?	• Flip Chart
10:00-10:15 Break			
10:15-11:30 (cont.) Facilitator helps team create Integrated Action Plan	• Create a monthly plan that combines key initiatives for Marketing, Sales, Operations, Maintenance, Finance, and HR	• What do we need to accomplish each month? • Where are our bottlenecks to getting work done?	• Flip Chart
11:30-12:15 Lunch			
12:15-3:15 Facilitator helps team create Integrated Scorecard	• Establish initial team goals, metrics, and benchmarks	• What are the team's challenges? • What does the team need to accomplish? • How will it track progress?	• Team Scorecard (p. 257)
3:15-3:30 Break			
3:30-4:15 Facilitator helps team review decisions and deliverables	• Review the session decisions and deliverables • Review details for next team meeting	• What did the team decide? • What does the team need to get done before the next session? • Who owns these deliverables? • When is the next team meeting?	
4:15-4:45 Closing remarks by team leader	• Key messages to communicate back to the business • Session pluses and minuses • Provide encouragement to participants	• What will the team tell the rest of the organization about the meeting? • What went well during the session? • What would make the next session even better?	

Facilitator's Agenda for Session 2

Time	Objectives	Key Questions	Activities and Materials
8:00-8:15 Opening remarks by team leader	• Outline objectives of the session • Review rules of engagement	• What do we need to accomplish at the off-site?	• Flip Chart
8:15-9:00 Facilitator leads deliverables review	• Get status update on deliverables from the last session	• What was accomplished since the last session?	• Deliverables Status Slides
9:00-9:15 Break			
9:15-10:45 Facilitator helps team review and finalize Team Scorecard	• Finalize team goals, metrics, and benchmarks	• What are the team's challenges? • What does the team need to accomplish? • How will it track progress?	• Team Scorecard Slides and Handouts
10:45-12:00 Facilitator helps team update Integrated Action Plan	• Review integrated plan that combines key initiatives for Marketing, Sales, Operations, Maintenance, Finance, and HR	• What did we accomplish last month? • Where do we need to do something different?	• Integrated Action Plan Slides and Handouts
12:00-12:45 Lunch			
12:45-2:30 Facilitator helps team solve high-priority issues	• Develop solutions to the top two problems emerging from Team Scorecard and Action Plan	• Where are the highest-priority issues for the business? • What will we do about these problems? • Who owns the solution? • What metrics will change as a result of these solutions?	• Flip Charts
2:30-2:45 Break			
2:45-4:00 Facilitator helps team create set of team Norms	• Establish rules for having an enterprise mindset, communication, accountability, and resolving conflict	• How should team members view business issues? • How should team members treat each other? • What happens if rules get violated?	• Team Norms (p. 303)
4:00-5:00 Facilitator asks team members to commit to team success	• Make public commitments to help the team operate at a higher level	• What will people keep doing to help the team succeed? • What will people start, stop, or do differently to help the team succeed? • How should team members be held accountable for their commitments?	• Personal Commitments (p. 347)

Time	Objectives	Key Questions	Activities and Materials
5:00-5:30 Facilitator helps team review decisions and deliverables	• Review session decisions and deliverables • Review details for next team meeting	• What did the team decide? • What does the team need to get done before the next session? • Who owns these deliverables? • When is the next team meeting?	
5:30-6:00 Closing remarks by team leader	• Key messages to communicate back to the business • Session pluses and minuses • Provide encouragement to participants	• What will the team tell the rest of the organization about the meeting? • What went well during the session? • What would make the next session even better?	

Facilitator's Agenda for Session 3

Time	Objectives	Key Questions	Activities and Materials
8:00-8:15 Opening remarks by team leader	• Outline objectives of the session • Review rules of engagement	• What do we need to accomplish at the off-site?	• Flip Chart
8:15-9:00 Facilitator leads deliverables review	• Get status update on deliverables from the last session	• What was accomplished since the last session?	• Deliverables Status Slides
9:00-9:15 Break			
9:15-10:45 Facilitator helps team review Team Scorecard	• Get status update on team goals, metrics, and benchmarks	• What did the team accomplish? • What is working well? • Where is the team falling short?	• Team Scorecard Slides and Handouts
10:45-12:00 Facilitator helps team update Integrated Action Plan	• Review integrated plan that combines key initiatives for Marketing, Sales, Operations, Maintenance, Finance, and HR	• What did we accomplish last month? • Where do we need to do something different?	• Integrated Action Plan Slides and Handouts
12:00-12:45 Lunch			
12:45-2:30 Facilitator helps team solve high-priority issues	• Develop solutions to the top two problems emerging from Team Scorecard and Action Plan	• Where are the highest-priority issues for the business? • What will we do about these problems? • Who owns the solution? • What metrics will change as a result of these solutions?	• Flip Charts
2:30-2:45 Break			

Time	Objectives	Key Questions	Activities and Materials
2:45-4:00 Facilitator helps team clarify decision-making rights for team members	• Establish rules for making team, sub-team, and individual decisions	• What decisions should be made by the team? Sub-teams? Individuals? People below the team? • Who should be involved, how should these decisions be made, and who is the final decision maker?	• Decision-Making (p. 315)
4:00-4:45 Facilitator helps team review decisions, deliverables, and Norms	• Review the session decisions and deliverables • Review details for next team meeting	• What did the team decide? • What does the team need to get done before the next session? • Who owns these deliverables? • When is the next team meeting? • How is the team doing against team Norms?	• Team Norms; Post-Exercise Activity (p. 303)
4:45-5:15 Closing remarks by team leader	• Key messages to communicate back to the business • Session pluses and minuses • Provide encouragement to participants	• What will the team tell the rest of the organization about the meeting? • What went well during the session? • What would make the next session even better?	

Facilitator's Agenda for Session 4

Time	Objectives	Key Questions	Activities and Materials
8:00-8:15 Opening remarks by team leader	• Outline objectives of the session • Review rules of engagement	• What do we need to accomplish at the off-site?	• Flip Chart
8:15-9:00 Director of operations leads deliverables review	• Get status update on deliverables from the last session	• What was accomplished since the last session?	• Deliverables Status Slides
9:00-9:15 Break			
9:15-10:45 Director of finance leads Team Scorecard review	• Get status update on team goals, metrics, and benchmarks	• What did the team accomplish? • What is working well? • Where is the team falling short?	• Team Scorecard Slides and Handouts
10:45-12:00 Director of engineering leads Team Integrated Action Plan review	• Review integrated plan that combines key initiatives for Marketing, Sales, Operations, Maintenance, Finance, and HR	• What did we accomplish last month? • Where do we need to do something different?	• Integrated Action Plan Slides and Handouts
12:00-12:45 Lunch			

Time	Objectives	Key Questions	Activities and Materials
12:45-2:30 Director of sales leads team problem-solving session	• Develop solutions to the top two problems emerging from Team Scorecard and Action Plan	• Where are the highest-priority issues for the business? • What will we do about these problems? • Who owns the solutions? • What metrics will change as a result of these solutions?	• Flip Charts
2:30-2:45 Break			
2:45-4:45 Facilitator helps team share Journey Lines	• Understand how past experiences shape current behavior	• What have been team members' key formulating experiences? • What did they learn from these experiences? • How do these experiences affect how they lead and interact with others?	• Journey Lines (p. 333)
4:45-5:30 Team leader helps team review decisions, deliverables, and Norms	• Review session decisions and deliverables • Review details for next team meeting	• What did the team decide? • What does the team need to get done before the next session? • Who owns these deliverables? • When is the next team meeting? • How is the team doing against team Norms?	• Team Norms; Post-Exercise Activity (p. 303)
5:30-6:00 Closing remarks by team leader	• Key messages to communicate back to the business • Session pluses and minuses • Provide encouragement to participants	• What will the team tell the rest of the organization about the meeting? • What went well during the session? • What would make the next session even better?	
6:00-8:00 Team dinner	• Provide informal time for socializing		

Facilitator's Agenda for Session 5, Day 1

Time	Objectives	Key Questions	Activities and Materials
8:00-8:15 Opening remarks by team leader	• Outline objectives of the session • Review rules of engagement	• What do we need to accomplish at the off-site?	• Flip Chart
8:15-9:00 Director of operations leads deliverables review	• Get status update on deliverables from the last session	• What was accomplished since the last session?	• Deliverables Status Slides

Time	Objectives	Key Questions	Activities and Materials
9:00-9:15 Break			
9:15-10:45 Director of finance leads Team Scorecard review	• Get status update on team goals, metrics, and benchmarks	• What did the team accomplish? • What is working well? • Where is the team falling short?	• Team Scorecard Slides and Handouts
10:45-12:00 Director of engineering leads Team Integrated Action Plan review	• Review integrated plan that combines key initiatives for Marketing, Sales, Operations, Maintenance, Finance, and HR	• What did we accomplish last month? • Where do we need to do something different?	• Integrated Action Plan Slides and Handouts
12:00-12:45 Lunch			
12:45-2:30 Director of sales leads team problem-solving session	• Develop solutions to the top two problems emerging from Team Scorecard and Action Plan	• Where are the highest-priority issues for the business? • What will we do about these problems? • Who owns the solutions? • What metrics will change as a result of these solutions?	• Flip Charts
2:30-2:45 Break			
2:45-4:15 Facilitator leads Team Feedback Session	• Gain consensus on the team's strengths and areas of improvement	• How does this team compare to other teams? • How has it changed over the past six months? • What are this team's strengths? • What are the team's biggest challenges?	• TAS Feedback Report • Team Feedback Session (p. 227)
4:15-5:45 Facilitator helps team clarify Context	• Gain alignment on the situation facing the team • Gain alignment on the team's key challenges	• Who are the team's key stakeholders? What are they likely to do in the next 12 months? • Who are the team's key influencers? What are they likely to do in the next 12 months? • What are the team's top challenges for the next year?	• Context Assessment Exercise (p. 237)
6:00-8:00 Team dinner	• Provide informal time for socializing		

Facilitator's Agenda for Session 5, Day 2

Time	Objectives	Key Questions	Activities and Materials
8:00-8:15 Opening remarks by team leader	• Outline objectives of the session • Review rules of engagement	• What do we need to accomplish at the off-site?	• Flip Chart
8:15-11:45 Directors of marketing and finance lead strategic planning discussion	• Understand the strategic planning process • Set business goals for the next year • Make strategic choices • Identify key cross-functional and functional initiatives	• What will we do next year? • What will we not do next year? • How are we defining success? • What are our major initiatives for the next year? • What are the budget implications for the strategic plan?	• Strategic Planning Slides • Flip Charts
11:45-12:30 Lunch			
12:30-2:45 (cont.) Directors of marketing and finance lead strategic planning discussion	• Understand the strategic planning process • Set business goals for the next year • Make strategic choices • Identify key cross-functional and functional initiatives	• What will we do next year? • What will we not do next year? • How are we defining success? • What are our major initiatives for the next year? • What are the budget implications for the strategic plan?	• Strategic Planning Slides • Flip Charts
2:45-3:00 Break			
3:00-4:00 Facilitator leads discussion on Personal and Team Learning	• Clarify what team members have learned over the past six months • Clarify what the team has learned over the past six months	• What did you personally learn over the past six months? • How has the team changed and what has it learned over the past six months?	• Personal and Team Learning (p. 373)
4:00-4:45 Team leader helps team review decisions and deliverables	• Review session decisions and deliverables • Review details for next team meeting	• What did the team decide? • What does the team need to get done before the next session? • Who owns these deliverables? • When is the next team meeting?	
4:45-5:15 Closing remarks by team leader	• Key messages to communicate back to the business • Session pluses and minuses • Provide encouragement to participants	• What will the team tell the rest of the organization about the meeting? • What went well during the session? • What would make the next session even better?	

Chapter 6

Combining Teams

Marco was a high-potential leader with a gift for engendering loyalty, building teams, and delivering the numbers. Still early in his career, he had already established a successful track record by growing the North American division of a European defense contractor. But when a reorganization to grow revenues and reduce costs gave him responsibility for leading a newly combined division of North American and European facilities, he struggled to get the new leadership team to gel.

The newly formed Executive Leadership Team (ELT) consisted of four Americans—Marco and the vice presidents of sales, maintenance, human resources, and legal, and four Europeans—the vice presidents of manufacturing, distribution, IT, and finance. Even though everyone on the team worked for the same company, they spoke different languages, literally and figuratively.

Team members' views of context were naturally influenced by where they sat, and they had different expectations of how the team should communicate, make decisions, and manage conflict. As might be expected, team members struggled to shift their loyalties to the new global team. Faced with these challenges, Marco hired a leadership coach. We helped Marco by conducting a diagnosis to see where the team was getting stuck and coaching him through the steps needed to turn his team around.

THINGS TO CONSIDER WHEN COMBINING TEAMS

According to multiple research studies collated by Harvard Business Review, the failure rate for mergers and acquisitions exceeds 70%. That statistic probably doesn't surprise anyone who's lived through an M&A. On a smaller scale, our experience indicates the failure rate for merging two teams is equally dismal.

Successfully integrating two teams into one high-performing team is extraordinarily difficult, in part due to the low base rate of effective teams. If the probability of *one* team being high performing is only 20%, then the probability of *both* teams being high performing is only 4%. Add to those sobering odds the fact that organizational change tends to add stress, increase dysfunction, and lower performance, and you are faced with almost impossible odds.

Even when starting with two healthy, high-functioning teams, merging them into one high-performing team is tough for several reasons. For one, among successful teams, members strongly identify with the team; they buy into the Mission, their activities are driven by well-defined goals, team Norms dictate how they get work done and get along, and team members know how they fit into the equation. When teams are merged, team members cling to the identity of their first team because the newly formed team has no real sense of unity. Also, when teams merge, there is often a dynamic of winners and losers. Individuals who previously felt like they were part of a winning team may now feel like they're losing. People don't know how they fit in and whether their skills and experiences add value or are expendable in comparison to others on the team. Third, in times of change, political jockeying tends to increase while trust decreases. In the worst-case scenario, team members may even work to sabotage the success of the newly merged team. These issues rarely go away on their own.

The Rocket Model provides a sound framework of necessary components for developing a high-performing team post-merger:

- *Context:* Establishing a common view of the situation, the challenges facing the combined team, and the rationale for the team merger.
- *Mission:* Defining the new team's purpose, goals, and plans.
- *Talent:* Examining Talent (redundancies, gaps) given the team's new Mission, clarifying roles and responsibilities, and identifying and dealing with team members who are struggling to accept the change (and perhaps engaging in poor followership behaviors).

- *Norms:* Leaving behind old ways of working and agreeing on how the new team will handle meetings, communication, decision-making, accountability, and the like.
- *Buy-In:* Building loyalty to the new team and confidence in its ability to succeed.
- *Resources:* Determining the ways in which pooling resources across teams can be beneficial.
- *Courage:* Understanding there will be some level of mutual distrust on newly combined teams. It will take time to create an environment where people feel safe challenging each other's ideas, especially across old team boundaries.
- *Results:* Investing considerable team leader energy to focus the new team on winning and learning *together* and getting past the disruptive aftershocks of the change.

DIAGNOSIS

Because this was a newly formed team, we felt its members had not spent enough time together to complete a Team Assessment Survey (TAS), and that interviewing team members was more likely to yield actionable insights. We interviewed all eight members and summarized what we heard in a Team Interview Summary (TIS), which was first shared with Marco and used to guide the design of the sessions.

As expected, Context was a major stumbling block. The American business was dependent on four large customers, whereas the European business was spread evenly cross 40 customers. Geopolitical, regulatory, and competitive realities were also in stark contrast across the two regions. A top priority was helping everyone understand both perspectives, then building a common, global view of the business.

The two regions also operated under radically different Norms. The Europeans were more consensus oriented in their decision-making, whereas the Americans preferred speed over consensus. Values used to make decisions also differed. The Europeans placed a higher value on quality, reputation, and long-term partnerships, whereas the Americans emphasized revenues, profitability, and transactional relationships with customers. They had different approaches to meeting frequency, length, and agendas. Highlighting those differences—all of which had worked well for the separate teams in the past—and establishing how the newly combined team wanted to work together moving ahead was also a high priority.

Buy-In varied greatly across the two regions. Because Marco was the first American to lead this part of the business, the Europeans experienced a sense of loss. They worked for a European company but now reported to an American.

Excerpt From the TIS

Talent. A successful team needs the knowledge and capabilities needed to accomplish goals. In addition to having the right expertise, team members need to be effective team players. High-performing teams are the right size, are organized to optimize team performance, and have clear roles and responsibilities.

High-performing teams say	Observations of this team
- We have the right number of people. - The team has the right organizational/reporting structure. - We have clear roles, responsibilities, and accountabilities. - The team has the right mix of skills and experience. - Everyone on the team is an effective team player.	- The team's size and structure seem appropriate. - There is a diverse slate of talent, and all bring unique knowledge and experience to the team. - There is a high degree of uncertainty about team members' roles. Who is responsible for that? - There is a lot of jockeying going on among team members. - Some are not happy with the reorganization.

Norms. Norms include formal processes and procedures as well as the informal rules teams use to get work done. Effective teams ensure their norms help (rather than hinder) team performance. Important norms include how the team conducts meetings, makes decisions, keeps members informed, and holds members accountable.

High-performing teams say	Observations of this team
- Team meetings make effective and efficient use of time. - We spend enough time working on proactive versus reactive issues. - We use effective decision-making processes that result in sound, timely decisions. - We communicate with each other openly and directly; gossiping rarely happens. - Team members are held accountable for their attitudes, behaviors, and deliverables. - We periodically take a step back and find ways to work together more effectively.	- Who should be involved in decisions? Who gets to make final decisions? - There is little ownership or accountability for results on the new team. - Team members are not proactively reaching out when things start to go south. There is a tendency to wait too long before asking for help. - Face-to-face interaction is important to some members of the team. - The team needs to establish a formal meeting schedule. - What are the rules guiding team behavior?

SOLUTION

We cautioned Marco about the effort and time it would take to get the newly combined team performing at a high level. Over the next several months, he would need to help the team create a common view of its challenges, clarify the team purpose and rules, and establish an environment where team members felt empowered to speak their minds. He would also need to hold everyone accountable for adhering to the team's agreements about its deliverables and Norms. Even beyond the start-up phase, Marco would need to be diligent about keeping the team on track and not backsliding. To achieve these ends, we facilitated the first session to get the combined team going. We then coached Marco and some of the members of his team on how to facilitate the different team improvement activities, the outcomes to be achieved, and why they were important for Sessions 2-4.

Marco opened the first off-site by sharing his expectations for the session and asking others to also share their hopes and fears. Then he talked about his vision for the team and encouraged a robust discussion of the team's reactions. Next, he walked the team through the Rocket Model, emphasizing its widespread use among European companies. He led the team through exercises to address the Context, Mission, and Buy-In components.

Sessions 2, 3, and 4 were half-day sessions tacked on to monthly ELT meetings. Marco ran Session 2, which involved finalizing the Team Scorecard and creating a Team Action Plan. Two members of the ELT led Roles and Responsibilities Matrix and Decision-Making activities in Session 3, and two different members led the team Norms and Operating Rhythm activities in Session 4. These sessions helped the team refine its purpose, goals, and plans; ensured the team put these insights into practice while working to address significant business challenges; led to the creation of new Norms; built trust; allowed Marco to develop select team members; and boosted Buy-In by allowing Marco to lead from behind.

THREE MONTHS			
Session 1	**Session 2**	**Session 3**	**Session 4**
• Opening Remarks • Leader's Vision and Feedback • Dream vs. Nightmare Teams • Rocket Model Overview • Review TIS • Context Assessment Exercise • Team Purpose • Team Scorecard • Journey Lines • Closing Remarks • Team Dinner	• Team Scorecard • Team Action Planning	• Roles and Responsibilities Matrix • Decision-Making	• Team Norms • Operating Rhythm

ACCOUNTABILITY MECHANISMS

Given the geographic dispersion and different worldviews, goals, roles, and Norms of the previous teams, it would be easy for this ELT to backslide into old behaviors. Marco helped the team agree on how they would hold themselves accountable for sticking to new ways of operating. This included reviewing session deliverables, the Team Scorecard, and Action Plan progress at the beginning of monthly meetings; evaluating team Norms at the end of monthly meetings; and completing a TAS four months after the initial session.

OUTCOME

The Team Effectiveness Quotient (TQ) score from the TAS results four months after the initial session was 43, which was reasonable given the newness of the ELT. Everyone felt good about the team Context, Mission, and Resources, but more work needed to be done to further clarify roles and responsibilities, decision-making rights, and communication Norms; deal with a bad follower who was not fitting in with the new team; and complete monthly deliverables and Action Plan activities. At the four-month point, it was too soon to tell whether the team was having any impact on the business unit's overall revenues or costs, but the ELT felt that the Team Scorecard and Action Plan, if fully realized, would yield the intended results.

CONCLUDING COMMENTS

The designs for helping other combined teams may look very different than the one outlined here. Team leaders and facilitators will be on the right path if their designs help combined teams develop a shared perspective; gain consensus on the team's purpose, goals, and plans; clarify team members' new roles; establish rules for working together; and put mechanisms in place to track progress on goals and adherence to commitments.

Facilitator's Agenda for Session 1

Time	Objectives	Key Questions	Activities and Materials
8:00-8:45 Team leader's vision and feedback	• Describe where the two businesses have been • Describe potential strengths and liabilities of the new business unit • Describe where the business needs to go and how it will get there • Get reactions and answer questions about the vision	• What is the vision for the business unit? • What are the expectations for ELT members? • What are the ELT's reactions to the vision? • What questions does the ELT have about the vision?	• Vision Statement (p. 247)
8:45-9:00 Facilitator leads Dream vs. Nightmare Teams exercise	• Engage participants in discussion about effective vs. ineffective teams • Ask participants about the prevalence of effective teams	• What are the characteristics of nightmare teams? Dream teams? • How common are dream teams? • How do you make dream teams happen?	• Dream vs. Nightmare Teams (p. 201)
9:00-9:30 Facilitator reviews Rocket Model	• Familiarize participants with eight components of effective team performance	• What does the team need to do to operate effectively?	• Rocket Model Slide Deck (p. 209)
9:30-9:45 Break			
9:45-11:00 Facilitator runs Team Feedback Session and TIS	• Provide teams with qualitative information about team functioning and performance	• What are the team's strengths, surprises, and areas of improvement?	• Team Feedback Session (p. 227) • TIS
11:00-12:15 Facilitator leads discussion of team Context	• Help team members understand diversity of perspectives on the team • Get everyone on the same page about stakeholder expectations and contextual issues facing the team	• What do stakeholders expect from the team? • What external factors affect the team? • What are the team's biggest challenges?	• Context Assessment Exercise (p. 237)
12:15-1:00 Lunch			

Time	Objectives	Key Questions	Activities and Materials
1:00–2:00 Facilitator leads discussion about Team Purpose	• Create shared understanding of why the team exists	• Why does the team exist?	• Team Purpose (p. 253)
2:00–3:45 Facilitator leads group through exercise to draft Team Scorecard	• Translate high-level goals into specific deliverables • Establish benchmarks for measuring team performance	• What are the meaningful and measurable goals for the team? • How does the team define winning?	• Team Scorecard (p. 257)
3:45–4:00 Break			
4:00–5:45 Facilitator leads group through Journey Lines	• Help team members learn about each other • Begin building camaraderie and trust	• What life experiences have shaped each team member?	• Journey Lines (p. 333)
5:45–6:00 Closing remarks by team leader	• Review what the team accomplished during the day	• What progress did we make today? • What do we need to get done at the next meeting?	
6:30–8:30 Team dinner	• Provide informal time for socializing		

Team Leader's Agenda for Session 2

Time	Objectives	Key Questions	Activities and Materials
8:00–8:05 Opening remarks by team leader and reflection	• Outline objectives of the session	• What do we need to accomplish at the session?	• Flip Chart
8:05–9:45 Team leader helps team finalize Mission	• Finalize Team Purpose, goals, and metrics	• What are the team's challenges? • Why does the team exist? • What does the team need to accomplish? • How will it track progress?	• Context Flip Charts • Team Purpose Flip Charts • Team Scorecard Flip Charts
9:45–10:00 Break			
10:00–11:45 Facilitator helps group create Action Plan	• Create a monthly plan that will drive the Team Scorecard	• How should the team achieve its goals? • What does the team need to accomplish each month? • What are the bottlenecks to getting work done? • Who is responsible for what?	• Team Action Plan (p. 261)
11:45–12:00 Closing remarks by team leader	• Leave the off-site with a common message • Session pluses and minuses • Provide encouragement to participants	• What are the key messages coming out of the off-site? How will they get communicated? • How did the session go? • What would make the next session even better?	

Team Member's Agenda for Session 3

Time	Objectives	Key Questions	Activities and Materials
8:00–8:05 Opening remarks by team member	• Outline objectives of the session • Set expectations for participation • Review session agenda • Review session ground rules	• What do we need to accomplish at the session?	• Flip Chart
8:05–9:45 Team member runs Roles and Responsibilities Matrix	• Clarify owners, task assignments, and workload balances for team members	• Who owns each of the action steps in the Team Action Plan? • What other team activities need owners (e.g., setting up and running team meetings, etc.)?	• Roles and Responsibilities Matrix (p. 265)
9:45–10:00 Break			

Time	Objectives	Key Questions	Activities and Materials
10:00-11:30 Team member helps clarify decision-making rights for team members	• Review and revise which topics need to be decided by the ELT • Review and revise rules for making team, sub-team, and individual decisions	• What decisions should be made by the team? Sub-teams? Individuals? People below the team? • Who should be involved, how should these decisions be made, and who is the final decision maker?	• Decision-Making (p. 315)
11:30-11:45 Closing remarks by team members	• Review session deliverables • Review details for next team meeting • Provide encouragement to participants • Session pluses and minuses	• What does the team need to get done before the next meeting? • Who owns these deliverables? • When is the next team meeting? • Who is running the meeting? • What worked well during the session? • What does the team need to do differently at the next session?	

Team Member's Agenda for Session 4

Time	Objectives	Key Questions	Activities and Materials
8:00-8:05 Opening remarks by team member	• Outline objectives of the session • Set expectations for participation • Review session agenda • Review session ground rules	• What do we need to accomplish at the session?	• Flip Chart
8:05-9:45 Team member helps team set up an Operating Rhythm	• Determine the frequency, timing, and rules for team meetings	• When should the team meet? • What should it talk about? • Who runs the meetings? • What are the rules during meetings?	• Operating Rhythm (p. 307)
9:45-10:00 Break			
10:00-11:30 Team member helps team set Norms	• Clarify rules for how team members will interact and communicate	• What are the team's rules? • What are the expectations around communication, assignments, and how team members treat each other?	• Team Norms (p. 303)
11:30-11:45 Closing remarks by team members	• Review session deliverables • Review details for the next team meeting • Session pluses and minuses	• What does the team need to get done before the next meeting? • Who owns these deliverables? • When is the next team meeting? • Who is running the meeting? • What worked well during the session? • What does the team need to do differently at the next session?	

Chapter 7

Virtual Teams

We recently worked with a virtual team responsible for corporate and brand communications. Ironically, they struggled with communication. Five of the nine members worked from corporate headquarters in Toronto, two were in the US, one was in the UK, and two, including the team leader, were based in Germany. The team had been created 12 months earlier as part of a larger reorganization. Although everyone on the team knew each other, the entire team had not met face-to-face since its inception due to budget constraints.

During our initial call with the team leader, she informed us that the team was six weeks behind schedule in delivering a revamp of the corporate website, its employee engagement scores were among the lowest in the company, and two team members had gone to HR to request a transfer out of the team. We also learned that the team had been so focused on meeting its aggressive goals that members hadn't wasted time on any of that team-building stuff. We reassured the team leader that we were there to improve performance, not to waste time on anything superficial. When we started talking about the off-site, we also discovered that the company had put a hold on all discretionary travel so our work with them needed to be conducted virtually.

VIRTUAL TEAM CONSIDERATIONS

Twenty years ago, virtual teams were the exception; now technology has enabled most teams to have one or more members working remotely. In today's global organizations, this often means working internationally and cross-culturally. (Although we would argue that teams mixing Manhattanites and Mississippians is as cross-cultural as mixing Canadians and Columbians.) As we've discussed in the previous chapters, high-performing teams are the exception to the rule, but high-performing virtual teams are an even bigger exception.

The Rocket Model components that are especially difficult for virtual teams to get right include:

- *Context:* People from different locations can be worlds apart in how they view the team's stakeholders and challenges because they literally see and hear different information daily.
- *Talent:* With fewer opportunities to observe team members and give real-time feedback, leaders often struggle to coach and develop remote team members. Hiring remote team members also proves challenging.
- *Norms:* Communication, decision-making, meeting management, and accountability mechanisms are tricky for virtual teams. E-mails and text messages strip out important nonverbal signals, which increases the odds of misinterpretation. Language and cultural differences can compound the problem. Finding meeting times that work for everyone can be downright impossible for teams spanning multiple continents. And let's be honest, multitasking during meetings is worse when no one is watching.
- *Buy-In:* First-team loyalty, or the team to which members most closely identify, is a common stumbling block for virtual teams because members are pulled between the people they see every day (their regional counterparts) and their teammates, whom they see infrequently or not at all. Distance does *not* make the heart grow fonder.
- *Resources:* When some of the team sits in a resource-rich location, and others sit in the hinterlands, uneven access to resources can breed resentment and hamper a team's performance. In addition, virtual teams are more reliant on technology to support their communication, meetings, and productivity.
- *Courage:* Different cultures take different approaches to expressing disagreement. Some are direct and straightforward, others are subtle. Mix

the two styles together and you rarely get good results. In addition, when team members don't spend time together or know each other well, creating an environment where everyone feels safe challenging each other's ideas is a tall order.

DIAGNOSIS

TAS Results

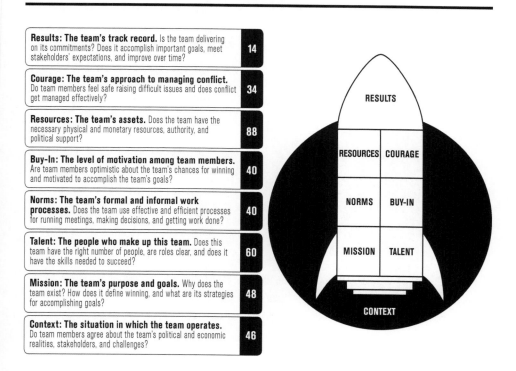

Results: The team's track record. Is the team delivering on its commitments? Does it accomplish important goals, meet stakeholders' expectations, and improve over time?	14
Courage: The team's approach to managing conflict. Do team members feel safe raising difficult issues and does conflict get managed effectively?	34
Resources: The team's assets. Does the team have the necessary physical and monetary resources, authority, and political support?	88
Buy-In: The level of motivation among team members. Are team members optimistic about the team's chances for winning and motivated to accomplish the team's goals?	40
Norms: The team's formal and informal work processes. Does the team use effective and efficient processes for running meetings, making decisions, and getting work done?	40
Talent: The people who make up this team. Does this team have the right number of people, are roles clear, and does it have the skills needed to succeed?	60
Mission: The team's purpose and goals. Why does the team exist? How does it define winning, and what are its strategies for accomplishing goals?	48
Context: The situation in which the team operates. Do team members agree about the team's political and economic realities, stakeholders, and challenges?	46

We administered the Team Assessment Survey (TAS) and interviewed all nine members of the team. During our discovery, we found two bright spots. First, the team's Talent score was relatively high. Digging in to the item-level data and interviews, we learned the team had the right skills, and roles and responsibilities were clear, but followership was uneven. Second, the team was not Resource constrained. In fact, this was their highest score. As tempting as it might be, they couldn't blame their lack of performance on insufficient Resources.

Other than that, they struggled. The four members at corporate head-quarters had a different view of stakeholder priorities than those who worked remotely. The two members in the US were team-killers, doing their best to drag everyone down. Because the six North American team members were in the same time zone, they frequently scheduled meetings that required their European counterparts to work in the evening. Because the Canadians, Americans, British, and Germans had vastly different styles of communicating, they often misread each other's intentions. In one instance, a Canadian team member thought she had been very direct in providing constructive feedback to her German colleague who had heard nothing but praise, and consequently ignored the advice. Team members in Toronto had more loyalty to colleagues in the same city than to the team and were often pulled off-task to help on other projects. Conflict was not constructive, and members blamed each other for the team failing to deliver the new website on time.

SOLUTION

Prior to the team sessions, the leader had a heart-to-heart with the two team-killers. One decided to leave the team, and the other committed to turning over a new leaf. We then started working with the team.

To accommodate the need to work virtually and time zone challenges, we advised the team to set up a series of nine monthly online meeting sessions with homework assigned between sessions. Prior to the first session, we sent everyone the TAS Feedback Report, Team Interview Survey (TIS), and a short article about the Rocket Model. In the first monthly online meeting session, the team leader provided some opening remarks stating that the team was on a journey and would be doing a series of activities over the next nine months to improve overall function and performance. We then did a quick overview of the Rocket Model, TAS Feedback Report, TIS, and broke into three-person sub-teams to identify what members saw as the team's strengths, weaknesses, and which results surprised them the most. The sub-teams held separate 45-minute online meeting sessions and got back on the large group online meeting to share virtual flip charts of their findings. The ensuing discussion helped clarify team development priorities and the activities to work on over the next eight sessions:

Month 1	Team Feedback Session: TAS and TIS
Month 2	Context: Context Assessment Exercise
Month 3	Mission: Team Purpose
Month 4	Mission: Team Scorecard
Month 5	Talent: Roles and Responsibilities
Month 6	Norms: Operating Rhythm and Master Calendar
Month 7	Norms: Communication and Accountability
Month 8	Buy-In: First-Team Loyalty and Personal Commitments
Month 9	Team Feedback Session (Time 2 TAS)

We also led the Month 2 session involving the Context Assessment exercise, and a team member was made responsible for consolidating the exercise results and sharing with the rest of the team for additional comments. Starting with the Month 3 session, we shifted our role from team facilitator to team coach. The team leader and a designated team member would read the instructions and associated support materials for the next month's team improvement activity. We then organized one-hour phone calls with the team leader and team member to review how to set up and facilitate the team improvement activity, answer questions, and discuss post-activity deliverables prior to the online meeting for Sessions 3-9. Different team members were responsible for leading the monthly team improvement activities, which fostered Buy-In and allowed the team leader to develop her staff and spend more time leading from behind. A second TAS was administered and the team leader reviewed the results with the team at the Month 9 session.

ACCOUNTABILITY MECHANISMS

Team members were responsible for creating electronic copies of team improvement activity results and circulating among the team prior to the next session. Sessions began with a review of this work to foster team engagement. The team also decided to complete a second TAS after the eighth monthly session to confirm team progress.

OUTCOME

The team delivered on all its major objectives and enjoyed much higher TAS scores for Context, Mission, Norms, and Results nine months later. Talent, Buy-In, and Courage also improved, but not to the same extent as the other Rocket Model components. The team still had issues with first-team loyalty, challenging each other in team meetings, and Talent shortfalls involving social media marketing.

CONCLUDING COMMENTS

Technology is allowing virtual teams to become increasingly commonplace, but organizations need to realize that virtual teams are much more challenging to lead than co-located teams. Building remote relationships, hiring and developing team members, establishing Norms, securing Resources, establishing psychological safety, and gaining Buy-In is more difficult with virtual teams, and it is easier for leaders to miss early warning signals of teams in trouble. It also takes more time and dedicated leadership attention to get virtual teams back on track. For this reason, we prefer to incorporate at least one face-to-face session in our work with virtual teams. We recognize there are times when budgets simply don't permit travel, but one or two days of face-to-face time with virtual team members can go a long way toward establishing relationships, common worldviews, and agreed-upon goals, roles, and rules.

Facilitator's Agenda for Session 1

Time	Objectives	Key Questions	Activities and Materials
15 minutes Opening remarks by team leader	• Outline objectives of the session • Set expectations for participation • Review the day's agenda • Set meeting ground rules	• What do we need to accomplish during the meeting?	
30 minutes Facilitator reviews Rocket Model	• Familiarize participants with the eight components of effective team performance	• What does the team need to do to operate effectively?	• Rocket Model Slide Deck (p. 209)
3 hours Facilitator runs Team Feedback Session—TAS and TIS	• Provide teams with benchmarking information about team functioning and performance	• How does our team compare to other teams? • What are our team's strengths, surprises, and areas of improvement?	• Team Feedback Session (p. 227) • TAS Feedback Report • TIS
15 minutes Concluding comments by team leader	• Review meeting deliverables • Get feedback on how the session went • Meeting pluses and minuses	• Who is responsible for creating an electronic copy of the team's strengths, surprises, and areas of improvement?	

Facilitator's Agenda for Session 2

Time	Objectives	Key Questions	Activities and Materials
20 minutes Opening remarks by team leader	• Outline objectives of the session • Set expectations for participation • Review the session agenda • Review meeting ground rules	• What do we need to accomplish during the meeting? • What are the comments and reactions to the TAS and interview results from the last session?	
2 hours Facilitator leads discussion of team Context	• Help team members understand the diversity of perspectives on the team • Get everyone on the same page about stakeholder expectations and contextual issues facing the team	• What do stakeholders expect from the team? • What external factors affect the team? • What are the team's biggest challenges?	• Context Assessment Exercise (p. 237)
15 minutes Concluding comments by team leader	• Review meeting deliverables • Get feedback on how the session went • Meeting pluses and minuses	• Who is responsible for creating an electronic copy of the team's stakeholders, influencers, assumptions, and challenges?	

Team Member's Agenda for Session 3

Time	Objectives	Key Questions	Activities and Materials
20 minutes Opening remarks by team member	• Outline objectives of the session • Set expectations for participation • Review the day's agenda • Review meeting ground rules • Get activity updates from team members	• What do we need to accomplish during the meeting? • What are the comments and reactions to the team Context results from the last session?	
1.5 hours Team member leads discussion about Team Purpose	• Create shared understanding of why the team exists	• Why does this team exist?	• Team Purpose (p. 253)
15 minutes Concluding comments by team member	• Review meeting deliverables • Get feedback on how the session went • Meeting pluses and minuses	• Who is responsible for creating an electronic copy of the Team Purpose?	

Team Member's Agenda for Session 4

Time	Objectives	Key Questions	Activities and Materials
20 minutes Opening remarks by team member	• Outline objectives of the session • Set expectations for participation • Review the day's agenda • Review meeting ground rules • Get activity updates from team members	• What do we need to accomplish during the meeting? • What are the comments and reactions to the Team Purpose results from the last session?	
3 hours Team member leads group exercise to draft Team Scorecard	• Translate high-level goals into specific deliverables • Establish benchmarks for measuring the team's performance	• What are the meaningful and measurable goals for the team? • How does the team define winning?	• Team Scorecard (p. 257)
15 minutes Concluding comments by team member	• Review meeting deliverables • Get feedback on how the session went • Meeting pluses and minuses	• Who is responsible for creating an electronic copy of the Team Scorecard?	

Team Member's Agenda for Session 5

Time	Objectives	Key Questions	Activities and Materials
20 minutes Opening remarks by team member	• Outline objectives of the session • Set expectations for participation • Review the day's agenda • Review meeting ground rules	• What do we need to accomplish during the meeting? • What are the comments and reactions to the Team Scorecard results from the last session?	
1.5 hours Team member leads group through Roles and Responsibilities Matrix	• Clarify owners, task assignments, and workload balances for team members	• Who owns each of the action steps in the Team Action Plan? • What other team activities need owners (e.g. setting up and running team meetings, etc.)?	• Roles and Responsibilities Matrix (p. 265)
15 minutes Concluding comments by team member	• Review meeting deliverables • Get feedback on how the session went • Meeting pluses and minuses	• Who is responsible for creating an electronic copy of the team's roles and responsibilities?	

Team Member's Agenda for Session 6

Time	Objectives	Key Questions	Activities and Materials
20 minutes Opening remarks by team member	• Outline objectives of the session • Set expectations for participation • Review the day's agenda • Review meeting ground rules	• What do we need to accomplish during the meeting? • What are the comments and reactions to the Roles and Responsibilities Matrix results from the last session?	
1.5 minutes Team member helps group set up new Operating Rhythm	• Determine the frequency, timing, and rules for team meetings	• When should the team meet? • What should it talk about? • Who runs the meetings? • What are the rules during meetings?	• Operating Rhythm (p. 307)
15 minutes Concluding comments by team member	• Review meeting deliverables • Get feedback on how the session went • Meeting pluses and minuses	• Who is responsible for creating an electronic copy of the team's Operating Rhythm and master calendar?	

Team Member's Agenda for Session 7

Time	Objectives	Key Questions	Activities and Materials
20 minutes Opening remarks by team member	• Outline objectives of the session • Set expectations for participation • Review the day's agenda • Review meeting ground rules	• What do we need to accomplish during the meeting? • What are the comments and reactions to the Operating Rhythm results from the last session?	
1 hour Team member helps group set Communication Norms	• Clarify rules around level of communication, communication modes, response times, etc.	• What information do team members need to get their assigned tasks completed? • How often should information be updated? • How should the information be communicated? • What are expected response times?	• Communication (p. 319)
45 minutes Team member helps group set Accountability Mechanisms	• Clarify expectations for team members	• What are the expectations for team member deliverables? • What are the expectations for team member behavior? • What are the consequences for noncompliance?	• Accountability Mechanisms (p. 323)
10 minutes Concluding comments by team member	• Review meeting deliverables • Get feedback on how the session went • Meeting pluses and minuses	• Who is responsible for creating an electronic copy of the team's communication and accountability rules?	

Team Member's Agenda for Session 8

Time	Objectives	Key Questions	Activities and Materials
30 minutes Opening remarks by team member	• Outline objectives of the session • Set expectations for participation • Review the day's agenda • Review meeting ground rules	• What do we need to accomplish during the meeting? • What are the comments and reactions to the Communication and Accountability results from the last session?	
1 hour Team member asks fellow members to commit to the team's success	• Make public commitments to help the team operate at a higher level	• What will people keep doing to help the team succeed? • What will people start, stop, or do differently to help the team succeed? • How should team members be held accountable for their commitments?	• Personal Commitments (p. 347)
15 minutes Concluding comments by team member	• Review meeting deliverables • Get feedback on how the session went • Meeting pluses and minuses	• Who is responsible for creating an electronic copy of the team's Personal Commitments?	

Team Leader's Agenda for Session 9

Time	Objectives	Key Questions	Activities and Materials
20 minutes Opening remarks by team leader	• Outline objectives of the session • Set expectations for participation • Review the day's agenda • Review meeting ground rules	• What do we need to accomplish during the meeting? • What are the comments and reactions to the Personal Commitments from the last session?	
1.5 to 2 hours Team leader runs a Team Feedback Session—TAS	• Provide teams with benchmarking information about team functioning and performance	• How does our team compare to other teams? • What are our team's strengths, surprises, and areas of improvement? • How has the team changed over time?	• Team Feedback Session (p. 227) • TAS Feedback Report
15 minutes Concluding comments by team leader	• Review meeting deliverables • Get feedback on how the session went • Meeting pluses and minuses	• Who is responsible for creating an electronic copy of the team's strengths, surprises, and areas of improvement? • What are the team's next steps?	

Chapter 8

Teams That Are Really Groups

Jose was excited about his new role as manager of talent acquisition for a midsize plastics company. A former collegiate football player, he believed in the value of teamwork. During the first meetings with his new direct reports, he shared his perspective on teams: "I owe all of my success to teamwork, and I expect all of you to be team players. Teamwork is an immensely powerful force that shows all of us how far-reaching our contributions can be. When we work as a team—each of us individually and all of us collectively—we enjoy greater enthusiasm and, ultimately, greater success." After his inspirational words, heads nodded and everyone smiled politely, then they all went back to filling their assigned job openings.

The five talent acquisition specialists who reported to Jose were assigned to five manufacturing facilities spread out across the United States. Given the demanding nature and hours of the jobs they were working to fill, they recruited in the local markets and only rarely filled positions outside of their assigned regions. Annual turnover in the plants exceeded 35% and a tight labor market made it difficult to achieve time-to-fill goals for hourly employees. Everyone on the team was feeling stressed.

In an effort to boost *esprit de corps*, Jose introduced weekly team activities, such as potlucks and happy hours. He organized team outings one afternoon every month, even paying out of his own pocket for everyone to attend a baseball game together. Jose also increased the frequency and duration of team meetings. Despite his efforts, Jose noticed people continued to work in silos rather than as a team. While everyone sat together, they didn't interact much outside of meetings. Jose didn't see any conflict between team members, just a lack of camaraderie. After six months on the job, Jose was disheartened to receive 360-degree feedback stating that his team-building efforts were largely viewed as a waste of time, and his team's performance on key metrics was headed in the wrong direction.

TEAM VS. GROUP CONSIDERATIONS

In Chapter 2, we introduced the distinction between groups and teams. *Groups* are collections of people who have individual goals, work independently, and are rewarded based on their individual accomplishments. *Teams* have common goals, members work interdependently, and everyone wins or loses together. These differences can be illustrated by comparing golf and soccer teams. The actions of individual golfers generally have little impact on the group they are golfing with; each golfer is trying to shoot the lowest score and achieves reward through individual accomplishments. In contrast, the actions of soccer goalies or midfielders directly affect others on the team; the team's overarching goal is to win the game and individual heroics will matter little if the opposition scores more goals. Asking golfers to operate as a team or soccer players to operate as a group will lead to disastrous results. Although many people assume that teams are better than groups, the nature of the goals and work to be accomplished determines which approach is best.

As discussed in Chapter 2, many teams fall along the Group Versus Team Continuum and have both team and group characteristics. A key question for hybrids is when they should function as a group and when they are better off working as a team. Clarifying collective goals, areas of interdependence, and common rewards determines what plans need to be put in place, how often team members should meet, what they should talk about, how they should communicate with each other, and how progress will be reviewed. Equally important is clarifying deliverables, decision-making rights, communication requirements, and behavioral expectations for team members' individual accountabilities. Hybrids should spend collective time working through team issues; leaders should spend one-on-one time with team members helping them achieve their individual goals.

DIAGNOSIS

Based on our initial call with Jose, we suspected his team was really a group, and this was borne out in the Team Assessment Survey (TAS) Feedback Report. Jose was stunned by the group vs. team TAS results. He viewed his direct reports as a team, whereas they saw themselves more as a group. Jose viewed goals as common across team members, but his direct reports' ratings indicated they were focused on their own individual goals. In further discussion with Jose, we learned that their common goals were merely a combination of individual goals. Jose believed his direct reports needed to work interdependently, but they saw their efforts as fairly independent. We told Jose that this made sense to us. They supported different manufacturing facilities and recruited in different areas of the country so there was little need for collaboration. Jose had a "one for all, and all for one" perspective about the team's fate (perhaps because his own rewards were tied to their overall performance). We pointed out that his direct reports were primarily rewarded for their own efforts. Jose was like many leaders in that he was not in touch with how his team was operating and assumed teams were better than groups.

TAS Group vs. Team Analysis

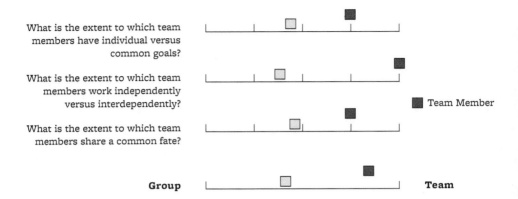

APPROACH TO GOALS

1. People have individual goals. Any common goals are simply a summation of everyone's individual goals.
2. Mostly people have individual goals.
3. People have a mix of individual and overarching or common team goals.
4. Mostly people have common goals, but there are a few individual goals.
5. There are no individual goals, only common goals.

WORK INTERDEPENDENCY

1. People work independently, and one person's actions have little effect on the team.
2. People mostly work independently, but there are a few areas where they work collaboratively.
3. There is an equal mix of activities where people work together versus independently.
4. People mostly work interdependently, but there are a few areas where they work independently.
5. People work interdependently, and what any person does greatly impacts others on this team.

FATE

1. People are rewarded solely on their own results and there are no rewards for team performance.
2. People are primarily rewarded for their own results, but there are some rewards based on team performance.
3. People are greatly rewarded for both their individual and the team's overall results.
4. People are primarily rewarded for the team's results, but there are some rewards based on individual performance.
5. People on this team win or lose together; there are no rewards for individual accomplishments.

After Jose got over his shock, we shared our perspective on the relative merits of groups vs. teams and asked him to consider which approach would produce the best results. Jose thought carefully about his efforts to promote teamwork, the reactions of his team, and their poor results, and said, "I guess we should operate as a group." It was an aha moment. Leaders need to identify whether they are managing a group or a team and adjust their style accordingly.

SOLUTION

During the diagnostic stage, we established that Jose's direct reports were more like a group than a team and that this was appropriate, given the work they needed to accomplish. With this information in mind, we started helping the group operate more effectively.

Using the Rocket Model as our framework, we walked Jose through the following recommendations:

- *Context:* We suggested working through a Context Assessment exercise. Having a shared understanding of organizational priorities, especially the company's plans for expanding manufacturing operations, had implications for all of them, as did macroeconomic and demographic trends. In addition, identifying common challenges would lay the groundwork for sharing best-practice solutions.
- *Mission:* We recommended tracking the group's performance on key metrics, identifying obstacles, and determining which obstacles were best solved across regions versus those that required region-specific solutions. Providing individuals with information about how their performance compared to fellow team members would also yield useful feedback.
- *Talent:* Chemistry isn't as important in groups as it is in teams, so we advised Jose to hire primarily for skills rather than team fit. With everyone sitting together, however, bringing in a team-killer could be very disruptive. To maximize the group's collective performance, it made sense to continue basing rewards on individual rather than group accomplishments.
- *Norms:* We recommended that the group spend time defining the rules by which they worked, starting with what meetings they needed to have and what they needed to cover during the meetings. We

suggested to Jose that the group meet less frequently and that he cut back on the fun activities to give everyone more time to accomplish their individual assignments. His leadership style needed to change from being consensus driven to more hub-and-spoke so that he could provide personalized support to his direct reports. Finally, because the company's values included mutual support, it made sense for the group to identify where they could help each other, even though they worked independently.

- *Buy-In:* The links between their own efforts and goal accomplishment were self-evident, but it was important to tee up a discussion about whether everyone thought their goals were attainable.
- *Courage:* Although Courage tends to be less important in groups than in teams, Jose wanted his team to feel comfortable raising concerns and challenging each other (and him). This point was especially important to Jose because none of his direct reports had raised their concerns with him about his team-building efforts until they could do so via anonymous feedback.
- *Results:* We recommended that the group stay focused on Results and improve their performance by sharing best practices.

After walking Jose through the TAS results and coaching him on group vs. team issues, we designed and facilitated a 1.5-day session that coincided with the kickoff of the team's annual goal-setting and budgeting process. Jose provided an update on where the company was headed over the next year and led a discussion on the talent acquisition implications for the five manufacturing facilities. The team then learned about the differences between groups and teams and how the Rocket Model worked for groups. They reviewed the TAS results, which were generally low except for the Talent and Resources components. These results were not surprising, as groups tend to score lower than teams on the TAS. The team then worked on creating a common view of the situation facing talent acquisition, as well as clarifying the situational challenges at each individual plant. They also spent time setting individual and collective talent acquisition goals, finalizing metrics and benchmarks, and establishing new norms to work together more effectively. The second day was spent updating the team's Operating Rhythm, which involved reducing the number of group meetings but increasing the number of one-on-one meetings with Jose. Time was also spent sharing best talent-recruiting practices for the plants.

1.5 DAYS	
Session 1: Day 1	**Session 1: Day 2**
• Company Update and Discussion • Groups vs. Teams • Rocket Model Overview from a Group Perspective • Team Feedback Session—TAS • Group and Individual Context Assessment • Group and Individual Goals • Team Norms	• Operating Rhythm • Sharing Best Practices

ACCOUNTABILITY MECHANISMS

Jose set the tone for accountability by asking his direct reports to provide a second round of 360-degree feedback six months into the new year. His boss and peer feedback results were still good, but his direct report feedback had greatly improved. His team appreciated the reduction of time spent on team-building activities and the additional support they were getting from Jose in one-on-one meetings. The team also reviewed and discussed individual and collective results at their monthly meetings, and evaluated adherence to team Norms once a quarter.

OUTCOME

As stated in the previous paragraph, by focusing more on groupwork and less on teamwork, Jose was perceived to be a more effective leader. The team started viewing the monthly results as a friendly competition that included a traveling trophy and a free lunch bought by fellow team members. Over time, this reduced the average number of days it took to fill open positions, increased the percentage of hires staying more than six months, and got the team numerous kudos from plant managers and staff about the quality of hires they were bringing into the facilities.

CONCLUDING COMMENTS

Frustration, wasted effort, and poor performance are the result of three common misperceptions about teams and groups. First, the labels team and group are often used interchangeably but, as described in Chapter 2, they represent two distinct methods of working. Second, many people believe teams are inherently superior to groups, but that's not the case. The nature of the work that needs to be accomplished dictates the best approach and pushing teamwork when groupwork is required almost always backfires. Third, leaders assume effective leadership looks the same in every situation, but what it takes to successfully lead a team is different from what it takes to lead a group. Few leadership development programs teach the distinction between leading groups versus teams.

There are several other important observations about teams and groups. First, some leaders lead their teams like groups, which is the converse of Jose's situation, but equally problematic. When leaders over-index on leading groups, they insert themselves into the center of team activities and interfere with team members effectively working together. Leaders may think they are adding value by coordinating team member communication and efforts, but the hub-and-spoke leadership model reduces efficiency, disempowers team members, and causes collective performance to suffer with teams. Second, even though Jose's direct reports all sat together and reported to the same boss, they functioned more as a group than a team. This is the opposite of many of the teams we encounter whose members are functionally or geographically dispersed, yet need to operate as a team. What makes a collection of people a team or a group is not where they're located, but the nature of their goals and how they get things done. Third, pure groups or teams are rare; most often people who work together fall somewhere in the middle of the continuum. A key for many leaders is identifying those issues where direct reports need to work as a team and those where a group approach is more effective.

Finally, we believe the distinction between groups and teams is a big deal, and leaders who fail to take these differences into account do so at their own peril. Failure to recognize and adjust for the differences between groups and teams is one reason leaders fail and so few teams become high performing. A summary of how the Rocket Model applies to groups and teams follows below.

Considerations for Groups vs. Teams

Components	Considerations for Groups	Considerations for Teams
Context	Group members need to have a strong understanding of the situation they individually face, such as local clients, competitors, and challenges.	Team members need to share a common view and set of assumptions around customers, competitors, macroeconomic conditions, challenges, and the like.
Mission	Group members need to have explicit and well-defined individual goals and define success by individual goal accomplishment. An overarching purpose and group goals are not as important.	Teams need a compelling purpose and common, well-defined team goals that require interdependent effort. Team Scorecards should be used to communicate how teams define winning and to track progress on goal accomplishment.
Talent	Group members should be hired for the specific requirements of the position; fit with other group members is not important. Selection and training will focus on hiring and developing those skills needed for the role. Roles need to be made explicit, and group size generally has a linear relationship with group performance. Rewards should focus on individual goal accomplishment.	Team members need to possess different but complementary skills and experience and fit with other team members is equally important. Team size is an important consideration, and rewards should be based on collective accomplishments. Selection and development should focus on the needs of specific roles, member interdependencies, and common team requirements. Reporting structures and bad followership will have a much stronger impact on team performance.
Norms	Group Norms should be set around meetings, communication, decision-making, and accountability. However, groups should meet and communicate less frequently than teams; decision-making will be more leader-centric (i.e., more authoritarian and information gathering) and group members should have explicit performance expectations for individual responsibilities and be held accountable for achieving them.	At a minimum, team Norms should be set around meetings, communication, decision-making, and accountability. Teams may also elect to set Norms around conflict management, After-Action Reviews, urgency, performance, customer centricity, and the like. Teams should meet and communicate more frequently than groups, decision-making will be more team centric (i.e., more information gathering and consensus), and team members should have explicit performance expectations for individual and team responsibilities and be held accountable for achieving them.
Buy-In	Group members need enough engagement and motivation to accomplish their individual goals and abide by the rules governing group behavior. The links between their own efforts and individual goal accomplishment are usually self-evident, and they are expected to provide only minimal support to each other.	Team members need a higher level of engagement and motivation than group members, as they need to accomplish both individual and team goals, execute team decisions, meet and communicate with each other more frequently, and abide by the rules governing team behavior. They also need to provide mutual support and understand how their tasks and responsibilities contribute to the team's overall success.
Resources	Group members need the requisite Resources to accomplish their individual goals. Group members often work out of remote locations, so they may need different Resources than team members.	Team members typically need more Resources than group members, as they need to accomplish individual and team goals, meet, communicate, do progress reviews, and share data and key learnings more frequently. Usually the latter can involve travel budgets, formal meeting space, improved telecommunications, or specialized software.

Components	Considerations for Groups	Considerations for Teams
Courage	It is not important that group members get along or have productive dialogues. Group leaders will still need to manage conflict effectively, however, as disagreements can occur around individual goals, sales pipelines, or territory or customer assignments.	Team leaders need to create psychologically safe environments for team members to raise difficult issues. The key for team leaders is to maintain a healthy level of productive conflict around team goals and processes and minimize interpersonal conflict.
Results	Group leaders define winning by individual group members' accomplishments, and group Results are simply the summation of individuals' accomplishments. Group leaders can improve capacity by sharing best practices and replacing low-performing group members.	Team leaders define winning by collective goal accomplishment and can teach their teams how to win by setting measurable team goals, articulating well-thought-out strategies for achieving team goals, setting clear expectations for individual performance, showing how individual efforts lead to team Results, and regularly reviewing progress against team goals and adjusting strategies accordingly.

Facilitator's Agenda for Session 1, Day 1

Time	Objectives	Key Questions	Activities and Materials
8:00–9:00 Group leader opens session and gives company update	• Outline objectives of the session • Set expectations for participation • Review the day's agenda • Set meeting ground rules • Provide an update on company Context and strategy for the next year	• What do we need to accomplish at the off-site? • Where is the company going? • How will it get there? • What are the implications for the group and group members?	
9:00–9:15 Facilitator leads Groups vs. Teams exercise	• Engage participants in discussion of groups vs. teams	• What are the characteristics of groups? Teams? • Which one is better? • Are we a group or a team?	• Groups vs. Teams Exercise (p. 205)
9:15–10:00 Facilitator reviews Rocket Model	• Familiarize participants with the eight components of effective group performance	• What does the group need to do to operate effectively as a group?	• Rocket Model Slide Deck (p. 209)
10:00–10:15 Break			
10:15–11:30 Team Feedback Session—TAS	• Provide benchmarking information about team functioning and performance	• How does our group compare to other groups? • What are our group's strengths, surprises, and areas of improvement? • Are we a group or a team?	• Team Feedback Session (p. 227) • TAS Feedback Report
11:30–12:15 Lunch			

Time	Objectives	Key Questions	Activities and Materials
12:15-1:45 Facilitator leads discussion of group and individual Context	• Help group members understand the diversity of perspectives on the group • Get everyone on the same page about stakeholder expectations and contextual issues facing the group • Help group members clarify the challenges for their specific situation	• What do stakeholders expect from the group? • What external factors affect the group? • What are the group's biggest challenges? • What are group members' biggest challenges?	• Context Assessment Exercise (p. 237)
1:45-3:45 Facilitator helps group members create individual and group goals	• Establish individual group member goals and benchmarks • Establish benchmarks for measuring the group's performance	• What are the meaningful and measurable goals for each group member? • How should each group member define winning? • What are the meaningful and measurable goals for this group? • How does this group define winning?	• Team Scorecard (p. 257)
3:45-4:00 Break			
4:00-5:00 Facilitator helps group create a set of group Norms	• Establish rules for having an enterprise mindset, communication, accountability, and resolving conflict	• How should group members view business issues? • How should group members treat each other? • What happens if rules get violated?	• Team Norms (p. 303)
5:00-5:15 Closing remarks by group leader	• Review what the group accomplished during the day • Remind the group what they will be doing on Day 2	• What progress did we make today? • What do we need to get done tomorrow?	
6:00-8:00 Group dinner	• Provide informal time for socializing		

Facilitator's Agenda for Session 1, Day 2

Time	Objectives	Key Questions	Activities and Materials
8:00-8:30 Opening remarks by group leader and reflection	• Outline objectives of the session • Understand key learnings and reactions from Day 1	• What do we need to accomplish at the off-site? • What were participants' reactions and learnings from Day 1?	• Flip Chart
8:30-9:45 Facilitator helps group set up Operating Rhythm	• Determine the frequency, timing, and rules for group meetings	• When should the group meet? • What should it talk about? • Who runs the meetings? • What are the rules during meetings? • When will one-on-one meetings with the group leader take place? What will they cover?	• Operating Rhythm (p. 307)
9:45-10:00 Break			
10:00-11:30 Facilitator leads group discussion on best practices	• Gain a common understanding of what is and is not working across group members	• What have group members done to achieve their goals? • Which activities are working better than others? • What activities do not seem to work?	• Flip Chart
11:30-12:00 Closing remarks by group leader	• Review session deliverables • Review details for the next group meeting • Provide reactions to the off-site • Provide encouragement to participants • Session pluses and minuses	• What do group members need to get done before the next session? • When is the next group meeting? • Who is running the meeting? • How did the session go? • What would make the next session even better?	

Chapter 9

Matrixed Teams

Luc was named president
of a $3 billion division of a large pharmaceutical company. The Executive Leadership Team (ELT) he inherited included four regional vice presidents, six product line vice presidents, and 11 functional vice presidents (finance, supply chain, R&D, legal, regulatory, HR, IT, marketing, consumer insights, communications, and new business development). In addition, Luc added a VP of strategy to the team. The VP of strategy and the six product line VPs reported directly to Luc; the four regional VPs reported indirectly to Luc, directly reporting to regional group presidents who oversaw marketing and sales for all the company's divisions within their respective regions. The 11 functional VPs reported indirectly to Luc and directly to the global heads of the functions that provided shared services across the enterprise.

Luc and his leadership team were responsible for setting strategy and managing the overall performance within the division. Although P&L responsibilities ultimately resided with his regional counterparts, Luc was accountable for hitting the division's top-line and market share growth targets.

Luc knew he had walked into a mess. Results for his division had been below plan for the previous five years. The division's history of underperformance led to high turnover among top leadership. Luc was the sixth person to lead the division in as many years. In addition, each of his predecessors had made changes to ELT membership during their short tenures, so most were relatively new. Team culture was another obstacle. In their efforts to turn the division around, Luc's two immediate predecessors became highly dictatorial. People who raised concerns were directly shut down in front of the group, which had a chilling effect on everyone's willingness to speak up. Looking more broadly at culture within the division, employee engagement and retention were serious problems. Few employees want to be part of a division in a five-year slump.

After holding several ELT meetings, Luc felt stuck. He couldn't get the team to make progress on the serious challenges they faced and was starting to think that the leadership team was incapable of helping him turn the business around. At the same time, he was fearful about being one more in a series of leaders who changed up team membership without changing the division's results. That's when we got the call.

DIAGNOSIS

Based on what we heard from Luc about the team's history and his concerns about the team's level of functionality, we agreed to interview all 22 members of the ELT. Not surprisingly, the interviews confirmed that the ELT needed to focus on the Rocket Model components of Mission, Talent, Norms, Buy-In, and Courage. More detail about what we learned during the interviews is provided below.

- *Mission:* ELT members agreed on their overall purpose, which was to determine the strategy for the division and ensure aligned execution across product lines, regions, and functions in order to outpace the market on revenue growth. Although they agreed on what they needed to accomplish, they did not have a plan for how to get it done. Their high-level aspirations did not translate into an aligned strategy with clear priorities. One executive expressed it best when he said:

    o *"We lack clear, aligned priorities. Having a strategy means deciding what you are not going to do. We say we're going to focus on a few key areas, but then continue spreading our resources to keep everyone happy. The sum of individual interests does not equal the best interests of the division."*

- *Talent*: Everyone on the ELT recognized their colleagues were experienced and talented, but many cited the size of the team as being a problem. (Of course, none of these people thought they should be the ones to leave.) Comments we heard during the interviews included:

  - *"We are too big to function effectively. If everyone weighed in on an issue, that one topic would take all day."*
  - *"There isn't room for everyone to sit around the table."*

  Another difficulty on the Talent front was role clarity. As one executive told us:

  - *"There is a lot of confusion between regions, product lines, and functions as to roles and responsibilities. We're tripping all over each other."*

- *Norms*: Ineffective Norms were one of the team's biggest opportunities for improvement. Specifically, ELT members called out decision-making, meeting management, and sense of urgency and accountability as problems. Decision-making was such a mess that it was a miracle any decisions were made at all. Product VPs had to get approval from regional VPs for marketing and sales resources; regional VPs then had to ask their bosses for approval. Regions felt they had no say in product decisions that would affect their P&L. Neither the product nor regional VPs felt they could make decisions without the approval of the functional VPs, who in turn had to get approval from their respective bosses at headquarters. Dissatisfaction about decision-making yielded the following comments:

  - *"We don't know where decision rights lie. A product line leader thinks he can do something in EMEA, but EMEA owns decisions affecting their region. We're stuck in the intersection."*
  - *"Because there's no clarity on who owns what, decisions take a long time. Everyone feels the need to weigh in on everything."*

ELT members all dreaded their monthly meetings and described them as a time sink. Meetings largely consisted of highly polished and overly positive presentations with few questions being asked, and agendas were packed with topics unlikely to generate controversy or have a significant impact on results. Comments that described the situation included:

- *"We don't have team meetings; we're more like a group of people who look at slides together."*

- *"We don't address burning issues. Instead, we give updates."*

- *"The boat is sinking, so please don't talk to me about the menu on the cruise."*

- *"We have too many items on the agenda, so we always fall behind. We've yet to make it through an entire agenda."*

- *"People are checked out during ELT meetings. They don't do the pre-reading, or they spend more time on their phones or laptops than they do participating in our meetings."*

ELT members also complained about the team Norms relating to a sense of urgency and accountability. Comments included:

- *"Our results are terrible, yet I don't get a sense of urgency about righting the ship."*

- *"We lack a sense of urgency, executional rigor, and accountability."*

- *"Perhaps it's because we've never actually agreed on any specific actions, but there is zero follow-up on what happened in past meetings. We have discussions, but nothing happens as a result, so we keep suffering through the same pointless discussions."*

- *Buy-In:* An interesting dynamic we heard throughout the interviews is that while each ELT member saw themselves as personally committed to the team's success, they saw their peers as lacking that same level of commitment. Comments we heard included:

  - *"The hearts and minds of ELT members are all over the place. We have highly capable, strong individual leaders but no sense of community and collaboration."*

- *"No one is willing to take a hit for the good of the team. People are managing their careers rather than doing what it takes to be an enterprise leader."*

- *"People continue to focus on optimizing their piece without connecting to the division's overall strategy."*

- *"Agreeing in the room and then doing what you want after the meeting is done—that's the standard operating procedure here."*

- *"Team members are pointing at each other, instead of pointing forward together."*

- *Courage*: The ELT suffered from artificial harmony, where difficult issues were not addressed, bad news was glossed over, debate was lacking, and problems never got resolved. One executive said it best:

  - *"We are too nice. We need to call bullshit when we see it."*

  Every member of the ELT alluded to artificial harmony as being part of the team's dysfunction. When asked why *they* didn't speak up, they blamed it on previous leadership or the organization's culture—none of them took personal responsibility for their role in this dynamic.

Overall, we were astonished by the level of learned helplessness we observed on a leadership team responsible for running a $3 billion business. They all saw the same problems, but none of them felt empowered to do anything about it. Instead, they felt and acted like victims of the matrix who were waiting for Luc to rescue them.

SOLUTION

Prior to the first session, we shared the Team Interview Summary (TIS) with Luc. Although he was not surprised by the themes in the feedback, he was caught off guard by the team's level of angst and helplessness. Luc acknowledged that he needed to reduce the size of the team, but he was not ready to make those changes prior to the off-site, which was just two weeks away.

Just as Luc didn't want to be seen by ELT members as the person who could solve all their problems, we told Luc we couldn't work miracles and that he should lower his expectations for what we could accomplish during that first off-site. With the goal of setting ourselves up for mutual success, we agreed with Luc on the following guidelines for the first session:

- We would not have an overly ambitious agenda (a common complaint about the ELT's typical meetings), instead focusing on a few critical business and teamwork issues.

- We would share the TIS to get concerns out on the table, but then refocus the team from whining about the past to tackling their problems head-on. (Surprisingly, talking about shared misery ended up being a bonding experience for the team.)

- Luc wanted to start instilling a sense of ownership, empowerment, and accountability.

- Luc needed to set the expectation that ELT members look at the big picture regarding issues, rather than view them through the lens of their function, geography, or product line.

- Most important, Luc needed the team to make tangible progress on one or two significant business challenges. This would require them to translate financial goals into real choices; make actual plans; work with a sense of urgency, ownership, and accountability; and have courageous conversations.

Setting team Norms and clarifying decision-making rights were important components of the first off-site, as sorting out these issues would help the team work more effectively in the future.

Between the first and second off-site, Luc decided to break up the ELT into two teams. The tiger team consisted of Luc, the four regional VPs, and six product line VPs. The tiger team continued to meet one day a month, while the full ELT met for a two-day session once per quarter. The tiger team focused on execution, and this involved identifying problems, developing potential solutions, and implementing decisions to drive day-to-day business results. The two-day quarterly ELT meetings consisted of reviewing division scorecards and working on topics that cut across the division, such as reviewing customer, competitor, regulatory, and market and geopolitical trends; developing strategy; evaluating potential acquisitions; making difficult product or investment choices; vetting potential tiger team decisions; and succession planning.

Session 2 included the full ELT and was a half-day addition to a quarterly two-day meeting. Luc opened the session by describing the rationale and roles of the tiger team and full ELT, then everyone worked on finalizing the Operating Rhythm for both teams. The session ended with members rating the extent to which the ELT was adhering to its Norms and having a robust discussion on what it needed to do to improve compliance.

Between Sessions 2 and 3, Luc came to the realization that one of his regional VPs, two of the product line VPs, and his VPs of marketing and supply chain needed to be replaced. Several were incapable of leading their functional teams, two were bad followers who failed to live up to team Norms, and one consistently failed to deliver results. Luc had to work with their respective bosses and expend a considerable amount of political capital to get these individuals replaced, but he managed to upgrade these positions before the end of the year. Fellow team members were well aware of the situation, and Luc's credibility improved greatly by dealing with these sticky personnel issues.

Session 3 took place at the next quarterly meeting and was the second day of a two-day off-site with the full ELT. By this time, the six problematic team members had been removed and four of the replacements were in place. ELT members completed a Hogan Personality Inventory (HPI) and a Team Assessment Survey (TAS) a few weeks before the meeting, and we reviewed the results with Luc before the off-site. The TAS results indicated that the ELT needed to revisit decision-making rights, devise rules on how to keep everyone informed, and spend time getting to know everyone better.

SIX MONTHS			
Session 1: Day 1	**Session 1: Day 2**	**Session 2**	**Session 3**
• Rocket Model Overview • Team Feedback Session—Interview Summary • Team Norms • Business Problem Resolution • Team Dinner	• Business Problem Resolution • Decision-Making Rights • Team Action Planning • Team Commitments • Team Deliverables	• Operating Rhythm • Team Norms Evaluation • Team Deliverables	• Team Feedback Session—TAS • Operating Level • Decision-Making Rights • Communication • HPI • Team Deliverables

ACCOUNTABILITY MECHANISMS

Because accountability came up as a major concern during the interviews, we pushed the ELT to include accountability in every meeting agenda. The tiger team and full ELT got crystal clear on defining the who, what, and when in their plans and began every monthly and quarterly meeting by reviewing plan progress and previous meeting deliverables. In addition, we had the team end every meeting summarizing the deliverables and owners and evaluating whether the agenda focused on the right issues, the team adhered to its Norms, etc. Finally, the ELT completed a TAS six months after the initial session to assess how well they were working as a team.

OUTCOME

The differentiation between the tiger team and full ELT, focusing both teams on the appropriate topics, replacing the more problematic ELT members, establishing a tiger team and ELT Operating Rhythm, and clarifying decision-making rights and communication rules did wonders for ELT morale and performance. Although the TAS results indicated that there was ample room for improvement, the ELT felt the results were much better than they would have been six months earlier. Over the next two years, the division's performance improved to the point where it was consistently meeting or exceeding its targets. Luc became the longest-serving president the division had seen for the past 10 years, and eventually got promoted to an even bigger role at corporate.

CONCLUDING COMMENTS

Although this is the sole chapter we've specifically devoted to matrixed teams, most of the teams featured in this book are matrixed to some degree. Likewise, in our consulting practice, most teams we see are at least partially matrixed. One reason may be the sheer prevalence of matrixed organizational structures today. In a recent study, Gallup found that 84% of the employees it surveyed worked in an organization that was at least somewhat matrixed. Another reason may be that consultants tend to get called when a team is underperforming and matrixed teams struggle more than most.

Organizations adopt matrixed structures to deal with environmental complexity. The premise behind these structures is that they allow organizations to address the diverse, often conflicting interests of geographies, functions, and product lines. But in our experience, matrixed structures do not lessen the impact of environmental complexity—they merely reflect it. In practice, matrix structures lead to overlapping responsibilities, a proliferation of information, messy decision-making (if decisions get made at all), conflict, and a loss of accountability. Making things even worse, the pace of environmental change and the frequency of changes in team membership means the ground is always shifting. This makes it difficult for matrixed teams to create a sense of psychological safety and build the trust necessary to tackle difficult issues.

Organizational structure alone cannot solve the problem of complexity. The right systems, processes, relationships, and behaviors also need to be in place. The Rocket Model offers a useful framework and the team improvement activities provide tools to help matrixed teams resolve the goal, role, rule, commitment, and conflict management problems they are likely to encounter.

Facilitator's Agenda for Session 1, Day 1

Time	Objectives	Key Questions	Activities and Materials
8:00-8:15 Opening remarks by team leader	• Outline objectives of the session • Set expectations for participation • Review the day's agenda • Set meeting ground rules	• What do we need to accomplish at the off-site?	• Flip Chart
8:15-9:00 Facilitator reviews Rocket Model	• Familiarize participants with the eight components of effective team performance	• What does the team need to do to operate effectively?	• Rocket Model Slide Deck (p. 209)
9:00-9:15 Break			
9:15-10:45 Facilitator conducts Team Feedback Session—TIS	• Provide teams with qualitative information about team functioning and performance	• What are our team's strengths, surprises, and areas of improvement?	• Team Feedback Session (p. 227) • TIS
10:45-12:15 Facilitator helps team set Norms	• Clarify the rules by which team members will interact, communicate, and treat each other	• What are the team's rules? • What are the expectations around communication, assignments, and how team members treat each other?	• Team Norms (p. 303)
12:15-1:15 Lunch			
1:15-4:45 Facilitator leads group through business problem resolution (includes a break)	• Develop potential solutions to a major business problem	• What are the biggest issues facing the division? • Which of these issues are under the team's control? • What is the best solution to the problem?	
4:45-5:00 Closing remarks by team leader	• Review what the team accomplished during the day • Remind the team what they will be doing on Day 2	• What progress did we make today? • What do we need to get done tomorrow?	
6:00-8:00 Team dinner	• Provide informal time for socializing		

Facilitator's Agenda for Session 1, Day 2

Time	Objectives	Key Questions	Activities and Materials
8:00-8:30 Opening remarks by team leader and reflection	• Outline objectives of the session • Understand key learnings and reactions from Day 1	• What do we need to accomplish at the off-site? • What were participants' reactions and learnings from Day 1?	• Flip Chart
8:30-11:45 Facilitator leads group through business problem resolution (includes a break)	• Develop potential solutions to a major business problem	• What are the biggest issues facing the division? • Which of these issues are under the team's control? • What is the best solution to the problem?	
11:45-12:45 Lunch			
12:45-2:15 Facilitator clarifies decision-making rights for team members	• Determine which topics need to be decided by the ELT • Establish rules for making team, sub-team, and individual decisions	• What decisions should be made by the team? Sub-teams? Individuals? People below the team? • Who should be involved, how should these decisions be made, and who is the final decision maker?	• Decision-Making (p. 315)
2:15-2:30 Break			
2:30-4:30 Facilitator helps team create Action Plan and gets members to commit to team success	• Review the session deliverables • Review details for the next team meeting • Get team members' commitment to the team's goals, plans, roles, and rules	• What does the team need to get done before the next session? • Who owns these deliverables? • When is the next team meeting? • Who is running the meeting? • What needs to get done before the next team meeting? • Are people committed to the team's success?	• Team Action Plan (p. 261) • Personal Commitment (p. 347)
4:30-5:00 Closing remarks by team leader	• Provide observations and reactions to the off-site • Provide encouragement to participants • Session pluses and minuses • Key messages to the field	• How did the session go? • What would make the next session even better?	

Facilitator's Agenda for Session 2

Time	Objectives	Key Questions	Activities and Materials
8:00-8:10 Opening remarks by team leader	• Outline objectives and agenda for the session	• What do we need to accomplish at the session?	
8:10-9:45 Facilitator helps team set up Operating Rhythm for the tiger team and ELT	• Determine the frequency, timing, and rules for team meetings	• When should the team meet? • What should it talk about? • Who runs the meetings? • What are the rules during meetings?	• Operating Rhythm (p. 307)
9:45-10:00 Break			
10:00-11:30 Facilitator helps group with team Norms evaluation	• Hold the team accountable for its Norms	• How is the team doing on its Personal Commitments and team Norms?	• Team Norms; Post-Exercise Activity (p. 303)
11:30-12:00 Closing remarks by team leader	• Review the session deliverables • Review details for the next team meeting • Provide observations and reactions to the off-site • Provide encouragement to participants • Session pluses and minuses	• What does the team need to get done before the next session? • Who owns these deliverables? • When is the next team meeting? • Who is running the meeting? • How did the session go? • What would make the next session even better?	

Facilitator's Agenda for Session 3

Time	Objectives	Key Questions	Activities and Materials
8:00-8:10 Opening remarks by team leader	• Outline objectives and agenda for the session	• What do we need to accomplish at the session?	
8:10-9:45 Facilitator conducts a Team Feedback Session—TAS	• Provide teams with benchmarking information about team functioning and performance	• What are our team's strengths, surprises, and areas of improvement?	• Team Feedback Session (p. 227) • TAS
9:45-10:00 Break			
10:00-11:45 Facilitator clarifies decision-making topics and rights for the tiger team and ELT	• Determine which topics need to be decided by the ELT vs. the tiger team • Establish rules for making team, sub-team, and individual decisions	• What decisions should be made by the tiger team? ELT? Sub-teams? Individuals? People below the team? • Who should be involved, how should these decisions be made, and who is the final decision maker?	• Operating Level (p. 311) • Decision-Making (p. 315)
11:45-12:45 Lunch			
12:45-1:30 Facilitator helps clarify communication rules for the team	• Determine the topics, mode, frequency of team communications	• What do team members need to know? • How should information get communicated? • What is the expected response time for requests?	• Communication (p. 319)
1:30-3:15 Facilitator leads group through HPI Feedback Session	• Provide individuals with HPI feedback • Review aggregated HPI results for the team	• What is personality? • How do personality traits affect team dynamics? • What adjustments are needed to the team Norms, Operating Rhythm, decision-making, and communication rules?	• HPI (p. 289)
3:15-3:30 Break			
3:30-4:00 Closing remarks by team leader	• Review the session deliverables • Review details for the next team meeting • Provide observations and reactions to the off-site • Provide encouragement to participants • Session pluses and minuses • Key messages to the field	• What does the team need to get done before the next session? • Who owns these deliverables? • When is the next team meeting? • Who is running the meeting? • How did the session go? • What would make the next session even better?	

PART III

Team Applications

Chapter 10

C-Suite Teams

With $8 billion in annual revenues, 7,000 employees, and operations in 15 countries, GroBiz had come a long way since its days as a scrappy tech start-up. When its founder and CEO announced his retirement, GroBiz's board initiated an extensive search to replace him. Helen Chen appeared to be the perfect candidate to take the business to the next level. Her resume checked all the boxes: an undergraduate degree in computer science from MIT, an MBA from Stanford, a high-powered career that included stops at SAP and Amazon, and experience as the chief marketing officer of GroBiz's main competitor, where she was widely credited with turning around the business. Helen was excited about taking the top job at GroBiz and energized by the problems she was hired to fix—a weak pipeline of new products, increasing customer defections, and stagnant growth.

Helen sized up the executive team and decided the chief marketing officer (CMO) and chief technology officer (CTO) lacked the experience and sophistication needed to turn around the business. These individuals had been with GroBiz from the start, so this caused some consternation within the ranks. Helen thought this would change once people saw what more sophisticated leaders brought to these functions. Leveraging her extensive network,

Helen was able to quickly fill these roles with executives who were up to the task. She kept the other 10 leaders on the Executive Leadership Team (ELT) in place.

Despite everyone's initial optimism, little turned out as planned. Two years later, GroBiz's new product launches were even further behind, customer defections had not changed, and top-line growth remained stagnant. The market had dramatically improved, but GroBiz's stock price had barely changed since Helen took over. Several large institutional investors were pressuring the board to improve stock performance. Helen was feeling the heat and asking herself how it was possible that the new CMO and CTO couldn't get a handle on new product launches. After all, she had filled these critical roles with some of the best and the brightest people in the industry.

Helen knew that there were problems with the ELT, as it was a well-known secret that Marketing, Product Development, and Sales were not getting along. They seemed to play nice during team meetings, but second-guessing, backstabbing, and finger-pointing were daily occurrences. Not only were these top leaders not getting along, but their functions were waging silo wars and actively undermining each other. Product Development was hiring marketing and sales staff to sell their new apps, Marketing was hiring programmers to develop their own apps, and Sales was hiring marketing staff to get better local support. Realizing the ELT's dysfunction was getting in the way of the turnaround GroBiz desperately needed, Helen reluctantly sought outside help.

C-SUITE TEAM CONSIDERATIONS

With all the time and attention spent on succession planning, one would think that C-suite teams would be the epitome of effective teamwork. Corporate Darwinism ensures only the best and brightest make it to the top, yet research shows only one in five C-suite teams are high performing. To paraphrase Peter Senge, how does a team with an average IQ of 140 manage to operate like it has an IQ of 80?

Our work with C-suite teams shows that most suffer from one or more common sins. The seven sins of top teams can be easily avoided; the trick for CEOs is to recognize when they occur and take action to ensure they don't continue.

THE SEVEN SINS OF C-SUITE TEAMS

- Team Size
- Cloning
- Alpha Paralysis
- Operating Level
- Artificial Harmony
- Myopia
- First-Team Loyalty

Team size. Most teams have tight budgets that limit team size, but many C-suite teams suffer from the Hotel California syndrome. Once someone gets on a C-suite team, they never leave. After a few years, an eight-person ELT morphs into a 16-member behemoth whose sheer size greatly diminishes effective teamwork. Because communication, relationships, and coordination complexity increase exponentially with team size, the best C-suite teams are made up of less than 10 people. We've run into C-suite teams consisting of 25 team members—most CEOs suffer from the disease of inclusivity and manage teams that are too big to be effective. Somebody may need to get voted off the island if effective C-suite teams are a priority.

Cloning. People who make it to the C-suite are more similar than different. Members wear the same clothes, use the same acronyms, and are the biggest promoters of the corporate agenda. This causes top teams to suffer from groupthink, discount information that runs contrary to prevailing views, and jump to conclusions. Ensuring that top team members have diverse educational and professional backgrounds, rather than simply checking the necessary diversity boxes, is the best way to absolve this sin.

Alpha paralysis. Most C-suite teams are populated with alpha males and females who have opinions on just about everything. Top team members have no problem offering perspectives on topics they know little about and teams end up spending inordinate amounts of time debating relatively minor issues. In order to keep everyone happy, CEOs only raise relatively minor issues in meetings so egos don't get bent out of shape. They avoid surfacing controversial topics and making tough choices in team settings. When CEOs complain about a lack of ownership and having to make all the decisions, rest assured their teams are suffering from alpha paralysis.

Operating level. About 20 years ago, Charan, Drotter, and Noel published *The Leadership Pipeline*, which describes where leaders need to spend their time, what to let go of, and what to do differently as they rise through the ranks from individual contributors to CEOs. This same concept applies to teams. First-line supervisors leading teams of individual contributors should be discussing tactical topics. C-suite teams should focus on external scanning and discussing strategic issues, yet most spend time resolving internal issues that are best handled by one or two team members or further down the organization. C-suite teams operating at too low a level micromanage the rest of the organization, which causes employee engagement and retention of top talent to suffer. With no one keeping tabs on critical customer, competitor, and technology trends, these teams are surprised when disruptors emerge.

Artificial harmony. Jerks and those who push the envelope get weeded out during the climb and, as a result, the need to get along trumps the need to win in most C-suites teams. Meetings are cordial, back-slapping affairs where members are full of compliments and controversial issues are never raised. Yet team members complain about each other outside of meetings. Polite teams get polite results, so if lively debates and strong disagreements are not regular occurrences in meetings, artificial harmony is at play.

Myopia. C-suite members who view the world through a functional or regional lens and fail to take an enterprise view of issues suffer from myopia. Most have climbed the ranks through a single function or region, so myopia is more common than you think. P&L allocations can contribute to this problem, as regions or product lines with top and bottom responsibilities can make decisions that optimize their bonuses but sub-optimize the larger organization. It's hard to build a team when the players all want to be on other teams.

First-team loyalty. C-suite team members are in tricky positions, as they are members of the top team but also lead functions or regions with tens to thousands of employees. When push comes to shove, does their primary loyalty reside with the C-suite team or the functions they lead? Do they make decisions for the good of the enterprise or to maximize the performance of their functions? There is no right answer to the first-team loyalty question, but differing opinions about this concept will lead to C-suite team dysfunction. This question never gets raised by CEOs, and making the implicit explicit can go a long way toward getting this issue resolved.

DIAGNOSIS

After meeting with Helen and the chief human resources officer (CHRO) to gain their perspectives and talk through the project, we administered a Team Assessment Survey (TAS) and scheduled phone interviews with members of GroBiz's ELT. What we learned through this process wasn't all bad; in fact, some of what we heard was quite encouraging. Because of their involvement in strategy formulation, the ELT seemed fairly aligned on the team's Context. They mostly saw eye-to-eye about the situation but had some disagreements on the top challenges facing the business. The ELT also indicated its Mission was clear; everyone understood the goals and had plans in place for achieving them. Because of several major cost-cutting initiatives, Resources were more constrained than in the past but weren't much of a problem either.

The news was mixed when it came to Talent. Individually, ELT members had the right skills and experience for their positions, but the size of the team (13 members) was a hindrance. Merely having each ELT member give a 30-minute update took an entire day, and that wasn't allowing time for a Q&A.

Followership was a major problem with the ELT. The CTO believed he was the smartest guy in the room and had no doubt the path to GroBiz's success was through the adoption of new technology and more sophisticated applications. According to him, the CMO and regional sales presidents were idiots. He offered suggestions on how his peers could improve their organizations and disparaged them behind their backs when they were not adopted. The CTO was nothing but smiles during ELT meetings, but outside of these gatherings he never responded to inquiries from any of his peers, although he always had time for Helen. The CMO believed the CTO and regional sales presidents were incompetent and hired staff to make up for her peers' shortcomings. The regional sales presidents thought the CTO and CMO lived in ivory towers and had no idea what they were dealing with in the field.

GroBiz's executive team, like many top teams, failed to put the interests of the enterprise ahead of their functional or regional interests. Because of myopia and first-team loyalty, the CMO, CTO, and regional sales presidents primarily saw problems through the lens of how their area could save the day, rather than how the team needed to work together. Each viewed the situation as a chance to be the hero and curry favor with the board, should Helen get ousted. None saw it as an opportunity to improve coordination between their functions.

Norms and Courage were also problematic. Team meetings were largely report-outs, and if there was time for any discussion, it was spent arguing over the data rather than exploring possible solutions. Members found data to support their points of view and tore apart information offered by others. There was never a single version of the truth. Artificial harmony and alpha paralysis ensured none of the major problems facing the business ever surfaced in team meetings. Critical issues got resolved in one-on-one meetings with Helen. She often changed her position depending on who she spoke with last, so decisions were in a constant state of flux. The ongoing CTO/CMO/Sales battle was the elephant in the room; everyone knew what was happening, but no one was willing to call it out. Silo wars and poor decision-making were having ripple effects across GroBiz.

When we met with Helen, she told us that ELT members were unfailingly polite and collaborative during their monthly meetings. When we spoke with ELT members confidentially, we learned Helen had a carefully curated view of the team. Helen had been unaware of the degree to which she was witnessing artificial harmony on the ELT. The CTO, CMO, and regional sales presidents were collegial and cooperative in front of her, but inwardly they were seething. Rather than working through their disagreements in team meetings, they took a passive-aggressive approach to conflict. This too is common on executive teams, where team members are politically skilled, keep their hands clean, and wage proxy wars through their loyal lieutenants.

TAS Results

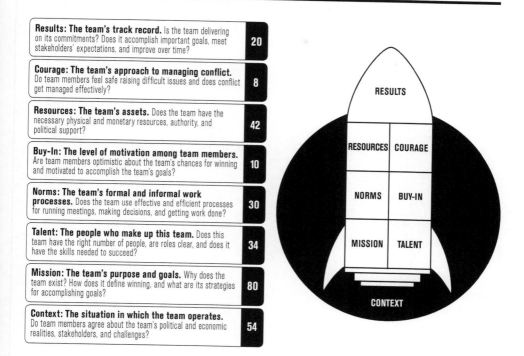

Results: The team's track record. Is the team delivering on its commitments? Does it accomplish important goals, meet stakeholders' expectations, and improve over time?	20
Courage: The team's approach to managing conflict. Do team members feel safe raising difficult issues and does conflict get managed effectively?	8
Resources: The team's assets. Does the team have the necessary physical and monetary resources, authority, and political support?	42
Buy-In: The level of motivation among team members. Are team members optimistic about the team's chances for winning and motivated to accomplish the team's goals?	10
Norms: The team's formal and informal work processes. Does the team use effective and efficient processes for running meetings, making decisions, and getting work done?	30
Talent: The people who make up this team. Does this team have the right number of people, are roles clear, and does it have the skills needed to succeed?	34
Mission: The team's purpose and goals. Why does the team exist? How does it define winning, and what are its strategies for accomplishing goals?	80
Context: The situation in which the team operates. Do team members agree about the team's political and economic realities, stakeholders, and challenges?	54

The Team Interview Summary (TIS) and TAS results indicated that team size, followership, Norms, Buy-In, and Courage were high-priority items to address if GroBiz was going to achieve the results it sought.

SOLUTION

When we met with Helen to share the TAS and TIS results, we reassured her that the results were not atypical of C-suite teams. Nonetheless, Helen was quite surprised by the findings. As seen here, Helen's ratings for the four Resources items are represented by the dark gray boxes, and the ELT's average ratings are represented by the lighter boxes. (Starting from the left, the five tick marks are associated with Strongly Disagree, Disagree, So-So, Agree, and Strongly Agree.) Helen saw team functioning quite differently from the rest of the ELT. Most CEOs, and team leaders in general, have overly optimistic views of team functioning and performance. Whether these boss-team perceptual gaps are due to team members telling leaders only what they want to hear, leaders ignoring inconvenient facts, or leaders spending relatively little time with their teams has yet to be determined, but this gap is a big contributor to why only 20% of teams are high performing. Leaders won't take action if they don't think there is a problem.

TAS: ELT vs. CEO Ratings

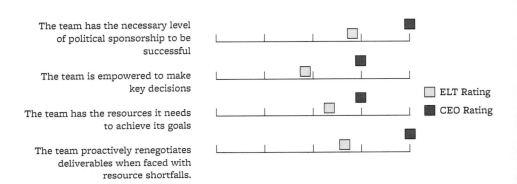

After getting over her initial shock, Helen asked for guidance to improve ELT performance. We recommended she make some team talent and structural changes and get the ELT to participate in several team-building sessions.

Talent and Structural Changes

- One of the most difficult decisions Helen made was firing the CTO she had personally recruited. Helen concluded that while he had the technical chops to do the job, he did not play nice with others. He had burned so many bridges that he needed to be replaced if the ELT was ever to become high performing. (The announcement of his departure was warmly received by his peers.)
- Helen created a new position, the chief commercial officer (CCO), which she filled with the president of sales for Europe, Middle East, and Africa. The regional sales presidents, CMO, and VP of product development all reported to the CCO, who was responsible for making sure new applications were built to meet customer needs specified by

Marketing; Product Development got new products properly launched; Marketing improved lead generation and delivered effective local marketing campaigns; and Sales quit making excuses for flat revenues. The CMO and regional sales presidents did not like this new structure, as they no longer reported directly to Helen. Helen told them she understood their concerns, but organizational changes were needed to address some of the ELT's underlying problems.

- We talked with Helen about reducing the size of the ELT, but with the new CTO and CCO structure, she was unwilling to make any more changes to her team. We made adjustments to the Operating Rhythm, decision-making, and communication norms to accommodate the larger team size.

SIX MONTHS			
Session 1: Day 1	**Session 1: Day 2**	**Session 2**	**Session 3**
• Leader's Vision and Feedback • Top Teams Facts • Rocket Model Overview • Team Feedback Session—TAS and TIS • Team Purpose and Scorecard Review • Operating Level • Team Dinner	• Decision-Making • Eavesdropping Exercise • Team Norms • Team Problem-Solving • Team Deliverables	• Team Problem-Solving • Operating Rhythm • Hogan Development Survey (HDS) • Personal Commitments • Team Norm Evaluations • Team Deliverables	• Team Feedback Session—TAS • Peer Feedback • Team Problem-Solving • Personal and Team Learning • Team Deliverables

We worked with Helen and the CHRO to design three off-sites to improve ELT functioning and performance. These started shortly after the CTO was fired and new commercial structure was put into place. Session 1 was a two-day event, and Sessions 2 and 3 were one-day events tacked on to the ELT's quarterly business reviews.

Session 1 was designed to help the ELT understand where it currently stood, where it needed to go, and what it needed to do to get there. Key goals for the session were to gain alignment on the ELT's current level of functioning; identify those topics it should be focusing on and those that should be handled lower in the organization; clarify who should be involved and final decision-makers for various topics; set rules for one version of the truth, ownership, accountability, enterprise mindset, and collaboration; and work on two critical challenges affecting the business. Team members left the session with a number of action items, and progress reviews were part of the monthly team meetings.

Session 2 began with the ELT working on two more critical issues affecting the business. Lively but respectful discussions took place as the team wrestled over possible solutions. No real consensus emerged for one issue, so Helen restated the three competing solutions and chose the one that she thought would be best for the business. Some were disappointed in her choice, but all were happy a decision finally got made. Everyone agreed that they would see the decision fully implemented in their functions and regions. Time was also spent revising the ELT's monthly, quarterly, board preparation, strategic planning, budgeting, and succession planning meetings; discussing how dark-side personality traits were causing team dysfunction as the company drove for results at the end of each quarter; making Personal Commitments to the team and business; and evaluating the extent to which it was adhering to team Norms.

A second TAS was completed and the results reviewed in Session 3. The talent and structure changes seemed to be paying off, as the Talent scores were 30 points higher. Norms, Buy-In, and Courage scores had similar improvements. Time was also spent providing peer feedback, working on another difficult business issue, and sharing Personal and Team Learnings from the past six months. By this point, the ELT was well on its way to becoming a high-performing team.

ACCOUNTABILITY MECHANISMS

Session 1, 2, and 3 deliverables were reviewed at the end of the sessions, and progress reviews were conducted at the ELT's monthly and quarterly meetings. The ELT also completed team Norms evaluations, provided peer feedback, and did a second TAS to review progress.

OUTCOME

The ELT noted improvements on the second TAS. Although it was not yet a high-performing team, it was well on its way to becoming one. New products included features that customers most wanted, were launched with great fanfare, and Sales was getting the proper support to drive revenue growth. GroBiz was a big ship that would take time to turn around, but all the pieces were in place to make it happen.

CONCLUDING COMMENTS

Because they are made up of some of the company's best and brightest leaders, one might assume that most C-suite teams are high performing. That's rarely the case. C-suite team members are five times more likely to describe their team as poor or mediocre than high performing. What happens in the C-suite sets the tone for the rest of the organization—high-performing top teams often lead organizations with highly engaged employees who achieve envious results. Dysfunctional C-suite teams lead organizations that ignore customers, dismiss competitors, point fingers, fight silo wars, shirk responsibility, hide behind bureaucratic rules, engage in artificial harmony, and focus attention inward rather than on market dynamics.

Many teams do not have the budget to hire external consultants, but this is not the case for C-suite teams. C-suite teams benefit by having a neutral referee, someone with no dog in the hunt who can help them become high performing. Consultants can provide advice on team size, reporting structures, staffing, Operating Rhythm and level, decision-making processes, and team dynamics. Facilitators can speak truth to power when trust is low and provide CEOs with feedback when they are over-indexing on leading from the front or behind. Facilitators can also hold up the mirror when teams violate Norms.

It can be hard finding consultants who are a good fit with the CEO and C-suite team. Many provide team-building services, but only a few are able to add value, operate at the C-suite level, and establish good chemistry with the CEO and his or her team.

Facilitator's Agenda for Session 1, Day 1

Time	Objectives	Key Questions	Activities and Materials
8:00–8:45 Team leader's vision and feedback	• Describe where the business has been • Describe the potential strengths and liabilities of the business • Describe where the business needs to go and how it will get there • Get reactions and answer questions about the vision	• What is the vision for the business? • What are the expectations for ELT members? • What are the ELT's reactions to the vision? • What questions does the ELT have about the vision?	• Vision Statement (p. 247)

Time	Objectives	Key Questions	Activities and Materials
8:45-9:05 Facilitator presents facts about C-suite teams	• Engage participants in discussion about effective vs. ineffective top teams • Tell participants about the common problems with top teams	• How prevalent are high-performing C-suite teams? • What are the common mistakes of C-suite teams?	• Curphy, G., & Nilsen, D. (2018, July). Your top talent is destroying your teams. Talent Quarterly, 36-40
9:05-9:45 Facilitator reviews Rocket Model	• Familiarize participants with the eight components of effective team performance	• What does the team need to do to operate effectively?	• Rocket Model Slide Deck (p. 209)
9:45-10:00 Break			
10:00-11:45 Facilitator runs Team Feedback Session—TAS and TIS	• Provide teams with qualitative information about team functioning and performance	• What are our team's strengths, surprises, and areas of improvement?	• Team Feedback Session (p. 227) • TAS • TIS
11:45-12:45 Lunch			
12:45-2:00 Facilitator leads discussion about Team Purpose	• Create a shared understanding of why the team exists	• Why does this team exist?	• Team Purpose (p. 253)
2:00-2:15 Break			
2:15-3:45 Facilitator leads group through exercise to revise the Team Scorecard	• Translate high-level objectives into meaningful and measurable goals • Establish benchmarks for measuring the team's performance	• Is the ELT measuring the right things? • How does this team define winning?	• Team Scorecard (p. 257)
4:00-5:45 Facilitator leads group through Operating Level discussion	• Help the ELT gain consensus on the time spent on various types of topics • Build a plan to help the ELT spend more time on strategic issues	• What topics take up most of the ELT's time? • What topics should be handled lower in the organization? • Which topics should be handled by the ELT?	• Operating Level (p. 311)
5:45-6:00 Closing remarks by team leader	• Review what the team accomplished during the day	• What progress did we make today? • What do we need to get done tomorrow?	
6:30-8:30 Team dinner	• Provide informal time for socializing		

Facilitator's Agenda for Session 1, Day 2

Time	Objectives	Key Questions	Activities and Materials
8:00–8:15 Opening remarks by team leader	• Outline objectives of the session • Review rules of engagement	• What do we need to accomplish at the off-site?	• Flip Chart
8:15–9:45 Facilitator leads decision-making exercise	• Clarify team decision-making rights	• Who should be involved in team decisions? • What decision-making style should be used? • Who is the final decision maker?	• Decision-Making (p. 315)
9:45–10:00 Break			
10:00–11:30 Facilitator runs exercise to clarify expectations for team members	• Publicly state expectations for team members	• What do people expect from fellow team members? • What are they willing to do to help the team succeed?	• Eavesdropping Exercise (p. 279)
11:30–12:30 Lunch			
12:30–2:00 Facilitator helps team create team Norms	• Establish rules for having an enterprise mindset, communication, one truth, accountability, and resolving conflict	• How should team members view business issues? • How should team members treat each other? • What happens if rules are violated?	• Team Norms (p. 303)
2:00–2:15 Break			
2:15–4:30 Facilitator helps team solve high-priority issues	• Develop solutions to two problems facing the business	• Where are the highest-priority issues for the business? • What will we do about these problems? • Who owns the solutions? • What metrics will change as a result of these solutions?	• Flip Charts
4:30–5:00 Facilitator helps team review decisions and deliverables	• Review the session decisions and deliverables • Review details for the next team meeting	• What did the team decide? • What does the team need to get done before the next session? • Who owns these deliverables? • When is the next team meeting?	
5:00–5:30 Closing remarks by team leader	• Key messages to communicate back to the business • Session pluses and minuses • Provide encouragement to participants	• What will the team tell the rest of the organization about the meeting? • What went well during the session? • What would make the next session even better?	

Facilitator's Agenda for Session 2

Time	Objectives	Key Questions	Activities and Materials
8:00-8:15 Opening remarks by team leader	• Outline objectives of the session • Review rules of engagement	• What do we need to accomplish at the off-site?	• Flip Chart
8:15-10:15 Facilitator helps team solve high-priority issues	• Develop solutions to two problems facing the business	• Where are the highest-priority issues for the business? • What will we do about these problems? • Who owns the solutions? • What metrics will change as a result of these solutions?	• Flip Charts
10:15-10:30 Break			
10:30-11:45 Facilitator helps team set up new Operating Rhythm	• Determine the frequency, timing, and rules for team meetings	• When should the team meet? • What should it talk about? • Who runs the meetings? • What are the rules during meetings?	• Operating Rhythm (p. 307)
11:45-12:45 Lunch			
12:45-2:15 Facilitator does HDS debriefing	• Determine what the team is likely to do when under stress • Develop mechanisms to help the team cope with stress	• What are dark-side personality traits? • How do dark-side traits affect leadership and teamwork? • What are the team's collective dark-side results? • How will the team mitigate its dark-side tendencies?	• HDS (p. 293)
2:15-2:30 Break			
2:30-3:45 Facilitator asks team members to commit to team success	• Make public commitments to help the team operate at a higher level	• What will people keep doing to help the team succeed? • What will people start, stop, or do differently to help the team succeed? • How should team members be held accountable for their commitments?	• Personal Commitments (p. 347)
3:45-4:15 Facilitator asks team to evaluate its Norms	• Hold the team accountable for its Norms	• How is the team doing against its Norms?	• Team Norms; Post-Exercise Activity (p. 303)
4:15-4:45 Facilitator helps team review decisions and deliverables	• Review the session decisions and deliverables • Review details for the next team meeting	• What did the team decide? • What does the team need to get done before the next session? • Who owns these deliverables? • When is the next team meeting?	

Time	Objectives	Key Questions	Activities and Materials
4:45-5:15 Closing remarks by team leader	• Key messages to communicate back to the business • Session pluses and minuses • Provide encouragement to participants	• What will the team tell the rest of the organization about the meeting? • What went well during the session? • What would make the next session even better?	

Facilitator's Agenda for Session 3

Time	Objectives	Key Questions	Activities and Materials
8:00-8:15 Opening remarks by team leader	• Outline objectives of the session • Review rules of engagement	• What do we need to accomplish at the off-site?	• Flip Chart
8:15-9:45 Facilitator runs Team Feedback Session—TAS	• Provide teams with qualitative information about team functioning and performance	• What are our team's strengths, surprises, and areas of improvement? • How has the team changed over time?	• Team Feedback Session (p. 227) • TAS
9:45-10:00 Break			
10:00-11:45 Facilitator runs peer feedback session	• Provide team members with feedback on the extent to which they are adhering to team Norms and fulfilling their team commitments	• Are team members abiding by team rules? • Are team members fulfilling their Personal Commitments?	• Peer Feedback (p. 227)
11:45-12:45 Lunch			
12:45-2:45 Facilitator helps team solve high-priority issues	• Develop solutions to two problems facing the business	• Where are the highest-priority issues for the business? • What will we do about these problems? • Who owns the solutions? • What metrics will change as a result of these solutions?	• Flip Charts
2:45-3:00 Break			
3:00-4:00 Facilitator helps team members reflect on key learnings	• Clarify personal and team lessons learned	• What have team members learned about themselves over the past six months? • What have team members learned about the team over the past six months?	• Personal and Team Learning (p. 373)

Time	Objectives	Key Questions	Activities and Materials
4:00-4:30 Facilitator helps team review decisions and deliverables	• Review the session decisions and deliverables • Review details for the next team meeting	• What did the team decide? • What does the team need to get done before the next session? • Who owns these deliverables? • When is the next team meeting?	
4:30-5:00 Closing remarks by team leader	• Key messages to communicate back to the business • Session pluses and minuses • Provide encouragement to participants	• What will the team tell the rest of the organization about the meeting? • What went well during the session? • What would make the next session even better?	

Chapter 11

New Team Leaders: Getting off to a Fast Start

Sarah was excited about her new role as the vice president of the Southeastern Region at Greentree Solutions, a company specializing in engineering, architectural, and environmental solutions. Leading 18 offices across 10 states, the position was a step up for Sarah, although Greentree was a smaller, less sophisticated company than the one she left.

Sarah's boss, Mike, had been honest with her from the start that this was a turn-around situation. Growth in the region had stalled and they had lost several large, long-standing accounts. In contrast, the company's other regions were seeing great success. Sarah came with a winning track record at one of Greentree's most formidable competitors, and Mike was confident that she was the right person for the job. Sarah had many ideas for changes she wanted to introduce, but she also realized that just because she was ready to make changes didn't mean her team was ready to accept them. Getting their buy-in would take time.

During Sarah's first week, she got to work learning about her team. She arranged meetings with several key clients to introduce herself and hear firsthand how they were feeling about working with Greentree in her region. She sought out information from her boss and three VPs in regions that shared clients with the Southeastern Region. Sarah also met with each of her direct reports individually. She asked them what was going well in the region, what they saw as pain points, and what their ideas were for improving Greentree. She also asked about their proudest accomplishments, how they spent their time, their goals, and what they needed from her. Although she was disappointed in some of their responses, she was careful to listen rather than to criticize or argue.

Having had a good experience with the Team Assessment Survey (TAS) at her previous employer, Sarah thought it could help provide insight into her new team's performance. Emphasizing the value of quantitative data to her engineering team, she asked them to complete the TAS so they could see how they stacked up against other teams.

DIAGNOSIS

Results. By looking at the TAS results for her team and spending one-on-one time with them, she learned that her managers thought the team was doing well—it was hardly a turn-around situation in their eyes. In fact, they claimed that the best, most creative work in the entire company was coming out of their region. When pressed about financial results, they admitted there had been a few bumps in the road. Sure, they lost a couple of clients, but that was to be expected because their primary contacts had left or retired. Economic headwinds were also a factor, so the team felt the region's performance problems were largely out of their control.

TAS Results

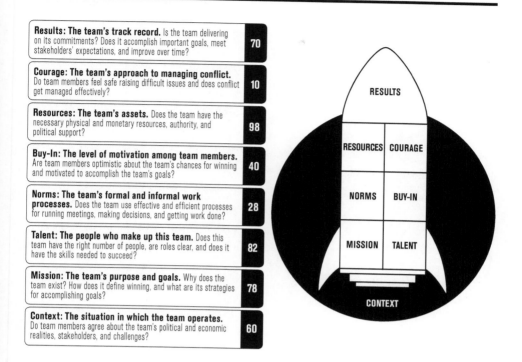

Results: The team's track record. Is the team delivering on its commitments? Does it accomplish important goals, meet stakeholders' expectations, and improve over time?	70
Courage: The team's approach to managing conflict. Do team members feel safe raising difficult issues and does conflict get managed effectively?	10
Resources: The team's assets. Does the team have the necessary physical and monetary resources, authority, and political support?	98
Buy-In: The level of motivation among team members. Are team members optimistic about the team's chances for winning and motivated to accomplish the team's goals?	40
Norms: The team's formal and informal work processes. Does the team use effective and efficient processes for running meetings, making decisions, and getting work done?	28
Talent: The people who make up this team. Does this team have the right number of people, are roles clear, and does it have the skills needed to succeed?	82
Mission: The team's purpose and goals. Why does the team exist? How does it define winning, and what are its strategies for accomplishing goals?	78
Context: The situation in which the team operates. Do team members agree about the team's political and economic realities, stakeholders, and challenges?	60

Puzzled by the disparity between her team's view of their results and those of her boss, Sarah asked Mike what he thought was going on. With a sigh, he said, "I'm sorry to say, none of this surprises me. Your predecessor was a complete cheerleader, big on praise and short on accountability. All they ever heard from him was how great they were doing."

From her colleagues and clients, Sarah heard that the Southeastern Region was indeed doing cutting-edge work, maybe too much so, because she also heard that members of her team were overly fond of their own ideas, erred on the side of elegance over pragmatism, and were quick to dismiss constructive feedback.

- *Context*: Sarah's one-on-one meetings with the managers on her team backed up the team's average scores. They were largely on the same page about stakeholder expectations, industry trends, and the impact of technology on the business.

- *Mission*: Sarah's team had a high score on Mission. On the positive side, they were crystal clear about the team's purpose and goals and regularly reviewed the financials. Areas to improve on included using leading, rather than just lagging, indicators of their performance. They also needed to get better at execution—they had been reviewing the numbers but not doing much about them.

- *Talent*: With all of the positive feedback they'd received from Sarah's predecessor, the team thought very highly of themselves and their score reflected it. On the other hand, Sarah's boss and peers shared serious doubts about two of the seven managers reporting to her. Sarah also learned from Mike that one of the operations managers reporting to her had applied for her job and was very unhappy about being passed over.

  Sarah learned a lot about her team from their responses to two of her questions: "How are you spending your time?" and "What are your goals?" There was a big disconnect between those answers for the two low-performers—they were spending their time on the wrong stuff. As part of her due diligence, Sarah also decided to put all eight of her managers through leadership assessments, which included the Motives, Values, Preferences Inventory (MVPI); the Hogan Personality Inventory (HPI); the Hogan Development Survey (HDS); 360-degree surveys; and a TAS for their respective teams.

- *Norms*: Item-level feedback on the TAS and Sarah's interviews with her team clarified that the reason for the low score was that they tended to be reactive, their meetings were inefficient, and they lacked standard processes and procedures for getting work done. The team also lacked a sense of ownership and any sense of responsibility for the region's substandard results.

- *Buy-In*: With the recent departure of their much-loved leader, team members were not feeling very engaged. In fact, they were worried about the changes this new outsider would try to force on them.

- *Resources*: A high point with a score of 98, the team felt they had the resources they needed to get the job done.

- *Courage*: Sarah's predecessor had put a premium on getting along and having fun together. Surfacing and working through disagreements just got in the way. The TAS pointed out that there were a number of tensions on the team that were simmering just below the surface.

SOLUTION

Sarah's approach coming into Greentree set the stage for turning the team around. Even though she was hired as a change agent, she didn't give in to the temptation of making changes on day one. Instead, she spent about a month getting the lay of the land—assessing the talent on her team, learning Greentree's culture, visiting offices, meeting clients, and identifying the low-hanging fruit so she could establish some early wins. She realized that without this baseline knowledge, she would have trouble adding value and face resistance from her team. She also knew that by asking questions and listening, she was starting to build her credibility.

Five weeks into the job, Sarah called the team together for its first off-site. Rather than disparaging the past, she started by acknowledging the positives she observed. Then she went on to share her vision for where she wanted to take the region and what she needed from her leadership team to get there.

Next, she shared the TAS results, along with key themes she heard from clients, her boss, and other regional VPs. The feedback had a chilling effect; the room went quiet and eye contact was minimal. Sarah realized that this was the first time her team had received such unflinching feedback and needed time to process, so she asked them to break into two groups and to analyze the TAS results and additional feedback they just received. The two groups were asked to identify the team's strengths and areas of improvement. In the debrief that followed, they prioritized two chief complaints. First, they thought team meetings left a lot to be desired. Second, they wanted to feel more comfortable raising difficult topics and working through disagreements together.

Sarah finished up the morning by running a Context Assessment exercise. This allowed the team to have robust conversations about the situation and challenges facing the team, and let the team practice working through disagreements. They discovered that members had fairly different expectations about headquarters, other regions, customers, employees, and competitors. The exercise also allowed Sarah to observe team dynamics and team members' level of engagement.

In the first part of the afternoon, Sarah worked with her team to establish Norms for more effective meetings. She was careful not to dominate the discussion and asked for a volunteer to document the team's decisions via flip chart. Together, they identified three types of team meetings: weekly meetings primarily focused on updates; monthly meetings to review performance metrics (and more importantly to talk about how to improve them); and special topics meetings with themes such as strategy, budgeting, and talent reviews. They then developed an annual calendar for meetings, determined meeting length and location, and set rules for agendas, prework, meeting behavior, and presentation protocol.

Returning after the break, her team came back into the room ready to tackle their second priority. When Sarah told them that teams learned to have difficult discussions through practice, that wasn't the answer they expected. She also stated that it was much easier to have these conversations if they knew her and each other better, and used the Journey Lines exercise to make that happen.

The team had their next scheduled monthly meeting, which was a morning session that consisted of a status update on the deliverables from the last monthly meeting, a Team Scorecard review, company updates, and team member report-outs. During the last hour of the session, Sarah asked the team to name one or two topics that were most in need of spirited debate. The response was nervous laughter. Sarah waited quietly until someone spoke up and once the ice was broken, the team came up with a long list of topics they had been avoiding. Sarah told the team that they would be working on one of the topics later that day.

Session 2 took place that afternoon and began with a lively discussion of the Team Scorecard. The team made decisions to add leading indicator goals, modify other goals, and scrap two goals that were easily measured but not being used to drive the business. The team then picked a difficult topic from the morning and spent the next 90 minutes sharing perspectives. Sarah encouraged input from everyone at the table and pushed the team for closure. At the end of the discussion, she asked the team how they thought they did, what went well during the discussion, and what ideas they had for improving future discussions.

Sessions 3 and 4 also took place the afternoons after regularly scheduled monthly team meetings. Sarah and her team worked through topics from their TAS feedback which included establishing team Norms around urgency, ownership, and accountability, and introducing the team to After-Action Reviews. In order to spend more time leading from behind, Sarah asked two team members to lead Sessions 3 and 4.

THREE MONTHS			
Session 1	**Session 2**	**Session 3**	**Session 4**
• Leader's Vision • Rocket Model Overview • Team Feedback Session—TAS • Context Assessment Exercise • Operating Rhythm • Journey Lines • Closing Remarks • Team Dinner	• Team Scorecard • Difficult Topics Discussion	• Team Norms • Difficult Topics Discussion	• After-Action Reviews

Outside of the team meetings, Sarah reviewed the leadership assessment results for her eight direct reports and met with them one-on-one to review the results and build development plans. Some of these meetings included courageous conversations with the two low-performing managers on her team. One got on board, the other decided to leave.

ACCOUNTABILITY MECHANISMS

Setting up an Operating Rhythm that regularly reviewed meeting deliverables, Team Scorecard results, and Action Plans set the tone for accountability. In addition, Sarah reviewed progress on each staff member's development plans in monthly one-on-one meetings and conducted After-Action Reviews at the conclusion of every major initiative. She also asked the team to complete a second TAS nine months later to measure progress.

OUTCOME

As the team started performing better, Sarah gained Buy-In and was able to introduce more changes that strengthened performance in the region. By the end of the year, the team was exceeding its annual revenue and margin targets and had realized noticeable improvements in TAS scores.

CONCLUDING COMMENTS

New team leaders, especially those coming from outside the organization, face three big hurdles. First, they need to get up to speed on what's what, who's who, and how things get done. Without this knowledge, they can't add much value. Second, until they've proven themselves and built solid relationships with their staff, they lack credibility. And while new leaders are busy getting the lay of the land, team performance can take a dip, making their job that much harder. Third, they need to determine what they need to do (or just as importantly, not do) to improve team performance. Because most teams are underperforming, new team leaders usually can implement a few activities that enable their teams to perform at higher levels. Some new leaders will luck into teams that are already high performing. In these situations, asking a team to do things in a radically different way because it fits better with how the leader does things will be a recipe for disaster.

Many leader transitions are longer and more painful than they need to be. Using the Rocket Model can help new leaders quickly learn about the teams they've inherited, build relationships, add value, establish credibility, overcome resistance, and improve the performance of their teams.

Team Leader's Agenda for Session 1

Time	Objectives	Key Questions	Activities and Materials
8:00-8:30 Team leader's opening remarks and Vision Statement	• Outline objectives of the session • Set expectations for participation • Review the day's agenda • Set meeting ground rules	• What do we need to accomplish at the off-site? • Where has the team been, what is it doing well/not so well, where does it need to go?	• Vision Statement (p. 247) • Flip Chart
8:30-9:00 Team leader reviews Rocket Model	• Familiarize participants with the eight components of effective team performance	• What does the team need to do to operate effectively?	• Rocket Model Slide Deck (p. 209)
9:00-9:15 Break			
9:15-10:45 Team leader conducts Team Feedback Session—TAS	• Provide teams with benchmarking information about team functioning and performance • Provide team with outside feedback on performance	• How does our team compare to other teams? • What are our team's strengths, surprises, and areas of improvement?	• Team Feedback Session (p. 227) • TAS Feedback Report
10:45-12:15 Team leader conducts Context Assessment exercise	• Help team members understand the diversity of perspectives on the team • Get everyone on the same page about stakeholder expectations and contextual issues facing the team	• What do stakeholders expect from the team? • What external factors affect the team? • What are the team's biggest challenges?	• Context Assessment Exercise (p. 237)
12:15-1:00 Lunch			
1:00-2:15 Team leader helps team set up Operating Rhythm	• Determine the frequency, timing, and rules for team meetings	• When should the team meet? • What should it talk about? • Who runs the meetings? • What are the rules during meetings?	• Operating Rhythm (p. 307)

Time	Objectives	Key Questions	Activities and Materials
2:15–2:30 Break			
2:30–4:45 Team leader facilitates Journey Lines activity	• Help team members learn about each other • Begin building camaraderie and trust	• What life experiences have shaped each team member?	• Journey Lines (p. 333)
4:45–5:00 Closing remarks by team leader	• Review what the team accomplished during the day • Clarify key messages from the session • Remind the team what needs to happen before the next monthly meeting	• What progress did we make today? • What will we tell our staff after the meeting? • What do we need to get done before the next meeting?	
6:00–8:00 Team dinner	• Provide informal time for socializing		

Team Leader's Agenda for Session 2

Time	Objectives	Key Questions	Activities and Materials
1:00–1:10 Team leader's opening remarks	• Set expectations for participation • Review the afternoon agenda • Review meeting ground rules	• What do we need to accomplish at the session?	
1:10–2:45 Team leader helps group revise Team Scorecard	• Translate high-level goals into specific deliverables • Establish benchmarks for measuring the team's performance	• What are the meaningful and measurable goals for this team? • What are the team's leading performance indicators? • How does this team define winning?	• Team Scorecard (p. 257)
2:45–3:00 Break			
3:00–4:30 Team leader facilitates difficult topics discussion	• Identify and resolve some of the more difficult topics facing the team	• What are the team's most pressing issues? • What should we do about one or two of them?	• Flip Charts
4:30–5:00 Closing remarks by team leader	• Review what the team accomplished during the day • Clarify key messages from the session • Remind the team what needs to happen before the next monthly meeting	• What progress did we make today? • What will we tell our staff after the meeting? • What do we need to get done before the next meeting?	

Team Member's Agenda for Session 3

Time	Objectives	Key Questions	Activities and Materials
1:00-1:10 Team member's opening remarks	• Set expectations for participation • Review the afternoon agenda • Review meeting ground rules	• What do we need to accomplish at the session?	
1:10-2:30 Team member helps team set Norms	• Clarify the rules around urgency, ownership, accountability, communication, and collaboration	• What are the team's rules? • What are the team's expectations for performance, how to treat fellow team members, communication, etc.?	• Team Norms (p. 303)
2:30-2:45 Break			
2:45-4:15 Team leader facilitates difficult topics discussion	• Identify and resolve some of the more difficult topics facing the team	• What are the team's most pressing issues? • What should we do about one or two of them?	• Flip Charts
4:15-4:45 Closing remarks by team leader	• Review what the team accomplished during the day • Clarify key messages from the session • Remind the team what needs to happen before the next monthly meeting	• What progress did we make today? • What will we tell our staff after the meeting? • What do we need to get done before the next meeting?	

Facilitator's Agenda for Session 4

Time	Objectives	Key Questions	Activities and Materials
8:00-8:45 Team leader's opening remarks and team member updates	• Company and region update • Set expectations for participation • Review the day's agenda • Review meeting ground rules	• What is happening across the company and region? • What do we need to accomplish at the session?	
8:45-9:00 Break			
9:00-10:30 Team leader facilitates After-Action Review	• Identify key learnings from a project that went reasonably well over the past three months • Practice productive dialogue	• What did team members do well or need to keep doing to enable the team to succeed? • What can team members do differently to improve performance? • How can the team apply key learnings to future projects?	• After-Action Reviews (p. 361)

Time	Objectives	Key Questions	Activities and Materials
10:30–11:00 Closing remarks by team leader	• Review what the team accomplished during the day • Clarify key messages from the session • Remind the team what needs to happen before the next monthly meeting	• What progress did we make today? • What will we tell our staff after the meeting? • What do we need to get done before the next meeting?	

Team Member's Agenda for Session 4

Time	Objectives	Key Questions	Activities and Materials
1:00–1:10 Team member's opening remarks	• Set expectations for participation • Review the afternoon agenda • Review meeting ground rules	• What do we need to accomplish at the session?	
1:10–3:00 Team member facilitates After-Action Review	• Identify key learnings from a project that went reasonably well over the past three months • Practice productive dialogue	• What did team members do well or need to keep doing to enable the team to succeed? • What can team members do differently to improve performance? • How can the team apply key learnings to future projects?	• After-Action Reviews (p. 361)
3:00–3:30 Closing remarks by team leader	• Review what the team accomplished during the day • Clarify key messages from the session • Remind the team what needs to happen before the next monthly meeting	• What progress did we make today? • What will we tell our staff after the meeting? • What do we need to get done before the next meeting?	

Chapter 12

Onboarding New Team Members

Faisal was excited about his new role with GreenWave Foods. Prior to joining GreenWave, he spent four years working at ColaCo, one of the world's largest packaged food and beverage companies. GreenWave was a much smaller company whose footprint was limited to North America, but Faisal was stepping into a much bigger role. However, working for GreenWave would require some adjustments on his part. On a personal level, he moved from the East Coast to Oregon and noticed people were a lot more laid-back in Portland—a welcome change from the rat race he left behind. On the career front, Faisal was coming from a global company known for its marketing sophistication, and he expected to have many opportunities to help his GreenWave colleagues elevate their game.

Faisal's boss was out of the office during his first week on the job. Jill had arranged for her executive assistant to show Faisal his cubicle and provide a list of onboarding activities he was to complete before the end of the week. These tasks included getting a security badge, laptop, and cell phone; signing up for insurance and retirement programs; and attending a one-day onboarding program to learn about the company's strategy, values, and code of conduct.

Faisal was excited to be heading into his first meeting with his new teammates on his third day at GreenWave. As he was accustomed to doing at ColaCo, he showed up to the meeting a few minutes late and was annoyed to find that his peers had started the meeting without him. He thought this was incredibly rude, but said nothing. During the meeting, the discussion turned to changes in customer preferences. At ColaCo, Faisal had been intimately involved in customer research, so he shared some insights from a recent study he had completed. Expecting his new colleagues to be grateful for the information he brought to the table, he was shocked when two of them started asking questions about his methodology. "Who do these rubes think they are?" Faisal thought to himself. Toward the end of the meeting, one of his colleagues summarized the decisions the team had made. Faisal had not agreed with any of these decisions, so he cautioned, "This seems premature. Shouldn't we run these by Jill?" His teammates looked at each other before one of them said, "We are fully empowered at GreenWave." With that, the team proceeded to nail down action items and assignments, some of which were allocated to Faisal. Although he didn't appreciate teammates assigning him work, he kept his disgruntlement to himself.

Working at home on Saturday morning, Faisal needed additional information to complete one of his assigned tasks. He sent an email to everyone on the team asking where he could access this information. By that evening he still hadn't received a response, so he sent the team a second email. Sunday came and went with no response, and Faisal was furious at being ignored and started to feel that he had made a big mistake coming to GreenWave.

A BETTER APPROACH TO ONBOARDING NEW TEAM MEMBERS

Faisal's story illustrates the gaps that occur in traditional onboarding processes that are limited to administrative tasks and learning about a company's history, products and services, organizational structure, and policies. Missing from Faisal's onboarding experience was the opportunity to learn about his new team's approach to making decisions, tradition of starting meetings on time, rules about answering emails on the weekend, and accepted practice of challenging each other. What Faisal interpreted as rudeness was actually his new team abiding by their norms.

The Rocket Model and related tools can be used to accelerate the onboarding process, reduce misunderstandings and potential friction, and help new team members add value sooner. Instead of letting Faisal figure things out on his own, Jill could have asked him and the rest of the team to go through a New Team Member Onboarding Checklist. By assigning different topics on the checklist to various members of the team, Jill also could have helped Faisal build relationships with his peers.

New Team Member Onboarding Checklist

Component	Key Actions	Who	Due Date
Context	• What does the team know about its key customers and competitors? • Who are the key internal and external stakeholders? • What are the team's political and economic realities? • What are the team's top challenges?	Bob	June 1
Mission	• What are the team's purpose and goals? How does it define success? • What are the team's 30-, 60-, 90-, and 120-day plans? • When is progress against goals and plans reviewed?	Kumar	June 2
Talent	• Who is responsible for what on the team? • Who does the new team member need to work most closely with? • How is the team rewarded for performance?	Julie	June 3
Norms	• What processes or systems does the team use to get work done? • When is the training for these processes and systems? • What are the key work handoffs? • What are the team's Operating Rhythm and meeting rules? • What topics get discussed/decided in team meetings? • How does the team make decisions? • What are the team's rules about returning emails? • What are the rules around ownership and accountability?	Ernesto and DeShawn	June 4-5
Buy-In	• How does the new team member contribute to team success?	Mary	June 8
Resources	• What resources are available? • What resources does the new team member need to succeed? • How much authority and political capital does the team have?	Alfredo	June 9
Courage	• What are the rules around team conflict? • When is it appropriate to challenge others? • Are there any topics that are taboo?	Moamar	June 10
Results	• How has the team performed over the past year? • How does the team win? • What has the team learned from past successes and mistakes?	Jill	June 11

CONCLUDING COMMENTS

Organizations pay a lot of money to get new employees hired and trained, yet some have shockingly high six-month turnover rates. No selection system is perfect, so some level of employee turnover is inevitable. Some of this retention problem is also due to the nature of the work to be performed, pay, and company values, but higher than expected turnover rates are a tremendous waste of time and money. Some employee turnover can also be attributed to poor team integration and, unlike company pay policies, this is a factor under a leader's immediate control. Leaders can bypass six months of rookie mistakes and mutual frustration and improve new staff retention by covering the eight Rocket Model components shortly after a new employee joins the team.

Chapter 13

Training Leaders to Build High-Performing Teams

Blue Tiger started selling niche products to teens and young adults about 30 years ago. Savvy marketing and execution excellence helped the company enjoy annual double-digit growth and become one of the world's most recognizable brands. P&L responsibility resides at the country level, and country leadership teams consist of a general manager (GM) and the directors of marketing, sales, supply chain, finance, IT, human resources, and legal services. A huge proponent of entrepreneurism and ownership, Blue Tiger's country leadership teams are given considerable latitude to hit their numbers.

To no one's surprise, the company's phenomenal success quickly spurred imitators. Numerous local competitors emerged, and some international competitors with deep pockets introduced new brands and leveraged well-established distribution channels. With more competitors entering the market, countries started struggling to meet annual sales and profitability targets. Senior leadership initially thought that increased competition was the culprit and believed that new products and better marketing campaigns would best remedy the situation. However, further analysis showed that country teams facing almost identical competitive pressures achieved dramatically different results. No doubt increased competition was causing headwinds, but there was more to the story. Digging deeper, Blue Tiger found that some leaders were consistently better at delivering good results; when they moved from country to country, improved performance followed. Intrigued, Michelle, Blue Tiger's chief human resources officer (CHRO), asked the talent analytics team to figure out what was causing these leaders to achieve consistently strong results.

DIAGNOSIS

The talent analytics team spent several weeks sifting through all the data they had on 200 past and current country GMs. Were high-performing GMs smarter, enabling them to put better strategies in place? Did they have different personality profiles? For example, were they more charismatic or focused on driving results? Did they have different experience profiles or educational backgrounds? The analytics team found that being smarter, more experienced, more ambitious, and keeping dark-side personality traits in check certainly helped, but these assets only had modest relationships with country performance. The team conducted interviews with GMs and staff in high-performing and low-performing countries and discovered that effective teamwork was the key difference between winning and losing.

SOLUTION

Michelle shared these findings with the CEO and Executive Leadership Team (ELT). Many questioned the results, but Michelle had her ducks in a row and was able to convince the top team that effective teamwork was a competitive advantage. The ELT started thinking about what Blue Tiger could do to improve teamwork—and not just within its country leadership teams. If effective teamwork made that much of a difference to Blue Tiger's results, then team-building capability was important at all levels of the organization. With more than 1,000 headquarters, regional, country, and functional teams, the ELT realized that hiring facilitators to work with each team was not a viable option. The CEO asked Michelle to develop a practical solution to improve teamwork across the company.

Michelle met with the HR Leadership Team (HRLT) to discuss options. After several hours of lively debate, the team decided an enterprise-wide leadership development program that taught team leaders how to build high-performing teams would be the best way to go. Because the vast majority of leaders were out in the field, the program needed to be highly practical—complex academic team models and concepts would get ripped to shreds by the audience. They wanted a program based on solid team research, but packaged in a way that was easily understood by participants. Providing leaders with feedback on team functioning and performance was also important, as this would give insight into team strengths, areas of improvement, and how the team compared to other teams; compel them to take action; and allow HR to look at team-building capabilities within and across functions and countries. But teaching team concepts and providing feedback on team performance by themselves were not enough. The program also needed to provide leaders with easy-to-use tools and techniques to improve team performance.

Having determined some of the overarching considerations for the leadership development program, Michelle asked Paola, the VP of talent management, to work out several other issues affecting program design and delivery. These issues included selecting a team framework, working out program length and logistics, and determining how to evaluate program impact.

TEAM-ORIENTED LEADERSHIP DEVELOPMENT PROGRAM DESIGN CONSIDERATIONS

- Choose a framework.
- What do participants need to learn?
- Who attends? Program size?
- What content and pedagogy?
- Program length?
- Program materials?
- Program logistics?
- Who delivers?
- Program impact?

Choose a framework. The first, and perhaps most important, decision was selecting a team-building framework for the leadership development program. Paola and the learning and development (L&D) team began by reviewing different team approaches, such as Tuckman's Forming-Storming-Norming-Performing Model, Lencioni's Five Dysfunctions of a Team, Wiley's Five Behaviors of a Cohesive Team, Hackman's Model of Team Effectiveness,

Whelan's Integrated Model of Group Development, and the Drexler-Sibbet Team Performance Model. After investigating different team frameworks, Blue Tiger's L&D team landed on the Rocket Model because it was practical and easy to understand, had strong research underpinnings, included a comprehensive and validated team assessment, came with over 30 field-tested team improvement tools, and had been used in leadership development programs attended by over 5,000 leaders.

What do participants need to learn? As Stephen Covey famously said, start with the end in mind. Paola and the L&D team needed to clarify what participants needed to learn and be able to do after they left the leadership development program. After considerable debate within the L&D team and in consultation with country GMs and headquarters staff, two major program objectives were to provide participants with insight on who they were as leaders and to explore how this played out with their teams. The final objectives for the leadership development program were:

1. Reflect on how past events shape who you are as a leader.
2. Understand how your personality affects your leadership style.
3. Develop a personal definition of leadership.
4. Understand the difference between groups and teams.
5. Understand the eight components of the Rocket Model of team performance.
6. Review the Team Assessment Survey (TAS) Feedback Report for your team.
7. Create a Followership Scatterplot for your team.
8. Practice implementing team improvement tools.
9. Build Action Plans to implement team improvement tools.

Who attends? Program size? Blue Tiger's CEO mandated that all 1,000 leaders were to attend the leadership development program. The top leaders at headquarters and country GMs would go first, as this would allow their staff to see some of the tools in action before they attended the program. Fifty programs consisting of 12-24 participants were scheduled in order to get all 1,000 leaders trained over a two-year period.

What content and pedagogy? The learning objectives drove the program content and included concepts and team improvement activities from this book, the TAS, and the Hogan Personality Inventory (HPI). To facilitate learning, participants sat in four-person learning pods that engaged in small group learning activities. The program was highly interactive and included a mix of lecturettes, individual and small group activities, large group report-outs and discussions, peer coaching, and team improvement activity teach-back sessions. A detailed program design is provided at the end of this chapter.

Program length? There was considerable debate about the length of the program, with some arguing for a shorter program to reduce cost and time away from work, and others arguing for a longer program to ensure learnings were applied back home. After these discussions, program length was set for two days.

Program materials? Each program attendee would receive a customized participant manual, an HPI Feedback Report, a TAS Feedback Report, *Ignition: A Guide to Building High-Performing Teams*, and electronic access to the team improvement activity support materials.

Program logistics? The L&D team put together a two-year training calendar for the 50 programs. They coordinated training locations as well as room setup, A/V, and meal and beverage requirements. Participant manuals were printed and participants were sent introductory emails that included a message from the CEO, a list of learning objectives, an agenda, the location, lodging details, and HPI and TAS instructions six weeks before each program.

Who delivers? To minimize costs, six L&D staff members and four HR business partners attended the pilot program and two-day train-the-trainer session. These individuals would deliver all 50 programs, with most using two facilitators.

Program impact? Participants were told that Blue Tiger was going to administer a second TAS once everyone had completed the leadership development program. A comparison of results between the first and second TAS would be used to measure program impact. Country operational, financial, customer, and employee metrics would also be used to evaluate program impact.

TWO DAYS	
Day 1	**Day 2**
• Introductions and Overview • What Is Leadership? • Learning from the Past: Journey Lines • Leadership and Personality: HPI • Who Do I Want to Be as a Leader? • Team Quiz • Groups vs. Teams • Rocket Model Overview and Puzzle • TAS Review	• Overview and Reflection • Peer Coaching • Followership • Team Teach-Back Preparation • Team Teach-Back Report-Outs • Team Action Planning and Peer Coaching • Next Steps

ACCOUNTABILITY MECHANISMS

A second TAS was going to be administered in order to check on team progress.

OUTCOME

The program was successfully delivered to 1,000 leaders. There were also a number of country managers who were able to use the TAS results and team improvement tools to turn their country teams around and record much stronger financial and operational results. These GMs were asked to share their stories across the company.

CONCLUDING COMMENTS

For some unknown reason, the idea of team building has become inextricably linked to internal and external consultants. Need to restructure a team? Call a consultant. Need to do a fun event with your team? Call a consultant. Need to launch a new team? Call HR for advice. We have come to believe that it is impossible to build teams without outside help.

It's true that team coaching engagements are powerful ways to get teams to the next level of performance. The problem is these interventions don't scale. Organizations consist of hundreds if not thousands of teams, yet a consultant can only work with a handful of teams at any given time. They also can't afford to have consultants work with all of their teams. Consultants add the most value by helping C-suite teams and those critical to strategy formulation and execution get to the next level of performance.

Most organizations train leaders on how to create strategies, manage performance, and communicate effectively. Why can't they teach leaders how to build high-performing teams? The Rocket Model, TAS Feedback Reports, and team improvement activities were designed to be easy to understand and practical to use. All of the materials needed to teach leaders how to build high-performing teams can be found in this book, so there is no excuse for letting them sink or swim when it comes to building teams. The ability to build teams is fundamental to leadership and should be viewed no differently than goal-setting or delegation skills when it comes to training leaders. It's a crime that organizations offer little formal training for building high-performing teams.

The program described in this chapter is by no means the final answer; we have developed and delivered a wide variety of one- and two-day leadership development programs for building high-performing teams. What is taught, who attends, and program length all depend on the problems an organization is trying to solve as well as budgetary and operational constraints. Because leaders tend to greatly overestimate their team-building skills and are infinitely interested in themselves, we recommend the TAS be part of any team-oriented leadership development program. The best designs include the Rocket Model, TAS, and team improvement activities.

Imagine what would happen to organizational performance if the percentage of high-performing teams jumped from 20 to 40 or 50%? Or if those teams critical to strategy implementation were high performing? The cost of getting leaders trained and holding them accountable for building effective teams is far less than the potential benefit. It's time we got on with it.

Program Prework

- HPI
- TAS
- TQ: *The Elusive Factor in Successful Teams* white paper

Trainer's Agenda for Day 1

Time	Objectives	Key Questions	Activities and Materials
8:00-8:30 Opening remarks by trainer	• Review learning objectives • Review program agenda • Set program ground rules • Do participant introductions	• What will we cover during the program? • Who is attending the program?	• PowerPoints • Flip Chart
8:30-9:00 Trainer leads discussion on leadership	• Review leadership definitions • Clarify the differences between leadership and management • Clarify the links between leadership and teams	• What is leadership? • What are the differences between leadership and management? • What is the relationship between leadership and teams?	• PowerPoints • Flip Chart
9:00-9:15 Break			
9:15-10:45 Trainer asks participants to complete Journey Lines	• Learn how the past affects who you are as a leader	• What have been the significant events in participants' lives? • How have these experiences shaped who they are as leaders?	• Journey Lines (p. 333)
10:45-12:00 Trainer helps participants interpret HPI	• Define personality • Learn how personality affects who you are as a leader	• What is personality? • How do personality traits affect leadership?	• HPI (p. 289)
12:00-12:45 Lunch			
12:45-1:45 Trainer helps participants create leadership credo	• Clarify one's personal definition of leadership	• What is your personal point of view about leadership? • What kind of leader do you strive to be?	
1:45-2:10 Trainer runs Team Quiz	• Clarify myths and misunderstandings about leadership and teamwork	• What do we know about leadership and teamwork?	• Team Quiz (p. 233)
2:10-2:30 Trainer clarifies difference between groups and teams	• Clarify the differences between groups and teams	• What are groups? • What are teams? • What does this mean for leaders?	• Groups vs. Teams (p. 205)
2:30-2:45 Break			
2:45-3:30 Trainer provides Rocket Model overview	• Familiarize participants with the eight components of effective team performance	• What does the team need to do to operate effectively?	• Rocket Model Slide Deck (p. 209)
3:30-3:50 Trainer runs Rocket Model Puzzle	• Familiarize participants with the eight components of effective team performance	• What does the team need to do to operate effectively?	• Rocket Model Puzzle (p. 211)

Time	Objectives	Key Questions	Activities and Materials
3:50-4:40 Trainer reviews the TAS Feedback Report	• Learn how to interpret a TAS Feedback Report	• What are my team's strengths, surprises, and weaknesses? • How does my team compare to other teams?	• TAS Feedback Report • Team Feedback Session (p. 227)
4:40-4:45 Trainer closes the day		• Any questions about the material covered today?	

Trainer's Agenda for Day 2

Time	Objectives	Key Questions	Activities and Materials
8:00-8:30 Opening remarks by trainer	• Review learning objectives • Review program agenda • Review ground rules • Reflect on key learnings	• What will we cover during the program? • What were the key learnings from Day 1?	• PowerPoints • Flip Chart
8:30-9:15 Trainer sets up peer coaching session	• Discuss TAS results with partners • Get coaching and guidance from partners	• What did I learn from my TAS results? • What are my team's strengths? • What do I plan to work on with my team?	• PowerPoints • TAS Feedback Report
9:15-9:30 Break			
9:30-11:00 Trainer asks participants to identify followership types	• Learn the four followership types • Assess followership types • Learn how leadership affects followership	• What is followership? • What kind of followers are on my team? • What will I do to improve followership?	• Followership Scatterplots (p. 271)
11:00-11:45 Trainer sets up team improvement activity teach-backs	• Practice facilitating Team Feedback Session • Practice facilitating Context Assessment exercise • Practice facilitating Roles and Responsibilities Matrix • Practice facilitating Operating Rhythm activity • Practice facilitating Decision-Making activity	• How can we teach the rest of the class how to set up and facilitate team improvement activities with their teams?	• Team Feedback Session (p. 227) • Context Assessment Exercise (p. 237) • Roles and Responsibilities Matrix (p. 265) • Operating Rhythm (p. 307) • Decision-Making (p. 315)
12:00-12:45 Lunch			

Time	Objectives	Key Questions	Activities and Materials
12:45-2:15 Trainer facilitates team teach-back report-outs	• Understand when to use and how to facilitate different team improvement activities	• When should I use different team improvement activities? • How should I facilitate different team improvement activities?	• Team Feedback Session (p. 227) • Context Assessment Exercise (p. 237) • Roles and Responsibilities Matrix (p. 265) • Operating Rhythm (p. 307) • Decision-Making (p. 315)
2:15-2:30 Break			
2:30-3:30 Trainer helps participants build Team Action Plans	• Build plans to improve team functioning and performance • Get coaching and guidance from partners	• What does the team need to do to operate effectively? • What team improvement activities will we use? • When will the team do them?	• Team Action Plans (p. 261)
3:30-4:00 Trainer closes the day	• Clarify program next steps • Encourage participants to share TAS results and implement team improvement activities • Provide encouragement	• What do you plan on doing with your team back home? • What were your key learnings from the program?	

Chapter 14

High-Potentials and Teams

When John Sully joined TelPro
as its chief human resources officer (CHRO), the company was in a crisis. The previous CEO had just taken an unexpected medical retirement and there were no internal candidates ready to take her place. After some pointed questioning, the board determined other critical roles also lacked ready-now successors. John's first task was to help TelPro implement a systematic approach for resolving TelPro's succession planning problem, and part of this solution included a process for identifying and developing high-potential talent. The identification process included a standard nine-box performance and potential framework and calibrated functional and regional talent discussions. The development process involved a six-month accelerated leadership development program that featured professors from top business schools and TelPro executives as facilitators. Using a combination of case studies and lectures, the program's three sessions covered market dynamics, business models, strategy, finance, investor relations, employee engagement, strengths, mindfulness, authenticity, and diversity and inclusion. The high-potential development program was a huge hit with executives and participants and won a nationally recognized award for training excellence.

The award was nice, but John knew expensive programs like these needed to demonstrate impact. John asked the talent analytics team to track the performance of the 10 participants after graduation, and was dismayed to hear grumbling about how some were faring. Faculty members agreed that Olga Wiener and Neville Schell were the best in the class, yet their performance after graduation was far from stellar. Because the high-potential program was one of his signature accomplishments and its two best and brightest graduates were struggling, John was eager to get things back on track.

DIAGNOSIS

John initially hired us to coach Olga and Neville. As part of our intake process, we asked both of their teams to complete a Team Assessment Survey (TAS). The Team Effectiveness Quotient (TQ) scores for their respective teams were 29 and 15. No wonder they were floundering.

We shared the results with John and told him we weren't surprised. Like many high-potentials, Neville and Olga had gone to the right schools, held jobs of increasing responsibility within their functions, were loyal, and left strong, positive impressions on those above them. High-potentials often succeed because of their own talent and efforts, but flounder when placed in positions where they need to build teams to succeed. Goals eventually become too big to be accomplished by a lone individual, no matter how talented he or she may be.

Based on these results, John decided to put the other eight graduates of the high-potential program through a TAS. The group's results showed only a third of the graduates had average or above average team-building skills; the rest were below average or downright bad when it came to building high-performing teams. The stars, Olga Wiener and Neville Schell, were at the bottom of the distribution. These results indicated TelPro's high-potential program was over-indexed on individual contributor skills. All were skilled at managing up, but most were clueless when it came to building teams.

TAS Results for TelPro's High-Potentials

NAME	CONTEXT	MISSION	TALENT	NORMS	BUY-IN	RESOURCES	COURAGE	RESULTS	TQ
Huang	84	28	88	58	78	70	78	40	66
McCartney	52	94	54	42	62	38	44	62	56
Pilar	46	22	60	57	42	62	56	56	50
Poon	34	32	60	46	40	42	40	48	43
Matumbo	68	66	30	16	20	68	20	40	41
Jiang	34	60	56	32	30	38	30	24	38
Whelan	32	32	20	22	38	50	38	46	35
Wiener	16	50	34	22	18	34	30	30	29
Takaki	4	4	38	16	38	20	26	40	23
Schell	16	20	28	22	16	4	6	8	15
Average	39	41	47	33	36	43	37	39	

SOLUTION

John made three decisions that profoundly impacted TelPro's next high-potential program.

High-potential eligibility. John, along with TelPro's Executive Leadership Team (ELT), decided that candidates had to be leading teams to be eligible for high-potential consideration. The stretch from individual contributor to a director or VP role after program graduation was proving to be too great. Candidates needed to have experience hiring, developing, and firing staff; getting people to work together towards common goals; and maintaining a track record of *team* success before they would be considered for mission-critical roles.

High-potential identification. John got the ELT to adopt a more rigorous, data-based process for identifying high-potential talent. The new process consisted of:

- The *Hogan Personality Inventory (HPI)*, which provides an overview of a person's typical day-to-day behaviors that can facilitate or inhibit their ability to achieve goals and get along with others. HPI Managerial Potential scores range from 0-100 and would factor into candidates' Overall Potential scores.
- The *Hogan Business Reasoning Inventory (HBRI)*, which measures a person's ability to correctly identify and solve problems. HBRI Critical Reasoning scores are a combination of problem identification and resolution capabilities, range from 0-100, and contribute to candidates' Overall Potential scores.
- A *TAS*, administered to candidates and his or her direct reports. TAS Team Effectiveness Quotient (TQ) scores range from 0-100, are an indicator of the extent to which candidates can build high-performing teams, and would be part of candidates' Overall Potential scores.
- The *Hogan Development Survey (HDS)*, which measures 11 performance risks, or derailment tendencies. The HDS can help candidates understand and manage their reactions to stres s and the results would be used to calculate Overall Risk scores.

Overall Potential scores ranged from 0-100 and were based on a combination of candidates' Managerial Potential, Critical Reasoning, and TQ scores. These three inputs were evenly weighted. Examples of Overall Potential score calculations for three high-potential candidates can be found below:

Overall Potential Calculation

HPI Managerial Potential Scores	HBRI Critical Reasoning Scores	TAS TQ Scores	Overall Potential Scores
68	38	22	43
39	88	35	54
66	77	70	71

John explained to the ELT that Overall Potential scores described the extent to which candidates had the right stuff. Smart, resilient, ambitious, earnest, innovative, and socially skilled candidates who could build teams would receive higher Overall Potential scores than those who were less career oriented, creative, socially skilled, and adept at solving problems or building teams.

John also told the ELT that Overall Risk scores determined the extent to which candidates had the wrong stuff. He gave real-world examples of dark-side traits, when they were likely to emerge, and how they interfered with a leader's ability to build teams and get work done through others. John also described research showing that the greater the number of HDS traits in the high-risk zone, the more likely leaders would exhibit counterproductive behaviors under stress.

Overall Risk Calculation

HDS Traits in the High-Risk Zone (>90)	Multiplying Factor	Overall Risk Scores
0	9	0
2	9	18
5	9	45

Overall Risk scores ranged from 0-99 and were calculated by multiplying the number of HDS trait scores in the high-risk zone (e.g., > 90) by nine. (There are 11 dark-side personality traits on the HDS.) Candidates with greater numbers of HDS traits in the high-risk zone would receive a higher Overall Risk score; those with fewer dark-side traits would have a lower score. John asked the previous group of high-potential candidates to complete the HPI, HBRI, and HDS and combined them with their TAS results. John told the ELT that Olga and Neville had moderate Overall Potential, but some of the group's highest Overall Risk scores. These two had done a great job at leaving a positive impression on the ELT, but their dark-side tendencies were alive and well when leading their teams.

John added the Overall Potential and Overall Risk scores to the one-page summaries that included pictures, job and educational histories, performance management ratings, and boss ratings for potential candidates. The additional information looked something like this:

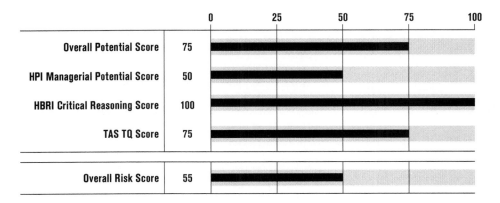

Dark-Side Traits >90

- Excitable
- Skeptical
- Cautious
- Reserved
- Diligent

Because it provided a more comprehensive view of promotion potential and risk and permitted better apples-to-apples comparisons between candidates, this new information became a prominent feature in ELT succession-planning and high-potential identification discussions. The 12 selected for the next accelerated leadership development had higher Overall Potential and lower Overall Risk scores than most of the other nominees.

High-potential development. Not only were different kinds of candidates identified as high-potentials, John also did a major revamp of the accelerated leadership program so that it focused more on building teams. John used an action learning framework to redesign the accelerated leadership development program, as it would give candidates hands-on exposure to parts of the business they may not be familiar with and get them thinking at an enterprise-wide level. This approach would also generate viable solutions to some of the organization's most vexing problems, develop the leadership and team-building skills of participants, and give executives a chance to observe high-potential talent in action.

FOUR MONTHS			
Session 1 **(3 days)**	**Session 2** **(2 days)**	**Session 3** **(2 days)**	**Session 4** **(1.5 days)**
• Opening Comments by CEO and CHRO • What Is Action Learning? • Journey Lines • Market Dynamics • Corporate Strategy • Scoping Documents • Personal Learning Goals • Team Action Planning • Roles and Responsibilities Matrix • Operating Rhythm • Communication • Team Deliverables	• Team Action Plan Review • Organizational Visit • HDS Review • Team Action Planning • Personal Learning Updates • Team Norm Evaluation • Team Deliverables	• Team Action Plan Review • Presentation Preparation • ELT Presentation and Feedback • Feedback Analysis • Team Action Planning • Personal Learning Updates • Team Norm Evaluation • Team Deliverables	• Presentation Preparation • ELT Presentation and Decision • Peer Feedback • Personal and Team Learning • Inheriting New Teams • Closing Comments

John asked Rocio, his VP of talent management, to lead the accelerated leadership development program redesign and delivery efforts. Rocio worked with the ELT to clarify program objectives, identify two action learning team topics, select action learning team sponsors, create scoping documents, spell out roles and responsibilities, and work out the designs for the four sessions. The first session was dedicated to getting the action learning teams launched. This involved introducing sponsors and team coaches, reviewing and asking questions about scoping documents and assigned problems, creating initial Team Action Plans, defining team member roles and responsibilities, establishing team Norms, and clarifying personal learning objectives.

The highlight of Session 2 was a visit to another company doing something related to the problem the action learning teams were tasked to resolve. For example, the team tasked with developing better customer service met with leaders at Disney to learn about their approach to customers.

Rocio designed Session 3 to be a progress review. By this time, the action learning teams had completed much of their due diligence and had started to explore potential solutions for their assigned problems. They submitted presentations on their preliminary analyses and potential solutions and were given feedback on how to best proceed. The teams then worked this guidance into their final deliverables for Session 4.

Each action learning team submitted a white paper on their problem background, data reviewed, final recommendations, cost/benefits analysis, and implementation plan to the ELT and the other action learning team before Session 4. They also completed a formal presentation on the assigned topic and received a final decision from the ELT on whether to move ahead with their recommended solution. During Session 4, time was also spent providing peer feedback, identifying what participants learned about themselves and teamwork, and preparing participants to take over new teams after graduation.

ACCOUNTABILITY MECHANISMS

Deliverables and Action Plan updates were regular components of action learning team gatherings. Team Norms evaluations were conducted at the end of Sessions 2 and 3, and Session 4 included a Team Feedback Session. Session 3 included a preliminary presentation and Session 4 included each action learning team's white paper and final presentation.

OUTCOME

The final recommendations for both action learning teams were accepted and put into place by the ELT. The customer service initiative was credited for improving net promoter scores from 22 to 33, reducing customer churn by 10%, and improving annual revenues by 3%. This improvement in business results made true believers out of the ELT and paid for the accelerated leadership development program many times over.

The second round of accelerated leadership development program graduates were also more skilled at building high-performing teams. Ten of the 12 participants had been transferred to other teams after graduation, and a year later their overall average TQ score was 68.

CONCLUDING COMMENTS

Lack of leadership bench strength has been a major concern of CEOs for at least 20 years. Based on what we are hearing from our clients, this remains one of the top challenges facing organizations today. Managing talent has become a major organizational imperative and we've come to believe that companies with the best talent are going to win. Yet Enron, GE, Motorola, and others populated with top players have either gone bankrupt or are shells of their former selves. We think that talent is only half of the answer; the most successful companies over the long term are those with *the best talent and the best teams*.

One of the reasons why organizations continue struggling with a lack of leadership bench strength is that their talent management systems measure the wrong things. You do not need to be a leader to be smart, innovative, resilient, hard-working, outgoing, and easy to get along with. These attributes just as easily describe good marketers, salespeople, customer service reps, accountants, and engineers as they do leaders. What differentiates individual contributors with the right stuff from leaders is the latter's ability to build high-performing teams. Organizations get what they measure, and their talent management systems over-index on individual contributor characteristics and say little about team-building capabilities. This is one reason why so few teams in organizations are high performing.

Talent management systems ensure organizations recruit and hire the right candidates, develop employees, evaluate and reward performance, identify high-potential talent, and support succession management. Systems that incorporate objective performance data and personality, mental ability, and 360-degree assessments are fairer and result in better talent decisions than those that rely on opinion and gut instinct. But these components alone are not enough, as they primarily measure individual contributor abilities and cannot determine the extent to which candidates can build high-performing teams. Consequently, many organizations end up promoting LINOs, or leaders-in-name-only. These individuals are smart, ambitious, hard-working, get things done, and are adept at strategic sucking-up; whether they can create loyal followings, build high-performing teams, and get things done through others is another matter.

CEOs would get more sleep if teams were included in talent management processes. Interview protocols that included teams could be used to evaluate new hires for leadership roles. Leaders could be trained on how to build teams and then be given feedback on team dynamics and performance. Performance reviews and promotion decisions could include a team component, and rewards could be based on team as well as individual accomplishments. These recommendations are not particularly difficult to adopt and Human Resources would add more value if teams were factored into their talent management systems.

Finally, there are many different ways to identify and develop high-potential talent. We described a robust, data-based approach that leveraged personality, mental abilities, and team information to make informed high-potential selection decisions. The Rocket Model was a subtle but important aspect of the accelerated leadership development program, as the Context, Mission, Talent, Norms, Buy-In, Resources, Courage, and Results components were addressed and associated team improvement activities were included in the program design. Any high-potential program that leverages information about team-building capabilities and teaches participants how to build high-performing teams will yield better results than programs that perpetuate the myth of the superstar individual contributor.

Facilitator's Agenda for Session 1, Day 1

Time	Objectives	Key Questions	Activities and Materials
8:00-9:15 Opening remarks by CEO and CHRO	• Describe the state of the business • Outline objectives of the program • Set expectations for participation • Review the program agenda • Set session ground rules	• What is the state of the business? • Where is the company going? • How will it get there? • What do the action learning teams need to accomplish?	• PowerPoints • Flip Chart
9:15-10:00 CLO leads discussion about action learning	• Describe the rationale for using an action learning approach • Describe the key components of action learning programs • Clarify participants' roles in the action learning teams • Clarify action learning team deliverables	• What is action learning? • What should participants expect to learn from the program? • What are the time commitments for participating in the program? • What will the action learning teams need to deliver?	• PowerPoints
10:00-10:15 Break			
10:15-11:45 Facilitator leads each action learning team through Journey Lines	• Help team members learn about each other • Begin building trust and camaraderie	• What life experiences have shaped team members?	• Journey Lines (p. 333)
11:45-12:45 Lunch			
12:45-5:00 CMO does interactive presentation on market dynamics (Includes a break)	• Create a common view of the situation facing the company	• Who are the company's biggest customers, competitors, potential disruptors, etc.? • What are the key market forces? • What are the company's biggest challenges? • What is the company's business model?	• PowerPoints
5:00-5:15 Closing remarks by CLO	• Review what was accomplished during the day • Tell the teams what they will be doing on Day 2	• What did we learn today? • What do we need to get done tomorrow?	
6:00-8:00 Dinner with ELT	• Provide informal time for socializing		

Facilitator's Agenda for Session 1, Day 2

Time	Objectives	Key Questions	Activities and Materials
8:00-8:30 Opening remarks by CLO	• Outline objectives of the program • Set expectations for participation • Review the program agenda • Review session ground rules	• What do the action learning teams need to accomplish?	• PowerPoints • Flip Chart
8:30-11:45 Professor leads interactive strategy discussion (Includes a break)	• Develop a common definition of strategy • Clarify the company's strategic choices and overarching strategy	• What is strategy? • What are the company's strategic choices? • What is the company's strategy? • How is the company's strategy different from competitors?	• PowerPoints
11:45-12:45 Lunch			
12:45-2:45 CLO introduces scoping documents to action learning teams	• Clarify the action learning team deliverables and due dates	• What problem does each action learning team need to solve? • What is in and out of scope? • What are the action learning team deliverables? • What budgets do the action learning teams have? • What other organizations struggle with these problems? • What questions do the action learning teams have for the ELT?	• PowerPoints • Scoping Documents
2:45-3:00 Break			
3:00-5:00 CLO facilitates an action learning team and ELT discussion	• Clarify the action learning team deliverables and due dates	• What problem does each action learning team need to solve? • What is in and out of scope? • What are the action learning team deliverables? • What budgets do the action learning teams have? • What other organizations struggle with these problems?	• PowerPoints • Scoping Documents
5:00-5:15 Closing remarks by CLO	• Review what was accomplished during the day • Tell the teams what they will be doing on Day 3	• What did we learn today? • What do we need to get done tomorrow?	
6:00-8:00 Team dinner	• Provide informal time for socializing		

Facilitator's Agenda for Session 1, Day 3

Time	Objectives	Key Questions	Activities and Materials
8:00-8:30 Opening remarks by CLO	• Outline objectives of the program • Set expectations for participation • Review the program agenda • Review session ground rules	• What do the action learning teams need to accomplish?	• PowerPoints • Flip Chart
8:30-11:45 CLO facilitates Team Action Plan development (Includes a break)	• Develop a Team Action Plan	• What does the team need to do to solve the problem it's been assigned? • What data needs to be gathered? • Who needs to be visited? • Whose support is needed?	• Team Action Plans (p. 261) • Flip Chart
11:45-12:45 Lunch			
12:45-1:45 CLO helps team members clarify personal learning goals	• Clarify personal learning goals	• What do team members want to learn and work on during the project?	
1:45-3:00 CLO helps action learning teams clarify roles	• Clarify the roles and responsibilities of action learning team members	• What do members want to work on? • What experiences are they looking to gain or what skills do they want to develop? • Who is responsible for what in the Team Action Plan? • What is the workload balance of team members?	• Team Action Plans (p. 261) • Roles and Responsibilities Matrix (p. 265)
3:00-3:15 Break			
3:15-4:15 CLO helps action learning teams create Operating Rhythm	• Determine the frequency, timing, and rules for action learning team meetings	• When should the team meet? • What should it talk about? • Who runs the meetings? • What are the rules for the meetings?	• Operating Rhythm (p. 307)
4:15-4:45 CLO helps action learning teams create communication norms	• Clarify rules around communication modes, response times, etc.	• How should team members keep each other informed? • How quickly do team members need to respond to others?	• Communication (p. 319)
4:45-5:05 CLO reviews session deliverables	• Review deliverables for Session 2	• What needs to get done and who is responsible for making it happen before Session 2?	
5:05-5:15 Closing remarks by CLO	• Review what was accomplished during the first session • Tell the teams what they will be doing during Session 2	• What did we learn today? • What do we need to get done tomorrow?	

Facilitator's Agenda for Session 2, Day 1

Time	Objectives	Key Questions	Activities and Materials
8:00-8:15 Opening remarks by CLO	• Outline objectives of the program • Set expectations for participation • Review the program agenda • Review session ground rules	• What do the action learning teams need to accomplish?	• PowerPoints • Flip Chart
8:15-11:45 CLO facilitates Team Action Plan review (Includes a break)	• Update the Team Action Plan	• What data have been gathered? • What analyses have been conducted? • What are the implications? • What additional data are needed? • Whose support is needed?	• Team Action Planning (p. 261) • Flip Chart
11:45-12:45 Lunch			
12:45-4:45 CLO helps team members with corporate field visit	• Understand how other companies handle a problem similar to the one assigned to the action learning team	• How do other companies view our problem? • How have they dealt with these issues? • What worked? Didn't work? • What can we learn from these companies?	• Corporate Field Visit
6:00-8:00 Team dinner			

Facilitator's Agenda for Session 2, Day 2

Time	Objectives	Key Questions	Activities and Materials
8:00-8:15 Opening remarks by CLO	• Outline objectives of the program • Set expectations for participation • Review the program agenda • Review session ground rules	• What do the action learning teams need to accomplish?	• PowerPoints • Flip Chart
8:15-9:30 CLO helps action learning team members interpret HDS results	• Help team members understand their dark-side traits and how they could affect team dynamics	• What are dark-side traits? • How do they get leaders into trouble? • What can leaders do to mitigate dark-side traits? • What are the team's collective dark-side traits?	• HDS (p. 293)
9:30-9:45 Break			

9:45-3:45 CLO facilitates Team Action Plan discussion and update (Includes lunch and a break)	• Update the Team Action Plan	• What data are still needed? • What analyses need to be conducted? • What are the implications? • Whose support is needed?	• Team Action Plans (p. 261) • Flip Chart
3:45-4:15 CLO facilitates personal learning discussion	• Update key learnings for each team member	• What have we learned so far?	
4:15-5:00 CLO facilitates team Norms evaluation and deliverables	• Ensure adherence to team Norms • Review session deliverables	• Are we living up to our Norms? • Who is doing what by Session 3?	

Facilitator's Agenda for Session 3, Day 1

Time	Objectives	Key Questions	Activities and Materials
8:00-8:15 Opening remarks by CLO	• Outline objectives of the program • Set expectations for participation • Review the program agenda • Review session ground rules	• What do the action learning teams need to accomplish?	• PowerPoints • Flip Chart
8:15-11:45 CLO facilitates Team Action Plan review (Includes a break)	• Update the Team Action Plan • Prepare initial presentation	• What data have been gathered? • What analyses have been conducted? • What are the implications? • What will we present to the ELT?	• Team Action Plans (p. 261) • Flip Chart
11:45-12:45 Lunch			
12:45-4:45 CLO helps teams present initial findings to ELT	• Get feedback from the ELT on data analyses and initial recommendations	• What data were gathered? • What did the data tell the team? • What are the team's initial recommendations?	• PowerPoints
6:00-8:00 Team dinner			

Facilitator's Agenda for Session 3, Day 2

Time	Objectives	Key Questions	Activities and Materials
8:00–8:15 Opening remarks by CLO	• Outline objectives of the program • Set expectations for participation • Review the program agenda • Review session ground rules	• What do the action learning teams need to accomplish?	• PowerPoints • Flip Chart
8:15–9:30 CLO helps action learning teams interpret presentation feedback	• Help team members understand the feedback from the ELT and other action learning team	• What did the ELT and other team like about the initial presentation? • What did the ELT and other team not like about the initial presentation? • What changes do we need to make?	
9:30–9:45 Break			
9:45–3:45 CLO facilitates Team Action Plan discussion and update (Includes lunch and a break)	• Update the Team Action Plan	• What data are still needed? • What analyses need to be conducted? • What are the implications? • Whose support is needed?	• Team Action Plans (p. 261) • Flip Chart
3:45–4:15 CLO facilitates a personal learning discussion	• Update key learnings for each team member	• What have we learned so far?	
4:15–5:00 CLO facilitates team Norms evaluation and deliverables	• Ensure adherence to team Norms • Review session deliverables	• Are we living up to our Norms? • Who is doing what by Session 4?	

Facilitator's Agenda for Session 4, Day 1

Time	Objectives	Key Questions	Activities and Materials
8:00–8:15 Opening remarks by CLO	• Outline objectives of the program • Set expectations for participation • Review the program agenda • Review session ground rules	What do the action learning teams need to accomplish?	• PowerPoints • Flip Chart
8:15–11:45 CLO facilitates Team Action Plan review (Includes a break)	• Prepare final presentation	• What are the team's final recommendations? • What is the rationale? • What is the implementation plan?	• PowerPoints

Time	Objectives	Key Questions	Activities and Materials
11:45-12:45 Lunch			
12:45-4:45 CLO helps teams present final recommendations to ELT	• Get final decision from the ELT on problem recommendations and implementation plan	• What are the team's final recommendations? • What is the implementation plan? • What are the costs/benefits?	• PowerPoints
6:00-8:00 Team dinner with ELT			

Facilitator's Agenda for Session 4, Day 2

Time	Objectives	Key Questions	Activities and Materials
8:00-8:15 Opening remarks by CLO	• Review session agenda	• What will action learning team members be doing?	• PowerPoints • Flip Chart
8:15-9:45 CLO helps facilitate Team Feedback Sessions	• Help team members understand how they were perceived by others during the project	• What did team members do well during the project? • What could team members do better during the project?	• Team Feedback Session (p. 227)
9:45-10:00 Break			
10:00-11:30 CLO facilitates personal learning discussion	• Update key learnings for each team member	• What were key learnings from the program?	• Personal and Team Learning (p. 373)
11:30-12:00 CLO closing remarks	• Clarify next steps for participants	• What are some things to consider when inheriting a new team?	• Chapter 11
12:00-1:00 Graduation lunch			

Chapter 15

Helping Organizations Foster Effective Teamwork

Compendia Consulting was a highly respected management consultancy with more than 40 offices around the world. Like many of their competitors, Compendia was organized into regions, practice areas, and functions. Teamwork was strong within local offices. Consultants enjoyed a strong sense of camaraderie, collaborated to support local clients, and took pride in hitting their office's P&L goals. Practice area employees, who were responsible for providing thought leadership and designing new products and services, were similarly supportive of colleagues within their respective practices. Functional employees, most of whom were based in the US, also enjoyed a strong sense of teamwork with their functional coworkers.

Although employees were organized into offices, practice areas, and functions, each of Compendia's top 25 accounts had dedicated client teams. Client teams were headed up by client managers (CMs), who were some of the company's top salespeople. CMs were responsible for cultivating close relationships with clients, retaining and growing their accounts, ensuring products and services were delivered when needed, and keeping clients happy. Client teams consisted of 8-15 people and were made up of office, practice area, and functional staff responsible for developing and delivering customized solutions across offices. Client team membership was not a full-time job for most employees; team members delivered top-25 client work as needed and spent the rest of their time servicing other accounts. Most found this other work more rewarding, as local client engagements enabled consultants to more easily achieve their individual productivity and sales goals.

Client managers assembled client teams when the company landed a new account. They communicated the products, services, locations, and scope of work that needed to be delivered to the appropriate office, practice area, and functional head, who then nominated employees for the client team. Because most team members were geographically dispersed, CMs would launch client teams through a series of teleconferences to get everyone up to speed on the client, customized solutions to be designed and delivered, and billable hour and travel considerations. CMs ran monthly review meetings with client teams once services started being delivered but because of competing priorities, most were poorly attended.

Ten years earlier, two of Compendia's strategic priorities were to establish an international footprint and service multinational accounts. It had successfully achieved these objectives and the company had a lot of positive momentum. Offices were opening around the globe, people were busy, and new products and services were regularly launched. Despite this flurry of activity, Compendia's growth rate and profitability had shrunk considerably over the past three years. After digging into the numbers, Finance pointed out that Compendia's offices served more than 1,000 clients, but 70% of their revenue and 85% of their profit came from the largest 25 accounts. Growing and retaining large multinational accounts was proving to be a struggle, and rectifying this situation became the company's top strategic priority.

Compendia executives received an earful during the most recent round of top-25 client visits. "We work with Compendia because your global footprint is a good match for our needs," one client explained, "but it's a theoretical match more than a real one. We can't count on receiving the same services across your offices. What we get in Shanghai looks very different from what we get in Chicago, and that isn't working for us." Other clients complained about local consultants not knowing their business, being unavailable to deliver work, or junior staff members being assigned to deliver more senior-level work.

The chief commercial officer subsequently called a global meeting of the 25 client managers who were embedded in Compendia's local offices. After sharing a summary of the client feedback, she asked them to share their thoughts. Following a few minutes of polite discussion, the CMs let loose:

- "I have to beg, borrow, and steal from other offices to get support for my clients. People don't show up for client team meetings to discuss client strategy or delivery problems."
- "The offices are exclusively focused on serving their local clients. They have zero loyalty to global clients."
- "There's no sense of ownership, except that my butt is on the line."
- "The practice areas design overly complex solutions, and then don't provide sufficient training across all the delivery offices. It's no wonder we can't execute globally."
- "Our technology investments aren't in sync with our clients' needs."
- "We lack the systems and processes to operationalize our solutions."

In short, a lack of teamwork was the key obstacle for Compendia's top strategic priority.

The chief commercial officer brought these issues back to the Executive Leadership Team (ELT). Although there was some acknowledgement of the problems the CMs brought forward, her peers on the ELT focused on different concerns:

- "Our CMs make promises to clients without involving the right people, and then wash their hands of the mess while the rest of the organization is forced to clean up behind them."
- "My staff are working many more hours than CMs let them bill to these projects. It's hard to generate enthusiasm when people get punished for doing what is right."
- "CMs sell client solutions that are too elaborate and not easily delivered. The amount of training given to consultants is woefully inadequate, and they only deliver this work a few times a year. How are they supposed to get good at this stuff?"

After several more minutes of complaints, the CEO decided he had heard enough and moved on to the next agenda item.

DIAGNOSIS

Compendia, like many organizations, talked a lot about teamwork and collaboration. Teamwork was one of the company's core values, yet they inadvertently did things that got in the way of fostering effective teamwork where it mattered most—serving their largest clients. When teams fall short, there is a tendency to blame team leaders, but organizations often bear part of the blame. Sometimes it is not the seed, but the soil that prevents effective teamwork from taking root. The answers to the following seven questions can help organizations determine the extent to which they are helping or hindering effective teamwork.

DOES YOUR ORGANIZATION FOSTER EFFECTIVE TEAMWORK?

- Have those teams critical to organizational success been identified?
- Is your C-suite team modeling effective teamwork?
- Does your organization have a common point of view about teamwork?
- Are teams part of your organization's talent management practices?
- Does your organization provide feedback on team dynamics and performance?
- Does your organization train leaders on how to build teams?
- Does your organization recognize and reward teamwork?

Have those teams critical to organizational success been identified? Compendia invested in teamwork in all the wrong places. The company sponsored twice-annual team days within offices, practice areas, and functions, which created a strong sense of teamwork within silos but detracted from teamwork on client teams that cut across organizational boundaries. Because retaining and expanding their largest accounts was Compendia's top strategic priority, the company erred by not helping client teams become high performing. Organizations should avoid treating all teams alike, and instead invest in those teams where high performance adds the most value to organizational outcomes. Organizations with an innovation-focused agenda will be better served having high-performing product development teams. Teams with revenue, P&L, or strategy execution responsibilities generally need to be higher performing than others. All teams may be equal, but some teams are more crucial to organizational success than others.

Is your C-suite team modeling effective teamwork? Compendia's CEO only wanted to hear good news. The ELT rarely worked through problems together and they were quick to challenge the data, point fingers, or shoot the messenger when contentious issues were raised. Because Compendia's C-suite team failed to work together effectively across organizational boundaries, there was little chance the leaders below them would act any differently. Regional and practice area leaders looked after their own, created buy-in for their own goals, and discouraged an enterprise mindset. As described in Chapter 10, effective teamwork starts at the top.

Does your organization have a common point of view about teamwork? Ironically, Compendia did. Being in the management consulting business, they were fond of models and had developed one for teams, so this was not one of their shortcomings. In contrast, most organizations lack a point of view on how to build teams. Ask any 20 leaders how to build high-performing teams and you will likely hear 20 different answers. To better promote teamwork, organizations would be well-served by providing leaders with a common framework or model for building high-performing teams. There are many models out there, including those by Tuckman, Hackman, Katzenbach and Smith, Drexler-Sibbet, Wheelan, Wiley, and Lencioni. Any model is better than none, and some are better than others. We believe the most comprehensive, adaptable, and well-researched framework is the Rocket Model.

Are teams part of your organization's talent management practices? In Chapter 1, we defined Team Effectiveness Quotient (TQ) as a leader's ability to build high-performing teams. Organizations can foster effective teamwork by incorporating TQ into their talent management systems. Leadership competency models, which are at the core of most talent management systems, are almost always over-indexed towards individual contributor competencies (e.g., integrity, dealing with ambiguity, or drive) or competencies that deal with direct reports on a one-on-one basis (e.g., coaching others, building relationships, or managing performance). Rarely, if ever, do leadership competency models include the ability to build high-performing teams. Although Compendia talked about teamwork, they hadn't incorporated the concept into the company's leadership competency model or talent management systems. Organizations can go a long way in promoting effective teamwork by considering team-building ability (TQ) in selection and succession decisions, building

TQ through leadership development programs, measuring TQ as part of annual performance management reviews, and rewarding leaders for fostering teamwork.

Does your organization provide feedback on team dynamics and performance? Like many other organizations, Compendia was big on using data and routinely administered 360-degree feedback and employee engagement surveys. These results compared well with global benchmarks but Compendia did not measure team dynamics and performance. If they had, they would have discovered that few client teams were high performing.

Aggregated employee engagement, 360-degree feedback, or personality results can provide good insight about *why* teams behave in a certain manner, but they say little about *what* teams are actually doing and *how* they are functioning. Organizations need team-level assessments in order to answer the *what* and *how* about teams. To paraphrase Peter Drucker, "If you don't measure it, then you can't manage it."

TQ Results by Function

NAME	CONTEXT	MISSION	TALENT	NORMS	BUY-IN	RESOURCES	COURAGE	RESULTS	TQ
Foundation	96	92	90	98	98	98	98	98	**96**
Business Unit #1	92	86	92	84	88	74	96	98	**89**
Corporate Services	78	50	82	92	94	60	92	92	**80**
Compliance	92	86	38	92	92	50	76	92	**77**
Audit	74	58	74	84	54	80	76	66	**71**
Legal	32	50	74	78	20	96	34	64	**56**
IT	60	84	52	62	34	64	18	62	**55**
Corporate Communication	30	8	12	24	30	36	46	70	**32**
Finance	12	26	6	22	38	60	28	40	**23**
Investment	6	10	32	36	32	38	34	56	**30**
HR	4	8	34	26	50	12	28	52	**27**
Business Unit #2	10	6	16	22	24	58	22	6	**20**
Average	**49**	**47**	**50**	**60**	**55**	**61**	**54**	**67**	**55**

Systematically collecting Team Assessment Survey (TAS) results allows organizations to do some interesting analyses. It can determine the extent to which those critical to strategy execution are high performing. These analyses can also determine if certain business units, functions, or geographies do a better job of fostering teamwork than others. The table provides an example of organizational feedback that is available by summarizing TAS results. Compendia's client teams would likely report very different results.

Another problem organizations experience by not providing team-level feedback is that leaders develop a false level of confidence in their own team-building abilities. They heartily agree that only one in five teams are high performing, and all believe theirs is the one on top. Our research shows that team leaders' TAS ratings average 1.0 to 1.5 points higher on a 5-point scale than team members. Team members are rarely surprised by TAS results; the same can't be said for team leaders. Compendia's CMs all thought they were great team leaders, unfortunately the rest of their teams didn't know it. This problem gets fixed by providing leaders with benchmarked feedback on their team's performance.

Does your organization train leaders on how to build teams? According to some estimates, organizations spend more than $15 billion annually on leadership development. Much of this training focuses on such things as self-insight, authenticity, executive presence, mindfulness, and coaching others. No doubt these are important topics, but most programs fail to teach leaders the blocking and tackling skills needed to build high-performing teams. No matter how well you dress or how much self-knowledge you possess, if you can't build teams, you're not a leader. Compendia did offer leadership training to those in formal leadership positions, but CMs were not considered formal leaders and were excluded from these programs. It may not have mattered all that much, as these programs did not address how to build high-performing teams. Organizations can tackle this issue by implementing the leadership development programs described in Chapter 13.

Does your organization recognize and reward teamwork? Most organizations say they value teamwork, but most compensation systems are built around individual performance. This can drive leaders to devote all of their energy and efforts to doing things themselves and giving lip service to teamwork. Steven Kerr, a former chief learning officer at Goldman Sachs and General Electric, called this "the folly of rewarding A while hoping for B." Compendia took pride in being a meritocracy and focused heavily on individual goals, performance, and rewards. Consultants were recognized for putting in billable hours and selling business to clients, yet Compendia's top 25 accounts offered consultants little opportunity in either of these categories. Organizations wanting to foster effective teamwork need to ensure their compensation systems reward rather than discourage teamwork.

CONCLUDING COMMENTS

There is a big gap between what organizations say and what they actually do when it comes to promoting collaboration and teamwork. We have asked more than 500 human resources, talent management, and organizational development professionals from around the globe to rate how well their organizations fared against the seven questions listed earlier in this chapter. On a 5-point scale, the average ratings across the seven questions ranged from 1.8 to 2.6. Clearly there is room for improvement. With the scarce support most organizations provide to those leading teams, it should be no surprise that only one in five is high performing.

There are three important lessons from this chapter. First, all teams are not equal when it comes to organizational impact. Organizations need to identify which teams have the biggest influence on customers, revenues, profitability, share price, and market share and differentially invest in their development. Many organizations differentially invest in their high-potential talent, they need to do the same for their most valuable teams. Organizations would get more bang for their development buck by giving those teams critical to organization performance the support they need to be high performing.

Second, the ability to build high-performing teams is a critical leadership skill that most organizations ignore. Few organizations have leadership competency models that include the ability to build high-performing teams, and fewer still factor TQ into their talent management processes. As a result, organizations hire, develop, and promote charismatic, socially skilled, and politically connected individuals at the expense of those who build teams and get things done. Changing talent management systems to include TQ is inexpensive and within the realm of Human Resources. Moreover, the payoff for doing this is quite substantial.

Third, providing leaders with feedback about actual team performance will go a long way toward improving teamwork across an organization. Once leaders learn what effective teamwork looks like, get feedback on how their teams compare to others, and implement team improvement activities to enhance team performance, organizations will be well on their way to creating a culture that truly promotes collaboration and teamwork. Imagine what happens to organizational performance, employee engagement, and top-talent retention when a majority of employees work on high-performing teams. With the Rocket Model, TAS, and this book, we have the technology to make it happen.

PART IV

Team Improvement Activities

Introduction:
Team Improvement
Activities

The next section of the book

provides step-by-step instructions for setting up and facilitating 40 different team improvement activities, many of which were listed in Chapters 3-15. A few of these activities are targeted at team leaders, but most are intended to be used with intact teams. The activities are designed to help teams have the right conversations and resolve their own issues. All have been field-tested and refined over the years, so we can confidently say they work.

Preparation is the key to running effective team improvement activities. Facilitators should set aside 30-60 minutes to review the instructions, become familiar with the support materials, make copies of handouts, and do one or two practice runs prior to a team engagement. Teams don't like facilitators who waste everyone's time fumbling through activities, so preparation time is time well spent.

The team improvement activities can be set up and run by outside consultants, HR staff, team leaders, or team members. We encourage leaders to delegate some of the activities to team members, as this allows leaders to spend more time leading from behind, observing direct reports in leadership roles, and developing their staff. Team leaders should meet with facilitators prior to any team engagement. This ensures facilitators are fully prepared to run the activities and aligns their expectations about the outcomes, flow, and roles during the session.

The team improvement activities include everything needed for flawless facilitation: step-by-step instructions, flip chart examples, handouts, forms, and PowerPoint presentations. All of the activities are organized as follows:

Purpose	What team problem does the activity try to resolve?
Preparation	What needs to be considered or assembled before the activity?
Review Data	What Team Assessment Survey or interview results indicate this activity might be helpful?
Key Considerations	What do facilitators need to know or consider when doing this activity? Is this activity only for team leaders? Any cautions when using this activity?
Time Needed	How much time is needed to do the activity? Time estimates provided are based on teams of 6-9 people. Larger teams will need more time.
Room Requirements	What are the room arrangements?
Materials Needed	What handouts, forms, reports, articles, or A/V systems are needed?
Facilitation	What are the step-by-step instructions for facilitating the activity? When should the PowerPoints, flip charts, or handouts be used? What should the completed forms or flip charts look like?
Post-Exercise Activities	What are the accountability mechanisms for this activity?

In general, the team improvement activities follow a similar pattern:
- Facilitators explain the purpose and provide an overview of how the activity will run.
- Sub-teams do initial work on the issue or question being asked.
- Sub-teams report their findings or recommendations to the entire team.
- The entire team discusses and makes a decision on how to resolve the issue.

The sub-team activities encourage candid conversations (team members are more likely to share honest perspectives in smaller versus larger groups), increase involvement and energy levels, and help teams be more efficient. Facilitators should mingle among the sub-teams to ensure they are having the right conversations and preparing for large team report-outs. Some sub-teams will work through assigned activities very quickly and others will need considerable cajoling.

Because sub-teams can offer different recommendations, the most important conversations happen in the ensuing large team discussions. Working through these differences can take time. People have a higher need to be heard than agreed with, so facilitators and team leaders need to ensure all perspectives are acknowledged. Some large team decisions will end up consensus-based and team leaders will need to make final calls when consensus seems out of reach. Most team members prefer making decisions to dithering, and most will implement decisions they may not agree with if their opinions have been heard.

The first nine activities do some level-setting or describe how to collect information about teams. The remaining 31 activities are associated with the different Rocket Model components. Team improvement activity support materials consist of handouts, forms, PowerPoint presentations, articles, and white papers for each of the 40 activities. These materials can be downloaded from the Rocket Model website: www.therocketmodel.com.

The activities are organized by Rocket Model components, but their use should not be limited by this framework. Journey lines have been used in team talent discussions, the Feedforward activity has been used to improve team courage, and stakeholder mapping is sometimes tied to team context. The key is understanding what problems need to be resolved and choosing activities that help teams have the right conversations.

TEAM IMPROVEMENT ACTIVITIES 1-40

Team Diagnostics and Teaching Aids

1. Team Quiz
2. Dream vs. Nightmare Teams
3. Groups vs. Teams Exercise
4. The Rocket Model Slide Deck
5. The Rocket Model Puzzle
6. Team Assessment Survey (TAS)
7. Team Interviews
8. Team Feedback Sessions
9. Organizational Teamwork Analysis

Rocket Model Activities

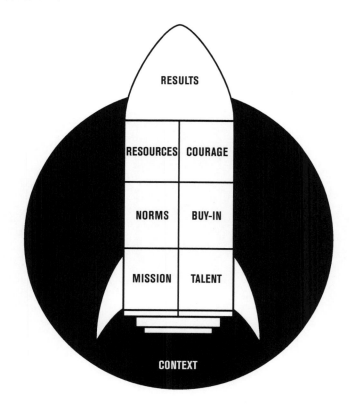

Results 40. Personal and Team Learning	
Resources 35. Resources Analysis 36. Stakeholder Mapping	**Courage** 37. After-Action Reviews 38. Team Journey Lines 39. Conflict Management Styles
Norms 24. Team Norms 25. Operating Rhythm 26. Operating Level 27. Decision-Making 28. Communication 29. Accountability Mechanisms 30. Self-Adjustment	**Buy-In** 31. Journey Lines 32. Motives, Values, Preferences Inventory (MVPI) 33. Expectancy Theory 34. Personal Commitment
Mission 12. Vision Statements 13. Team Purpose 14. Team Scorecard 15. Team Action Plans	**Talent** 16. Roles and Responsibilities Matrix 17. Followership Scatterplots 18. Feedforward Exercise 19. Eavesdropping Exercise 20. Wingfinder Assessment 21. Hogan Personality Inventory (HPI) 22. Hogan Development Survey (HDS) 23. New Team Member Checklist
Context 10. Context Assessment Exercise 11. SWOT Analysis	

See the Tools & Services tab on the Rocket Model website to download the PowerPoints, handouts, forms, templates, and articles needed to run these activities: www.therocketmodel.com

1

Team Quiz

PURPOSE

Increase Knowledge

Clarify some of the common myths and misunderstandings about leadership, groups, and teams.

Build Energy

Sharing knowledge and perspectives about leadership and teams raises participants' engagement levels. In addition, the quiz also serves as a mini example of teamwork. How did sub-teams approach the task, share information, make decisions, etc.?

PREPARATION

Key Consideration

The Team Quiz is not usually treated as a stand-alone exercise but as part of an introduction to effective teamwork. It generates a lot of discussion about groups and teams and serves as a good setup for giving an overview of the Rocket Model.

Time Needed

This activity takes 25-30 minutes, depending on the number of participants.

Room Requirements

The room should be conducive to sub-group conversations.

Materials Needed

1 copy of the Team Quiz for each team member and an LCD projector for the slides.

FACILITATION

		Materials
Step 1 2 min.	Introduce the quiz. The quiz assesses participants' general knowledge of leadership, groups, and teams.	Team Quiz PPT 1
Step 2 12 min.	Pass out the Team Quiz to participants.	Team Quiz PPT 2
	Organize participants into sub-teams of 4-6 people.	Team Quiz Handout
	Tell sub-teams they have 10 minutes to come to a consensus for each question on the Team Quiz. They should note final answers on one of the quizzes.	
	Circulate among the sub-teams to answer questions about quiz items.	
Step 3 10-15 min.	Once sub-teams have finished, go over the answers one at a time and conduct a large team discussion of the Team Quiz. Ask sub-teams to tally up their scores and recognize those with the highest score. Tie the answers to the content being covered later in the session.	Team Quiz PPT 3

POST-EXERCISE ACTIVITIES

None.

TEAM QUIZ ANSWERS

Correct answers in black. Wrong answers in gray.

1. Research shows that when people work together to complete a task, the job will probably:

   a. get done faster.

   b. take longer to finish.

   c. not get done.

2. Fill in the blanks: ___ of employees think collaboration is important, but only ___ report working on effective teams.

   a. 90%, 25%

   b. 75%, 10%

   c. 100%, 50%

   d. 90%, 5%

3. Research shows ___ of people in positions of authority have difficulty engaging employees, building teams, or getting results through others.

   a. 20%

   b. 40%

   c. 60%

   d. 80%

4. Research shows that those colleagues seen as the best sources of information are the:

   a. most engaged.

   b. most engaged and satisfied with their careers.

   c. least engaged.

   d. least engaged and satisfied with their careers.

5. True or False: All things being equal, groups outperform individuals and teams outperform groups.

6. Research shows the odds of a collection of people successfully transforming into a high-performing team are:

   a. less than 20%.

   b. 40%.

   c. 50%.

   d. 60%.

   e. greater than 75%.

7. True or False: Team-building activities (ropes courses, BBQs, etc.) are effective ways to improve team performance.

8. Which are common characteristics of executive leadership teams? (circle all that apply)

   a. High performance

   b. Cloning

   c. Alpha paralysis

   d. Artificial harmony

Team Quiz Rationale

1. This question is from a student achievement test for 4th graders in Ohio. According to educators, A is the correct answer. However, research done by Richard Hackman and cited in his *Harvard Business Review* article shows B and C are more likely to occur.

2. This comes from research done by Scott Tannenbaum for NASA.

3. There are 11 different bodies of research indicating that only 1 out of 3 leaders is perceived to be effective. This research is reviewed in articles by Bob Hogan and Rob Kaiser, and Gordy Curphy, Bob Hogan, and Rob Kaiser.

4. This finding comes from an article entitled "Collaboration Overload" in *Harvard Business Review* by Cross, Rebele, and Grant.

5. The correct answer depends on the nature of the work to be performed. Sometimes individuals or groups are the best ways to get things done.

6. This research comes from Richard Hackman and Ruth Wageman. Also, if you ask participants to estimate the percentage of teams that are high performing within their organizations, the average hovers between 10-20%.

7. This comes from work done by Curphy and Hogan and Curphy and Nilsen. This is one reason why team building gets a bum rap, as it usually consists of activities that have little to do with building high-performing teams. The best way to build teams is by having teams do real work.

8. This comes from Curphy and Nilsen's article in *Talent Quarterly*.

Total Possible Team Quiz Score = 11
Average Team Score = 6

2

Dream vs. Nightmare Teams

PURPOSE

Increase Knowledge

Gain alignment on the characteristics of high- and low-performing teams.

Increase Awareness

Estimate the total number of teams in organizations and the percentage of which are high performing.

PREPARATION

Key Consideration

This is not usually treated as a stand-alone exercise but as part of an introduction to effective teamwork. It generates a lot of discussion about teams and serves as a good setup for a Rocket Model overview.

Time Needed

This activity takes 15-20 minutes.

Room Requirements

The room should be conducive to large group conversations.

Materials Needed

An LCD projector for the slides, a flip chart, and a set of markers.

FACILITATION

		Materials
Step 1 2 min.	Introduce the activity, which is to identify the characteristics associated with high- and low-performing teams.	Dream Team PPT 1
Step 2 10 min.	Refer to the Dream vs. Nightmare Teams Flip Chart. Ask participants to think about the best team they were ever on. Then ask them to share the characteristics of that team in the large group. Record the characteristics under the Dream Teams column on Flip Chart #1. Ask participants to think about the worst team they were ever on. Then ask them to share the characteristics of that team in the large group. Record the characteristics under the Nightmare Teams column on Flip Chart #1.	Dream Team PPT 2 Flip Chart #1
Step 3 5-7 min.	Ask participants to share estimates of the total number of teams in their respective organizations with the large group. Then share that research shows the total number of teams in an organization = 30-40% of the total number of employees. This means that if a company has 10,000 employees, they will likely be organized into 3,000-4,000 teams. Then ask participants to share estimates of the percentage of teams in their organizations they would consider to be Dream Teams (i.e., high performing). These estimates will likely range from 10-20%, which is consistent with the team effectiveness research. Finally, ask participants to share ideas on why good teamwork is so rare and how they could make Dream Teams happen. Good teamwork requires a common framework for building teams, feedback on team functioning, and tools to improve team performance. This is why the Rocket Model, the Team Assessment Survey, and team improvement activities were created.	Dream Team PPT 2

POST-EXERCISE ACTIVITIES

None.

Dream vs. Nightmare Teams
Flip Chart #1

Dream Teams	Nightmare Teams

Team Improvement Activity
3

Groups vs. Teams Exercise

PURPOSE

Increase Knowledge

Understand the distinctions between groups and teams.

Increase Awareness

Identify where teams fall on the group vs. team continuum.

PREPARATION

Key Considerations

This is not usually treated as a stand-alone exercise but as part of an introduction to effective teamwork. The topic generates a lot of discussion about groups and teams and serves as a good setup for a Rocket Model overview.

Team leaders and facilitators should review the Team or Group? section in Chapter 2 prior to beginning this exercise.

Time Needed

This activity takes 20-25 minutes.

Room Requirements

The room should be conducive to large group conversations.

Materials Needed

1 copy of the Groups vs. Teams Exercise Handout for each team member or participant, an LCD projector for the slides, a flip chart, and a set of markers.

FACILITATION

		Materials
Step 1 2 min.	Introduce the activity, which is to clarify the differences between groups and teams.	Groups vs. Teams PPT 1
Step 2 5 min.	Pass out the Groups vs. Teams Exercise Handout. Ask participants to think about their boss's team—the one in which they are a team member along with their peers. Ask them to rate this team on a scale of 1-5 on the nature of its goals, degree of interdependence, and rewards. Provide examples of 1, 3, and 5 scores when explaining each of the three dimensions. They should record their answers on the handout. Ask participants to tally up a total score for the three items—the scores will range from 3-15. They should use an X to indicate their total score on the scale at the bottom of the handout.	Groups vs. Teams PPT 2 Groups vs. Teams Handout
Step 3 10-15 min.	Ask participants to share their total scores with the large group. Record these scores on the flip chart. Do a large group discussion about the range of scores and clarify the differences between groups and teams, the implications for leaders when selecting staff, conducting meetings, etc. Describe what happens when leaders treat groups like teams and teams like groups. A key issue for executive leadership teams and matrixed teams to resolve is determining when they need to work as teams and when they are better off working as groups. What topics need alignment and consensus and which topics are better handled by individuals or sub-groups? Also, state that these dimensions provide insight into the structural changes leaders may need to make if they want to foster teamwork or groupwork. Note: Teams can rate themselves using this handout, and this can lead to some interesting discussions. However, the Team Assessment Survey Feedback Report also provides a group vs. team analysis.	Groups vs. Teams Flip Chart #1 PPTs 3-5

None.

Example of Groups vs. Teams Flip Chart #1

```
                              X   X
                              X   X   X
                  X   X   X   X   X   X   X   X   X   X
Group    I--------------- I--------------- I--------------- I----------------I    Team
         3              6               9              12              15
```

4

The Rocket Model
Slide Deck

PURPOSE

Increase Knowledge

Provide a high-level overview of the Rocket Model and its eight components.

PREPARATION

Key Considerations

This is usually treated as a lead-in to a Team Feedback Session.

Team leaders and facilitators should read Chapter 1 prior to delivering this presentation. They may also want to review pages 5-12 from a Team Assessment Survey Feedback Report, as they describe each component of the Rocket Model, what high and low scores look like, and the survey items that make up the components.

Time Needed

This activity takes 20-40 minutes, depending on the amount of time spent explaining each Rocket Model component.

Room Requirements

The room should be conducive to large group conversations.

Materials Needed

An LCD projector for the slides.

FACILITATION

		Materials
Step 1 2 min.	Introduce the activity, which is to describe a roadmap for building high-performing teams.	Rocket Model PPT 1
Step 2 5 min.	Review the Rocket Model graphic. The model describes eight components teams need to attend to if they want to be high performing. It is a prescriptive model: When launching new teams, it is best to start at the bottom of the model and work toward the top. It is a diagnostic model: When working with existing teams, it can tell you what components are relatively strong and where teams need to improve.	Rocket Model PPT 2
Step 3 15-30 min.	Review each of the eight components of the Rocket Model, starting with Context and then working up through the model. Provide personal examples for each component.	Rocket Model PPT 3-10
Step 4 2 min.	Wrap up the presentation by asking participants if they have any questions about the eight Rocket Model components, how they fit together, where to start, etc.	Rocket Model PPT 11

POST-EXERCISE ACTIVITIES

None.

5

The Rocket Model Puzzle

PURPOSE

Increase Knowledge

Improve understanding of the Rocket Model and its eight components.

PREPARATION

Key Consideration

This is a good exercise to do right after a Rocket Model presentation and right before a Team Feedback Session.

Time Needed

This activity takes 15-20 minutes.

Room Requirements

The room should be large enough to assemble two to four puzzles on the floor and conducive to large group conversations.

Materials Needed

- 1 Rocket Model Puzzle for each two- to seven-person sub-team and an LCD projector for the slides. Puzzle order forms can be found at the end of the activity.
- Facilitators may want to shoot a short video of puzzles being assembled.

FACILITATION

		Materials
Step 1 2 min.	Introduce the activity, which is to improve understanding of the Rocket Model and what it takes to build high-performing teams.	Puzzle PPT 1
Step 2 10 min.	Break into two- to seven-person sub-teams. Position teams around the room so they can assemble their puzzles fairly independently. Pass out a Rocket Model Puzzle to each sub-team. Tell teams they are in a competition. The champion will be the first team to properly assemble the puzzle and assign the 16 items to the proper Rocket Model component. There are two items for each Rocket Model component.	Puzzle PPT 2 Rocket Model Puzzles Smartphone to video the teams
Step 3 7 min.	Conduct a large group debriefing on the Rocket Model Puzzle. Which items were more difficult to assign? What questions do people have about the Rocket Model? Option: If the team did not elect to do a Team Assessment Survey, then one way to gain insight into team dynamics is to ask team members to rate the team using a scale of 1 = Low, 3 = So-So, and 5 = High on each of the eight Rocket Model components after completing the puzzle. Draw the Rocket Model on a flip chart and ask team members to write down their scores in each of the eight components. Compute average component scores and discuss the results. (40 minutes)	Puzzle PPT 3

POST-EXERCISE ACTIVITIES

None.

Completed Rocket Model Puzzle

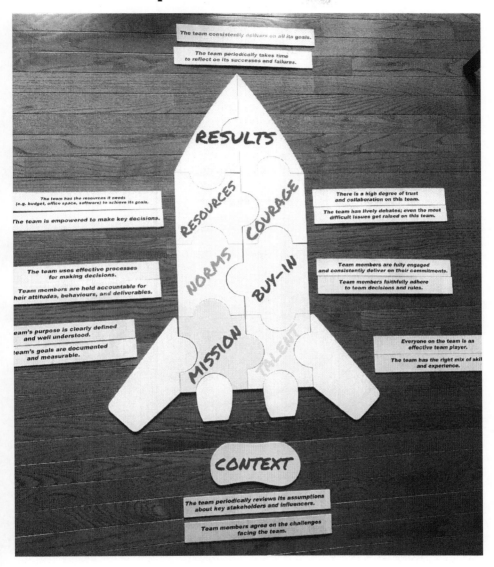

The Rocket Model Puzzle Order Form

First Name:	
Last Name:	
Company:	
Street Address:	
State:	
Country:	
Phone Number:	
E-Mail Address:	
Comments:	

Number of Puzzles	Type and Price	Total Amount
	Plastic Puzzles @ 250 EUR/Puzzle	
	Wooden Puzzles @ 450 EUR/Puzzle	
	VAT (20%, if applicable)	
	Shipping and Handling	

Please send completed Rocket Model Puzzle Order Forms to Rastislav Duris (Rastislav.Duris@spoluhrame.sk). He will confirm the order; puzzle arrival date; VAT; shipping and handling fees; and make payment arrangements. Please allow three to four weeks for shipment and handling.

Team Assessment Survey (TAS)

PURPOSE

Increase Awareness

Provide teams with qualitative, quantitative, and benchmarking feedback on team functioning and performance.

Build Trust

Initiate candid conversations about team strengths, surprises, and areas of improvement.

PREPARATION

Key Consideration

The Team Assessment Survey (TAS) is usually done as prework for Team Feedback Sessions or team-oriented leadership development programs. Please allow two to four weeks to set up and administer surveys, collect data, and generate Team Assessment Survey Feedback Reports.

Time Needed

- It takes team leaders 45-60 minutes to complete Team Assessment Survey Rater Lists, modify and send out Team Assessment Survey introduction e-mails to raters, and complete the leader version of the Team Assessment Survey.
- It takes team members 15-20 minutes to complete Team Assessment Surveys.

Materials Needed

- Completed Team Assessment Survey Rater List to be sent to TAS administrator.
- Team Assessment Survey introduction e-mail to be sent out to participants.

FACILITATION

		Materials
Step 1 10 min.	Team leaders and facilitators should read the Team Assessment Survey Administration Instructions.	TAS Administration Instructions
Step 2 15 min.	Team leaders or facilitators should complete a Team Assessment Survey Rater List and save the list as a .csv file.	TAS Rater List
	Team leaders should send completed Team Assessment Survey Rater Lists, the company name, team name, due date, and report recipient e-mail address to their designated TAS administrator or Gordy Curphy (gcurphy@curphyleadershipsolutions.com).	
Step 3 10-15 min.	Team leaders or facilitators should modify and send out Team Assessment Survey introduction e-mails to all TAS raters when the TAS Rater List is sent to Curphy Leadership Solutions. This will let raters know about the survey and improve response rates.	TAS Introduction E-mail
Step 4 15-20 min.	Team leaders should complete their Team Assessment Surveys.	TAS

POST-EXERCISE ACTIVITIES

- Monitor Team Assessment Survey completion rates.
- Review the All Team Member and Team Member vs. Team Leader versions of the Team Assessment Survey Feedback Report.
- Prepare for a Team Feedback Session.

Team Interviews

PURPOSE

Increase Knowledge

Provide teams with qualitative feedback about team dynamics and performance.

Increase Awareness

Help facilitators gain insight into a team's history, context, challenges, goals, players, norms, etc.

PREPARATION

Key Considerations

- Team interviews are done as prework before Team Feedback Sessions and are best conducted by someone outside the team.
- Team leaders need to give team members a heads-up about the interviews.
- Team facilitators will need to schedule the interviews with the team leader and team members.

Time Needed

Each interview takes 30-60 minutes.

Room Requirements

None. Most interviews are conducted over the phone.

Materials Needed

- 1 copy of the Team Interview Protocol for each interviewee.
- 1 copy of the Team Interview Summary Template.

FACILITATION

		Materials
Step 1 5 min.	Review the Team Interview Protocol prior to conducting interviews. Team facilitators do not need to ask team members every question, but they should make sure they have answers to all of the questions at the conclusion of the interviews.	Team Interview Protocol
Step 2 20-30 min.	Schedule interviews with the team leader and members.	
Step 3 30-60 min.	Conduct interviews using the Team Interview Protocol to take notes.	
Step 4 30-90 min.	Consolidate the interview notes and identify key themes for each Rocket Model component.	Team Interview Summary Template
Step 5 60-90 min.	Write a Team Interview Summary.	*See a sample of a completed Team Interview Summary on p. 221*

POST-EXERCISE ACTIVITIES

- Review the Team Interview Summary with the team leader before conducting Team Feedback Sessions.
- Prepare for a Team Feedback Session (Team Improvement Activity 8).

Example of a Completed Team Interview Summary

Team Interview Summary

US Leadership Team

Aug 2019

Prepared by: Gordon Curphy, Ph.D.
gcurphy@curphyleadershipsolutions.com
Office: 651.493.3734
St. Paul, Minnesota

Overview

This report provides information about the team's functioning across eight areas that have been shown to differentiate between high- and low-performing teams. Observations included in this report are based on information gleaned from interviews conducted with 14 members of the United States Leadership Team (USLT). The report does not represent a formal assessment of team effectiveness; rather it is meant to be a starting place for a robust team discussion. The team should review and validate (or dispute) the observations and determine those areas it wants to address.

Context. A team does not operate in a vacuum. Stakeholder expectations, industry and societal trends, government regulations, economic realities, and other external factors have implications for the team. When team members have conflicting views of contextual issues, team functioning is negatively impacted.

High-performing teams say:	Observations of this team:
• We are all on the same page about the political and economic realities facing the team. • We share a common understanding of the concerns and priorities of key stakeholders (e.g., other department heads, labor unions, city council, employees, HRG teams). • We have a good handle on the external factors affecting our work (e.g., demographic trends, regulatory changes, technology). • We agree on the top challenges facing the team.	• There is a seasonality to this business, with Q4 being critically important to the region's overall results. • As the pressure goes up in Q4, the USLT may spend more time in the weeds and micromanaging their functional teams. • The geographic dispersion of some functional leaders makes it more difficult to resolve issues, gain alignment, and build trust. • There have been a number of USLT membership changes over the past 10 years, and in the division during the past 18 months. • The division has shifted from top-line to bottom-line growth, and as a result is more focused on processes, standardization, and centralization than in the past. • With Bill's retirement, the USLT needs to devise a strategy for managing the division. • Is this a team or a group?

Mission. Teams are most effective when members agree on what success looks like: what needs to get done and by when. Goal clarity is the first step toward successful execution and is foundational to ensuring day-to-day activities are connected to key priorities.

High-performing teams say:	Observations of this team:
• We agree on what team success looks like. • Our goals are well-understood and used to prioritize day-to-day activities. • We regularly review progress against team goals and plans; a Team Scorecard is in place. • The team has effective strategies to overcome obstacles and achieve its goals. • We have a documented set of actions with owners for the next 30-120 days.	• The USLT has a clear set of plans for achieving YE numbers. • There is good alignment on what needs to get accomplished in 2018. • Team members agree on the overall direction of the business. • Although there is agreement on the what, there are disagreements on how things need to get accomplished. • The USLT is trying to do too many things, has too many initiatives, and does not have an agreed-upon set of strategic priorities for the rest of 2018.

Talent. A successful team has the knowledge and capabilities needed to accomplish goals. In addition to having the right expertise, team members need to be effective team players. High-performing teams are the right size, are organized to optimize team performance, and have clear roles and responsibilities.

High-performing teams say:	Observations of this team:
• We have the right number of people. • The team has the right organizational/reporting structure. • We have clear roles, responsibilities, and accountabilities. • The team has the right mix of skills and experience. • Everyone on the team is an effective team player.	• USLT members are smart, know the business, and have deep expertise in their respective functions. • The USLT is populated with disruptive thinkers who devise innovative ways to get things done. • Team members have a strong "get it done" attitude. • With Bill's impending retirement, are there increased retention risks to the USLT and their staff? Will loyalty shift from we to me? • Does the company really care about people, or are employees simply taken for granted? Why do so many employees leave after two years? • HR needs to play a bigger role in the US. • There are some who are not effective team players. • Jerry will need to change his perspective and modify some of his behaviors to be effective in the interim president role.

Norms. Norms include formal processes and procedures as well as the informal rules teams use to get work done. Effective teams ensure their norms help (rather than hinder) team performance. Important norms include how the team conducts meetings, makes decisions, keeps members informed, and holds members accountable.

High-performing teams say:	Observations of this team:
• Team meetings make effective and efficient use of time.	• Team members get along, are accessible and highly collaborative, and work well together.
• We spend enough time working on proactive versus reactive issues.	• People are generally kept informed of key events.
• We use effective decision-making processes that result in sound, timely decisions.	• At times, the USLT has robust debates about issues.
• We communicate with each other openly and directly; gossiping rarely happens.	• The group really comes together when facing challenges.
• Team members are held accountable for their attitudes, behaviors, and deliverables.	• The lack of process can be both refreshing and frustrating.
• We periodically take a step back and find ways to work together more effectively.	• Team meetings need to be improved. They are changed too often and there is usually not enough time to discuss or work through issues. Team members agree in meetings, but then do follow-up meetings or lobby Bill to get decisions made or changed.
	• There is a constant need to revisit decisions.
	• How will decisions get made after Bill retires?
	• Are there too many cooks in the kitchen? Does everyone need to be in every meeting or weigh-in on every decision? People seem afraid to take risks and make decisions without getting sign-off from the entire USLT.
	• Is the USLT operating at the right level? It spends a lot of time in the weeds, poring over details, and making decisions that should be made one or two levels lower in the organization.
	• The USLT needs to be more cognizant of the image it is projecting to employees. Some of the actions outlined above indicate a lack of alignment and disempowerment to employees.
	• The USLT needs to do a much better job holding functions accountable for their plans. Sales get a considerable amount of scrutiny, but the same is not true for the other functions.

Buy-In. For a team to be effective, its members need to be committed to the team's success. Buy-In is concerned with the level of engagement and motivation team members bring to the team's goals, roles, and rules.

High-performing teams say:	Observations of this team:
• Team members are fully engaged and consistently deliver on their commitments. • Team members faithfully adhere to team decisions and rules. • The team believes success is possible and works with a high degree of optimism. • Team members understand how their actions contribute to the department's overall success. • Team members are actively involved with team goal- and priority-setting, action planning, decision-making, etc. • A team first versus me first attitude pervades this team.	• Bill was able to foster a great sense of belonging within the USLT. Will this fade away with his retirement? • Team members are optimistic about what the US can do and are proud to be on this team. • There is some uncertainty about the first team. Are primary loyalties with the division, the USLT, or the functional organizations being led? • Can the USLT cultivate a loyal following across employees in the region?

Resources. To be successful, teams need the appropriate resources, which can include budget, software, data, authority, and political support.

High-performing teams say:	Observations of this team:
• We have the necessary level of political sponsorship to be successful. • The team is empowered to make key decisions. • We have the resources we need (e.g., budget, tools) to achieve our goals. • We proactively renegotiate deliverables when faced with resource shortfalls.	• Team members have to get approval for many of the things they want to do from the division. This slows down the decision-making process and is very disempowering. • Team members are held accountable for results but lack the authority needed to achieve them. • The region lacks much of the infrastructure normally associated with businesses this size. This makes it difficult to manage the business efficiently. • Rather than providing the support that is truly needed, the division tends to meddle in local issues that they know little about.

Constructive Courage. Successful teams raise difficult issues and resolve differences in an effective manner. Low-performing teams either promote artificial harmony (i.e., avoid controversial issues and difficult topics) or they engage in destructive conflict, making issues personal.

High-performing teams say:	Observations of this team:
• There is a high degree of trust and collaboration on this team. • We feel safe challenging each other. • We have lively debates; even the most difficult issues get raised on this team. • We do not let issues fester; we actively surface and work through disagreements.	• There is a lot of mutual respect on the USLT. • There is a good, natural tension between Marketing, Sales, and Finance. • There are no sacred cows on this team; team members speak plainly and raise contentious issues. • More time could be spent challenging each other in order to reach better solutions. We have too many post-meeting discussions to flesh out final decisions. • The fact that team members feel compelled to sit in so many meetings and ensure all decisions are blessed speaks volumes about the real level of trust on this team.

Results. Effective teams get stuff done! They deliver on goals, meet stakeholder expectations, and approach their work with an emphasis on continuous improvement.

High-performing teams say:	Observations of this team:
• The team consistently delivers on all its goals. • The team consistently exceeds the stakeholders' expectations. • The team periodically takes time to reflect on its successes and failures. • The team's ability to perform has improved over time.	• The US hit its numbers in 2017, which was a good thing. • The team is behind where it needs to be in 2018. • There is a path to win in 2018, but a considerable amount of work still needs to get done.

8

Team Feedback Sessions

PURPOSE

Increase Knowledge

Understand how to interpret Team Assessment Feedback Reports and/or Team Interview Summaries.

Drive Alignment

Gain consensus on a team's strengths and areas of improvement.

Build Trust

Encourage the right conversations about teamwork.

PREPARATION

Key Considerations

- Team Feedback Sessions are conducted after teams have completed Team Assessment Surveys and/or completed team interviews.
- What data were collected? What/who are this team's key influencers, stakeholders, history, challenges, goals, members, norms, etc.? How many people are on the team?

- Team leaders and facilitators should review the Team Assessment Survey Feedback Report and/or Team Interview Summary prior to the feedback session. They should be familiar with the team's strengths and weaknesses and make sure the team identifies these issues during the feedback session. If using a team facilitator, then team leaders and facilitators should review the team results prior to the session.
- Will the Team Assessment Survey Feedback Report and Team Interview Summary be sent out as prework? There is no right or wrong answer to this question, but generally speaking, these reports are not sent out as prework and are reviewed for the first time during feedback sessions.
- Team Feedback Sessions are usually done right after a Rocket Model overview (see Team Improvement Activity 4 – The Rocket Model Slide Deck).

Time Needed

Usually 90-120 minutes.

Room Requirements

The room should be conducive to sub-team breakouts and large group report-outs, and should have an LCD projector for the slides and flip charts and markers for sub-teams.

Materials Needed

- 1 copy of *TQ: The Elusive Factor Behind Successful Teams* (Curphy & Nilsen, 2018) sent out as prework to all team members.
- 1 copy of the Team Interview Summary for each team member.
- 1 copy of the All Team Member Team Assessment Survey Feedback Report for each team member.

FACILITATION

Materials

Step	Description	Materials
Step 1 2 min.	Introduce the activity, which is to gain consensus on the team's strengths and areas of improvement.	Team Feedback PPT 1
Step 2 15 min.	Pass out All Team Member Team Assessment Survey Feedback Reports and/or Team Interview Summaries.	TAS Feedback Reports Team Interview Summaries
	Review how to interpret a Team Assessment Survey Feedback Report and/or Team Interview Summary. Tell team members they will have time to analyze the results after the presentation, so they should follow along rather than paging ahead in order to fully understand how to interpret the reports.	Team Feedback PPTs 2-8
Step 3 35-50 min.	Break out into three- to five-person sub-teams. Ask the sub-teams to review the documents and create three flip charts that identify the team's strengths, areas of improvement, and any surprises (see page 17 in a Team Assessment Survey Feedback Report for an example). Sub-teams should work through the documents using the same process (e.g., everyone on the sub-team looks at and discusses findings from page 3 of the Team Assessment Survey Feedback Report, then goes to page 4 to note and discuss findings, etc.).	Team Feedback PPT 9 Flip Charts
Step 4 20-40 min.	Ask the sub-teams to present large group report-outs. Begin by having one sub-team share team strengths. Then ask the next team if they would add any other team strengths, and repeat for the other sub-teams. Ask the large group to comment on, ask questions, and share reactions to the sub-teams' lists. Use the same process for the team surprises, and again ask the large group to comment on, ask questions, and provide reactions to the sub-teams' lists. Finish the report-outs using the same process for areas of improvement, and ask the large group to comment on, ask questions, and provide reactions to the sub-teams' lists.	Flip Charts
	Team leaders and facilitators should create a consolidated list of team improvement areas on a flip chart and check with the team to ensure all the areas have been included.	Flip Chart
Step 5 10-15 min.	Show the Rocket Model graphic and remind the team that it is best to work from the bottom up when prioritizing improvement areas. Given this recommendation, work with the team to prioritize areas of improvement.	Rocket Model Graphic
	Tell the team that subsequent sessions will take place to improve team functioning in these areas.	

POST-EXERCISE ACTIVITIES

- Create an electronic copy of the prioritized team improvement list and circulate it among team members for additional feedback.
- Select the team improvement activities needed to help the team get to the next level of performance.
- Set up team meetings to address team improvement areas. Team leaders may opt to have team members facilitate some or all of these sessions.

Team Improvement Activity

9

Organizational Teamwork Analysis

Increase Knowledge

Understand the extent to which organizations foster effective teamwork.

Drive Action

Identify actions organizations can take to improve teamwork.

Key Considerations

- How important are teamwork and collaboration to an organization? Are they part of the organization's values or leadership competency models? Does the organization measure and reward good teamwork?
- This activity provides insight into what organizations can do to foster effective teamwork. It is usually completed in Team Improvement Workshops, keynote presentations on teamwork, or when working with organizations wanting to foster effective teamwork.

- How many people will be doing the activity? Are they from the same or different organizations?
- Facilitators and speakers using this activity should be familiar with the "Organizations That Get Teamwork Right" article from the May 2018 edition of *HR People + Strategy* magazine.

Time Needed

This activity takes 50-90 minutes, depending on the depth of the material covered.

Room Requirements

The room should be conducive to large group conversations.

Materials Needed

- 1 copy of the "Organizations That Get Teamwork Right" article from the May 2018 edition of *HR People + Strategy* magazine for each participant.
- 1 copy of the Organizational Teamwork Analysis Handout for each participant, an LCD projector for the slides, and a flip chart and a set of markers for each table or sub-team.

FACILITATION

		Materials
Step 1 2 min.	Pass out the "Organizations That Get Teamwork Right" article and introduce the activity, which is to determine the extent to which organizations actually value teamwork. Most organizations say they want or value teamwork and collaboration, but whether they do anything to make this happen may be a different story.	Teamwork Analysis PPT 1 "Organizations That Get Teamwork Right" Article
Step 2 10-30 min.	Pass out the Organizational Teamwork Analysis Handout to participants and tell them they'll be analyzing their organizations using the framework in the "Organizations That Get Teamwork Right" article. Taking each category one at a time, explain what the category is about, tell one or two stories or examples about the category, and ask participants to provide a 1-5 rating for the category. Repeat this process for the remaining five categories.	Organizational Teamwork Analysis Handout Teamwork Analysis PPT 2

		Materials
Step 3 20 min.	Once all six categories have been rated, ask sub-teams to share and discuss their ratings. They should note key themes across the ratings, and create a flip chart that lists the six categories, the individual ratings, and the average rating for each category.	Teamwork Analysis PPT 3-5 Flip Chart #1 *See a sample of a completed Flip Chart #1 on p. 234*
Step 4 20-40 min.	Ask the sub-teams to do large group report-outs. Ask the participants to comment on common themes from the table team report-outs and flip charts. Share global results for the Organizational Teamwork Analysis. How do the organizational results compare to global norms? What do these results say about organizations fostering effective teamwork? What is the relationship between these results and the fact that only 20% of teams in organizations are considered high performing? What role do organizations play in team dysfunction? Where should organizations get started if they want to do a better job of fostering teamwork?	

POST-EXERCISE ACTIVITIES

- If working with a single organization, then create an electronic copy of the overall Organizational Teamwork Analysis results (i.e., consolidate the results for all the flip charts).
- Set up meetings to address improvement areas.

Example of an Organizational Teamwork Analysis
Flip Chart #1

Component	Ratings
Top Team 1 = A dysfunctional top team. 3 = A team that gets along but is not a high-performing team. 5 = A high-performing top team.	1, 2, 1, 3, 3, 4 Avg = 2.3
Team Roadmap 1 = There is no common framework for building teams. 3 = There is a common framework, but it is not well-known or used. 5 = A team-building framework has been widely adopted across the organization.	1, 2, 1, 1, 2, 2, Avg = 1.5
TQ and Talent Management 1 = The ability to build teams is not considered when making hiring, development, performance management, promotion, or high-potential selection decisions. 3 = The ability to build teams gets mentioned when making hiring, development, performance management, promotion, or high-potential selection decisions. 5 = The ability to build teams is an important factor when making hiring, development, performance management, promotion, or high-potential selection decisions.	2, 3, 3, 4, 3, 2 Avg = 2.8
Team Feedback 1 = Team leaders are not provided with any team-level feedback. 3 = Team leaders get employee engagement feedback. 5 = Team leaders get benchmarked feedback on team dynamics and performance.	3, 2, 3, 2, 4, 3 Avg = 3.0
Team Training and Improvement Tools 1 = Team leaders are not provided any training or tools to build teams. 3 = Team leaders are provided some team-building tools, but most of the training is targeted at working with employees on a one-on-one basis. 5 = Team leaders are provided with training specifically designed to improve team dynamics and performance.	1, 2, 1, 1, 2, 3 Avg = 1.8
Rewards for Teamwork 1 = Rewards are administered based on individual accomplishments. There are few if any rewards for building high-performing teams. 3 = Leaders get rewarded based on individual and team accomplishments. 5 = Leaders get rewarded for building high-performing teams.	3, 4, 2, 3, 3, 4 Avg = 3.2

Organizational Teamwork Analysis Results
Global Averages (based on 250 organizations)

Component	Rating
Top Team 1 = A dysfunctional top team. 3 = A team that gets along but is not a high-performing team. 5 = A high-performing top team.	2.1
Team Roadmap 1 = There is no common framework for building teams. 3 = There is a common framework, but it is not well-known or used. 5 = A team-building framework has been widely adopted across the organization.	1.8
TQ and Talent Management 1 = The ability to build teams is not considered when making hiring, development, performance management, promotion, or high-potential selection decisions. 3 = The ability to build teams gets mentioned when making hiring, development, performance management, promotion, or high-potential selection decisions. 5 = The ability to build teams is an important factor when making hiring, development, performance management, promotion, or high-potential selection decisions.	2.4
Team Feedback 1 = Team leaders are not provided with any team-level feedback. 3 = Team leaders get employee engagement feedback. 5 = Team leaders get benchmarked feedback on team dynamics and performance.	2.2
Team Training and Improvement Tools 1 = Team leaders are not provided any training or tools to build teams. 3 = Team leaders are provided some team-building tools, but most of the training is targeted at working with employees on a one-on-one basis. 5 = Team leaders are provided with training specifically designed to improve team dynamics and performance.	2.3
Rewards for Teamwork 1 = Rewards are administered based on individual accomplishments. There are few if any rewards for building high-performing teams. 3 = Leaders get rewarded based on individual and team accomplishments. 5 = Leaders get rewarded for building high-performing teams.	2.6

10

Context Assessment Exercise

PURPOSE

Gain Alignment

Get everyone on the same page about the team's key stakeholders, influencers, and challenges.

Build Trust

Talking about issues outside of the team itself is less threatening and more likely to get everyone actively participating in the conversation. In addition, this exercise promotes insight into how other team members view issues and increases understanding of others' perspectives.

PREPARATION

Review Data

Review Context score and relevant comments on the Team Assessment Survey or Team Interview Summary.

Time Needed

This activity takes 60-90 minutes, depending on the size of the team.

Room Requirements

The room should be conducive to sub-team conversations, have an LCD projector for the slides, and flip charts and markers for sub-teams.

Materials Needed

1 copy of the Context Assessment Exercise Handout for each team member, flip charts, markers, and an LCD projector.

FACILITATION

		Materials
Step 1 5 min.	Introduce the activity and its purpose, which is to get everyone on the same page about the situation facing the team.	Context PPT 1
Step 2 10 min.	Create Context Assessment Flip Chart #1. Write the team's name in the middle of a flip chart. Ask team members to identify the team's key stakeholders. Examples could include customers, other internal teams, headquarters, the board of directors, or employees. Write the stakeholders around the team's name on the flip chart. Ask members to identify the team's key influencers—who or what impacts the team? Examples could include competitors, sponsors, regulators, market conditions, demographic trends, geopolitics, vendors, suppliers, or channel partners. Write the influencers around the team's name on the flip chart.	Flip Chart #1 *See a sample of a completed Context Assessment Flip Chart #1 on p. 240*

		Materials
Step 3 10 min.	In most cases, the team will have listed more than six stakeholders and influencers on Flip Chart #1, in which case, we recommend having the team identify those that will have the most impact on the team over the next six months. This works best by individual voting. Have everyone put check marks near those stakeholders and influencers that they believe will have the most impact. Everyone gets six votes and can allocate their votes any way they want; for example, giving all six votes to one stakeholder group or influencer. The team leader should vote last. Once voting is done, identify the top 6-8 stakeholders and influencers by tallying up the votes and doing a large group discussion of the results. Team leaders should consider the group's input but have the final say on which 6-8 stakeholders and influencers are the most influential.	
Step 4 10-20 min.	Break the team into sub-teams of 2-4 people. Assign stakeholders and influencers to the sub-teams with the *least* knowledge about them. Review the instructions and example of Flip Chart #2. Explain what 12-month assumptions and predictions are for a stakeholder or influencer, and then ask sub-teams to create Flip Chart #2 for each assigned stakeholder and influencer. Review instructions on PowerPoint 10.2 and an example of a completed Flip Chart #2 on PowerPoint 10.3.	Context PPT 2-3 Flip Chart #2 *See a sample of a completed Context Assessment Flip Chart #2 on p. 241*
Step 5 30-60 min.	Refer to the instructions on PowerPoint 10.4 to guide the sub-team report-outs to the large group. The larger team should ask questions, share information, make comments, and provide input to finalize the predictions and assumptions for each stakeholder or influencer. Note any changes to the predictions and assumptions on Flip Chart #2 before repeating the process for the remaining stakeholders and influencers.	Context PPT 4 Flip Chart #2
Step 6 20 min.	Distribute the Context Assessment Exercise Handout and state that the updated flip charts make up the first two rows of the handout. The next step is for them to synthesize the information to identify the team's top challenges for the next 12 months. Challenges can pertain to a specific stakeholder or cut across all stakeholders and influencers. Given this context, ask the large group to name the team's challenges and list them on a flip chart. Then ask the group to prioritize the challenges either by voice vote or by placing check marks on the flip chart. Tally up and do a large group discussion on the results. The team leader should vote last and have the final say on the team's top challenges.	Context Assessment Exercise Handout *See a sample of a completed Context Assessment on p. 242* Flip Chart Context PPT 5

POST-EXERCISE ACTIVITIES

- Create an electronic copy of the completed form and circulate it among team members for additional comments.
- Share the information when onboarding new team members.
- Revisit and update the team's context at least once a year.

Example of Context Assessment Exercise
Flip Chart #1

*Who and what impacts this team, and who
and what does this team influence?*

Headquarters

Demographics

Market Conditions

Midsize Customers

Local Competitors

Marketing and Sales

Quality Assurance

Contract Labor

Regulators

Finance

IT Team

Employees

Hardware Vendors

Geopolitics

Trade Wars

Software Vendors

Large Competitors

Large Customers

Example of Context Assessment Exercise
Flip Chart #2

Stakeholder/Influencer: Market Conditions

Top Assumptions or Predictions for the Next 12 Months

1. US GDP will grow at 2.5%, Europe at 1%, and China and India at 6%.

2. Continued shortage of mid-level programmers due to high demand.

3. General reductions in IT budgets next year.

4.

Example of a Completed Context Assessment Exercise

1. Stakeholders/ Influencers	Market Conditions	Competitors	Customers	Quality Assurance	Marketing and Sales
2. Assumptions	1. US GDP will grow at 2.5%, Europe at 1%, and China and India at 6% 2. Continued shortage of mid-level programmers due to high demand 3. General reduction in IT budgets next year	1. VGWare and CDC likely to merge, putting downward pressure on pricing 2. Mom and pop shops will grow and affect mid to small market pricing 3. XFer new entrant to the field, could be a major threat in two years	1. Application decisions moving to CMO, CFO, and COO 2. Looking for providers who understand their business, not just technology 3. More emphasis on end-to-end solutions and user experience	1. Short-staffed and getting backed up with other projects; will take longer to do QC 2. Past releases had poor quality; more pressure to reduce bugs before releases	1. Will continue to push for more features with lower price points 2. Continued emphasis on quality and timing of releases 3. Moving from event-driven to consultative sales approach
3. Challenges	1. Continued pressure to provide applications with more features, at higher quality, on time 2. Shortfall in software talent will make it difficult to meet application criteria 3. QA will be a major choke point if not addressed					

SWOT Analysis

PURPOSE

Gain Alignment

Get everyone on the same page about the team's key strengths, weaknesses, opportunities, and threats.

Build Trust

Talking about issues affecting the team is likely to get everyone actively participating in the conversation. In addition, this exercise promotes insight into how other team members view issues and increases understanding of others' perspectives.

PREPARATION

Review Data

Review Context score and relevant comments on the Team Assessment Survey or Team Interview Summary. What is the situation facing the team? Has it changed over time?

Time Needed

This activity takes 60-90 minutes, depending on the size of the team.

Room Requirements

The room should be conducive to sub-team conversations, have an LCD projector for the slides, and flip charts and markers for sub-teams.

Materials Needed

1 copy of the SWOT Analysis Handout for each team member.

FACILITATION

		Materials
Step 1 5 min.	Introduce the activity and its purpose, which is to get everyone on the same page about the situation facing the team.	SWOT PPT 1
Step 2 10 min.	Pass out the SWOT Analysis Handout and review the four quadrants of a SWOT. Take care not to fill in the quadrants for the team while reviewing the SWOT, but provide examples of the types of characteristics that typically get included in each quadrant.	SWOT Handout SWOT PPT 2
Step 3 15-20 min.	Break into four sub-teams and allocate a quadrant to each sub-team. Ask sub-teams to identify and note an initial set of characteristics or attributes for their assigned quadrant on flip charts.	SWOT PPTs 3-4 Flip Chart #1 *See a sample of a completed SWOT Flip Chart #1 on p. 245*
Step 4 30-60 min.	Ask sub-teams to do large group report-outs. Team members should share information, make comments on, and make edits to the characteristics or attributes for each quadrant. Finalize each set of characteristics before moving on to the next quadrant. Once the SWOT has been finalized, the team should discuss how the situation affects the team's purpose, goals, action plans, team member roles, norms, etc.	SWOT PPT 5

POST-EXERCISE ACTIVITIES

- Create an electronic copy of the completed SWOT Analysis and circulate it among team members for additional comments.
- Share the information when onboarding new team members.
- Revisit and update the team's context at least once a year.

Example of a Completed SWOT Analysis
Flip Chart #1

Team Strengths

Experienced team players

Low turnover

Clear team purpose

Sufficient budget

Team Improvement Activity
12

Vision Statements

PURPOSE

Gain Alignment

Get everyone on the same page about where the team has been, how it is currently functioning, and where it needs to go.

Inspire Others

Motivate team members to put forth the effort needed for the team to succeed.

PREPARATION

Review Data

Review Mission and Buy-In scores and relevant comments on the Team Assessment Survey or Team Interview Summary. Do team members know the team's why? Are they passionate about the team's purpose? Do they know what they need to do to help the team succeed?

Time Needed

It takes 60-90 minutes to prepare and 20-50 minutes to deliver and de-brief a Vision Statement.

Room Requirements

The room should be conducive to private conversations, have an LCD projector for the slides, and flip charts and markers for sub-teams.

Materials Needed

None.

Prepare the Presentation

Use the Vision Statement Form to organize thoughts about the team's why. Use data and specific examples to honor the past, be realistic about the present, and provide hope for the future. Use stories and analogies to emphasize key points.

Create a 5-10 slide presentation for the Vision Statement. The slides should be organized along these lines:

- Opening slide
- Honor the Past: Significant team milestones and past wins
- Be Realistic About the Present: Team strengths
- Be Realistic About the Present: Team areas of improvement
- Provide Hope for the Future: Where does the team need to go?
- Provide Hope for the Future: How will the team get there?
- Provide Hope for the Future: Expectations for team members
- Closing slide

See the example on page 250 for ideas on how to complete the Vision Statement form and presentation.

Leaders need to be brutally honest about the team's current strengths and areas of improvement, as failing to do so will impugn their credibility. They also need to convey emotion in order to inspire others; if they are not excited about where the team is going, then it will be hard to get the team excited about the journey. Shorter presentations and fewer slides are better, and team leaders should make liberal use of graphics and pictures in their presentations, as they convey stronger messages than text.

FACILITATION

		Materials
Step 1 10-20 min.	Deliver the Vision Statement to the team.	Leader's Vision PPTs
Step 2 10 min.	Break into three sub-teams. Ask sub-teams to identify and flip chart two reactions and two questions about the Vision Statement.	Vision PPT 1-3 Flip Chart #1 *See a sample of a completed Reactions and Questions Flip Chart #1 on p. 251*
Step 3 20 min.	Ask sub-teams to do large group report-outs. Team leaders should acknowledge team members' reactions and answer all questions as best they can.	

Note: CEOs and other executive leadership team leaders can create vision statements for their organizations, or they can do this as a team activity. The entire team can weigh in on Honoring the Past, Being Realistic About the Present, and Providing Hope for the Future. This presentation can then be delivered by top leaders to audiences across the organization.

POST-EXERCISE ACTIVITIES

- Circulate the Team Vision Statement presentation among team members for additional questions and comments.
- Share the Team Vision Statement when onboarding new team members.
- Revisit and update the Team Vision Statement at least once a year.

Example of a Completed Vision Statement Form
Retail President of a Kitchen Equipment Company

Honor the Past	
What has the team done well in the past? Be specific.	**Slide 1:** Picture of the first store - # employees, revenues, SKUs, etc. **Slide 2:** Graph of revenues, stores, and major events over the past 50 years - Comment on store geographic expansion, advent of catalogue and e-commerce sales, expanding # SKUs, expanding revenues and new revenue mixes, number of employees, private label brands, major trade deals, key people who made all this happen, etc.
Be Realistic About the Present	
What is the team currently doing well? Be specific.	**Slide 3:** Picture of a dated, but well-appointed kitchen - Comment on what is good about the kitchen and strengths of the brand. These include the three-pronged approach to sales (stores, catalogues, and e-comm); # SKUs, knowledgeable sales team, customer focus, and brand reputation.
Where does the team need to improve? Be specific.	**Slide 4:** Picture of the same kitchen, but dirty and messy - Comment on the kitchen and make analogies to what is currently wrong with the brand. Misaligned marketing campaigns, no mobile marketing and sales strategy, technology gaps, aging customer base, threats by traditional and nontraditional competitors, etc.
Provide Hope for the Future	
Where does the team need to go?	**Slide 5:** Picture of a state-of-the-art kitchen - Comment that this is where the brand needs to go over the next five years.
What goals does the team need to accomplish? How should the team measure success?	**Slide 6:** Describe the specific revenue, profit, and market share targets that need to be achieved in five years, and what will come from store, catalogue, and e-commerce sales.
What does the team need to do to accomplish these goals? How does the team win or have an impact?	**Slide 7:** Describe how the team needs to operate differently, including integrated and aligned marketing campaigns, greater empowerment and accountability, mobile strategy, and cross sales enhancements.
What are the expectations for team member behavior?	**Slide 8:** Members of the leadership team set the tone for the rest of the organization. They need to be inclusive, decisive, take responsibility for making decisions, and set the tone for teamwork and accountability.
Bumper sticker or tag line.	**Slide 9:** Picture from slide 5 with this tag line: "We will own the heart of the home!"

Example of a Completed Vision Statement
Flip Chart #1

Reactions

Excited

Anxious

Questions

Can we really do this?

Where will we get the resources needed to achieve these goals?

Team Purpose

PURPOSE

Gain Alignment

Create a common understanding of the team's why.

Inspire Others

Motivate team members to put forth the effort needed for the team to succeed.

Build Trust

Help the team have a productive dialogue on why it exists and what it needs to accomplish.

PREPARATION

Review Data

Review Mission and Buy-In scores and relevant comments on the Team Assessment Survey or Team Interview Summary. Do team members know the team's why? Are they passionate about the Team Purpose? Do they know what the team needs to do to succeed?

Time Needed

This activity takes 45-90 minutes, depending on the size of the team.

Room Requirements

The room should be conducive to private conversations, have an LCD projector for the slides, a flip chart, and wall space for Post-It notes.

Materials Needed

1 Post-It notepad for each team member.

FACILITATION

		Materials
Step 1 1 min.	Introduce the activity, which is to get everyone on the same page about the Team Purpose. Why does this team exist? How does it succeed?	Purpose PPT 1
Step 2 15 min.	Pass out Post-It notepads to everyone on the team. Ask individuals to jot down their answers to the question: "Why does this team exist?" If they have more than one answer, they should write them on separate Post-It notes. Team members should also write down their definition of success for the team. If they have more than one criterion for success, then they should write them on separate Post-It notes.	Post-It Notepads Purpose PPT 2
Step 3 30 min.	Ask individuals to do large group report-outs for the Team Purpose, and when everyone has finished, put the Post-Its up on a wall. Team members should gather around the Post-Its, discuss the contents, and group them into common themes. The team should come to a consensus on Team Purpose by the end of the session and note it on a flip chart.	Flip Chart
Step 4 30 min.	Ask individuals to do large group report-outs of their definitions of success for the team, and when everyone has finished, put the Post-Its up on a wall. Team members should gather around the Post-Its, discuss the contents, and group them into common themes. The team should come to a consensus on the team's success measures by the end of the session and document them on a flip chart.	Flip Chart

POST-EXERCISE ACTIVITIES

- Create an electronic draft of the Team Purpose and definition of success and circulate it among team members for additional comments.
- Share the Team Purpose and definition of success when onboarding new team members.
- Revisit and update the Team Purpose and definition of success at least once a year.

Team Scorecard

Provide Direction

Understand what teams need to do to succeed.

Drive Alignment

Shared goals drive unified actions.

Review Data

What was the team's Mission score on the Team Assessment Survey? Were there any comments in the Team Assessment Survey or Team Interview Summary conveying confusion about the team's goals?

Key Consideration

Does the team currently have a set of goals in place? Are they meaningful, measurable, and benchmarked?

Time Needed

This activity takes anywhere from 60-300 minutes, depending on whether the team already has well-defined goals in place, needs to create team goals, or needs to gather data in order to set team goals and benchmarks. The time needed to set team goals is sometimes split between two off-sites, where initial goal-setting work is done at the first off-site, relevant data is gathered and reviewed between off-sites, and goals finalized at a second off-site.

Room Requirements

The room should be conducive to private conversations, have an LCD projector for the slides, and flip charts and markers for sub-teams.

Materials Needed

1 copy of the Team Scorecard Handout for each team member.

FACILITATION

		Materials
Step 1 1 min.	Introduce the activity, which is to create a set of meaningful, measurable, and benchmarked team goals.	Scorecard PPT 1
Step 2 15 min.	Pass out Team Scorecard Handouts to everyone on the team. Review the SMART-B components, a sample Team Scorecard, and the four benchmarks.	Team Scorecard Handout Scorecard PPTs 2-4
Step 3 15-20 min.	Given the team's key stakeholders, influencers, challenges, and purpose, ask team members to identify the broad areas where the team needs to set goals to determine if it is being successful, having an impact, or winning. These might include customers, quality, productivity, financials, employees, adoption rates, test scores, safety, social media, etc. Write these on a flip chart. Combine areas where it makes sense and check in with the team on the final set of goal areas.	Flip Chart
Step 4 45 min.	Assign different goal areas to sub-teams and set a common measurement period for all goals (e.g., weekly, monthly, quarterly, etc.). Ask each sub-team to use flip charts to document 1-5 SMART-B goals for their assigned areas. For example, the sub-team assigned with the financial goal area may come back with monthly revenue, profitability, cash flow, days in A/R, etc.	Scorecard PPT 5 Flip Charts

Step 5 60-120 min.	Ask sub-teams to do large group report-outs on their draft SMART-B goals. Team members should share information, comment on, and make edits to each SMART-B goal. Determine whether a SMART-B goal is ready to be added to the Team Scorecard or needs more work before moving on to the next goal.	Flip Charts
Step 6 (If Needed) 60-120 min.	Teams may need to gather additional information before they can set metrics and benchmarks for some of the SMART-B goals. Those goals needing additional work should be assigned to sub-teams who are responsible for gathering data and creating updated drafts of their goals. Once the second draft of the SMART-B goals is completed, teams should then repeat **Step 5** at a later team meeting or off-site to finalize the Team Scorecard.	Flip Charts

POST-EXERCISE ACTIVITIES

- Create an electronic draft of the Team Scorecard and circulate it among team members for additional comments.
- Share the Team Scorecard when onboarding new team members.
- Review and update the Team Scorecard on a regular basis.

Team Action Plans

PURPOSE

Drive Action

Translate team goals into action steps with owners and due dates.

Drive Accountability

Set clear expectations for team member deliverables.

Improve Buy-In

Help team members see the links between their actions and team goals.

PREPARATION

Review Data

Review the Mission score and relevant comments on the Team Assessment Survey or Team Interview Summary. Was there any uncertainty about what the team needed to do to achieve its goals?

Time Needed

This activity takes 60-240 minutes, depending on the number of team goals and the size of the team.

Room Requirements

The room should be conducive to private conversations, have an LCD projector for the slides, and flip charts and markers for sub-teams.

Materials Needed

1 copy of the Team Action Plan Handout for each team member.

FACILITATION

		Materials
Step 1 5 min.	Introduce the activity and its purpose, which is to build action plans for the team's goals.	Action Plan PPT 1
Step 2 10 min.	Pass out copies of the Team Scorecard and Team Action Plan Handout. Review the components of a Team Action Plan and state that action plans should be built for team goals, whenever teams are working on a project, or when taking action to resolve a difficult challenge. Also review the Team Action Plan Checklist, which is used to confirm the robustness of team plans.	Team Scorecard Team Action Plan Handout Action Plan PPTs 2-3
Step 3 30-60 min.	Divide the team's goals among sub-teams and ask them to flip chart action plans for their assigned goals. There should be one action plan/flip chart per team goal. The plans should include all the major action steps and sub-steps, owners, and due dates. Also let all the sub-teams know when action plan completion status will be reviewed, such as during team monthly or quarterly meetings. These reviews should be built into Team Action Plans.	Action Plan PPTs 4-5 Flip Chart #1 *See a sample of a completed Action Plan Flip Chart #1 on p. 263*
Step 4 60-90 min.	Ask the sub-teams to do large group report-outs on their draft Team Action Plans. Team members should use Team Action Plan Checklists when reviewing plans and share information, comment on, and make edits to Team Action Plans as needed. Team leaders should have the final say on Team Action Plans.	Flip Charts
Step 5 10-30 min.	Because the plans have been built independently, the large group should discuss if any road blocks, capacity constraints, or bottlenecks are likely to occur once the plans are put together. Adjust action steps, owners, and due dates as needed to alleviate constraints.	

- Create an electronic copy of the Team Action Plan and circulate it among team members for additional comments.
- Share the Team Action Plan when onboarding new team members.
- Regularly review progress and update the Team Action Plan in team meetings.

Example of a Completed Team Action Plan
Flip Chart #1

Problem/Challenge/SMART-B Goal: To improve service station operating margins from 8% to 12% by December 2022.

Major Activities/ Sub-Steps	Due Date	Accountable Party	Completion Status
1. Communicate operating margin strategy to all employees.	Feb 1	Steve	Done
- E-mail with margin goal and rationale sent to all employees.	Jan 7	Steve, Marty	Done
- District manager briefing kits prepared and distributed.	Jan 7	Marty	Done
- District manager meetings held with all store managers.	Jan 14	Jen	Done
- Store manager meetings with employees.	Jan 21	Jen	Done
- Town hall meetings with all employees.	Jan 28	Steve	Done
2. Upgrade the 6 oldest stations.	Jun 1	Mitch	In progress
- New store design finalized.	Jan 21	Mitch, Steve	Done
- Remodeling vendor selected.	Feb 15	Mitch, Steve	Done
- Remodeling schedule finalized.	Mar 15	Mitch, Steve	In progress
- Remodeling completed.	May 15	Mitch, Steve	In progress
- Stations restocked and fully operational.	Jun 1	Steve, Jen	In progress

Roles and Responsibilities Matrix

PURPOSE

Gain Alignment

Create a common understanding of who is responsible for what on a team.

Drive Accountability

Clarify expectations for team members.

Improve Buy-In

Help team members see the links between their responsibilities and team goals.

PREPARATION

Review Data

Review Talent scores and relevant comments on the Team Assessment Survey or Team Interview Summary. Do team members know what they are responsible for? Is no one taking ownership, or are issues or tasks falling through the cracks? Are there duplicative efforts? Are too many decisions bubbling up to team leaders?

Key Consideration

Does the organization use the RACI model for assigning responsibilities? If so, then that model should be used for this activity.

Time Needed

This activity takes 60-120 minutes, depending on the number of team goals and the size of the team.

Room Requirements

The room should be conducive to private conversations, have an LCD projector for the slides, and a flip chart and set of markers.

Materials Needed

- 1 copy of the Team Scorecard for each team member.
- 1 copy of the Team Action Plan for each team member.
- 4 copies of the Roles and Responsibilities Matrix for each team member.

FACILITATION

		Materials
Step 1 1 min.	Introduce the activity, which is to clarify members' roles and responsibilities for the team.	R&R Matrix PPT 1
Step 2 15 min.	Pass out blank copies of the Team Scorecard and Team Action Plan (if available) and Roles and Responsibilities Matrix (P/S or RACI versions). Create a Roles and Responsibilities Flip Chart and write members' names across the top row. Ask team members to do the same on their handouts. Taking one team goal at a time, write down the major activities needed to accomplish this goal in the left column of the Roles and Responsibilities Matrix Flip Chart. Ask team members to write them down in the same order on their Roles and Responsibilities Matrix Handouts. Repeat this process for all remaining team goals, and add any other team tasks or responsibilities that cause confusion or do not fall neatly under one of the team's goals.	Team Scorecard Team Action Plan Roles and Responsibilities Matrix Handout Flip Charts

		Materials
Step 3 5-10 min.	Explain either the P/S or RACI rating scheme: - *P = Primary Owner.* There can only be one P per task. - *S = Support.* These individuals work on or provide input and support for the task, but they are not primarily responsible for task completion. There can be more than one S per task. - *R = Responsible.* Team members who do the work to complete the task. There can be multiple Rs for any task. - *A = Accountable.* The team member ultimately responsible for task completion. There can only be one A per task. - *C = Consulted.* These team members are solicited for opinions but do not do any of the work associated with the task. - *I = Informed.* These team members are kept abreast of task progress but are not solicited for input, and do not do any of the work associated with the task.	R&R Matrix PPT 2 or 3
Step 4 10-20 min.	If doing the P/S version of the Roles and Responsibilities Matrix, then ask team members to individually note Ps and Ss for each task on their handouts.	R&R Matrix PPT 4
Step 5 20-60 min.	Taking one task/row at a time, do a large group report-out by having team members share their Ps and Ss. Discuss and come to a consensus on final Ps and Ss for a task before moving to the next task. Note the final Ps and Ss on the flip chart and repeat the process for the remaining tasks. Team leaders get the final say on Ps and Ss for each task.	Flip Charts
Step 6 10-20 min.	Ask the large group to look down the columns to review the Ps and Ss for each team member. Are team workloads properly balanced? Does the team have any capacity constraints? Adjust Ps and Ss as needed to alleviate workload imbalances or capacity issues.	
RACI Option 45-90 min.	If doing the RACI version of the Roles and Responsibilities Matrix, start with doing Steps 1-3. Then take one task at a time and ask the team to identify the Rs, A, Cs and Is for each task. Note RACIs on the flip chart and repeat the process for the remaining tasks. Team leaders get the final say on the Rs, A, Cs and Is for each task.	R&R Matrix PPT 5 Flip Charts

POST-EXERCISE ACTIVITIES

- Create an electronic draft of the Roles and Responsibilities Matrix and circulate it among team members for additional comments.
- Share the Roles and Responsibilities Matrix when onboarding new team members.
- Adjust the Roles and Responsibilities Matrix when setting new goals, taking on new projects, onboarding new team members, restructuring the team, combining teams, etc.

Example of a Completed
Roles and Responsibilities Matrix
P/S Version

Critical Tasks/ Responsibilities	Team Members							
	Bob	Tom	Jill	Fred	Xi	Rajiv	Said	Luis
Run weekly update meetings						P		
Run monthly review meetings		S		S				P
Run annual strategic planning meetings	S	S			P			S
Conduct market research on key competitors			P				S	
Conduct customer research on potential app features	P		S		S		S	S
Create app requirements	S		S				P	
Review app requirements with team	S		S				P	
Build app project plan		S		P		S		
Initial feature review			S	P	S		S	S

P = Primary Responsibility   S = Support

Example of a Completed
Roles and Responsibilities Matrix
RACI Version

Critical Tasks/ Responsibilities	Team Members							
	Bob	Tom	Jill	Fred	Xi	Rajiv	Said	Luis
Run weekly update meetings		C	C			R		A
Run monthly review meetings	C	C	C	C	C	C	R	A
Run annual strategic planning meetings	C	C	C	C	R	C	C	A
Conduct market research on key competitors	C	C	A	R	R	I	I	I
Conduct customer research on potential app features	A	R	R	R	C	C	I	I
Create app requirements	R		R				A	
Review app requirements with team	R	C	A	C	C	C	C	C
Build app project plan		A		R		R		
Initial feature review			A	R	R		C	I

R = Responsible   A = Accountable   C = Consulted   I = Informed

Followership Scatterplots

PURPOSE

Assess Talent

Determine team members' levels of engagement and critical thinking.

Develop Staff

Devise plans to improve team followership.

Review Data

What was the team's Talent score on the Team Assessment Survey? Were there any comments in the Team Assessment Survey or Team Interview Summary conveying frustration with fellow team members?

Key Considerations

This exercise should not be done in team settings. Followership Scatterplots are usually completed by team leaders in leadership development programs that focus on team-building skills, or by working with team facilitators in one-on-one meetings. If doing the latter, the facilitators should do Steps 1, 2, 3, 6, 7, 8, and 9 described below.

Leaders, facilitators, and trainers using this activity should be familiar with the Followership (Curphy & Roellig, 2011) white paper.

Time Needed

Usually 45-120 minutes; Followership Scatterplots take more time to do in leadership development programs than when done as a solo effort.

Room Requirements

If the activity is done as part of a leadership development program, then the room should be conducive to sub-team breakouts, large group report-outs, have an LCD projector for the slides, and flip charts and markers for sub-teams.

Materials Needed

- 1 copy of the Followership (Curphy & Roellig, 2011) white paper for each team leader.
- 1 copy of the Followership Scatterplot for each team leader.

FACILITATION IN LEADERSHIP DEVELOPMENT PROGRAMS

		Materials
Step 1 1 min.	Introduce the activity, which is to identify the types of followers leaders have on their teams.	Followership PPT 1
Step 2 5 min.	Review the critical thinking and engagement/enthusiasm aspects of followership by describing the characteristics associated with high and low scores for each dimension.	Followership PPT 2
Step 3 10 min.	Do a brief overview of the four followership types. For example, when describing Self-Starters, point out where they fall on the Critical Thinking and Engagement dimensions, and then add one or two sentences about what these individuals are like. Repeat this process for the other three followership types.	Followership PPT 3
Step 4 15 min.	Break into four sub-teams and assign one of the followership types to each sub-team. Ask sub-teams to create a flip chart with the followership type listed at the top, common behaviors or characteristics for this type, and motivational strategies to keep Self-Starters in the upper right quadrant or to convert Slackers to Self-Starters, Criticizers to Self-Starters, or Brown-Nosers to Self-Starters.	Followership PPT 4 Flip Chart #1 *See a sample of a completed Followership Type Flip Chart #1 on p. 274*

		Materials
Step 5 20-30 min.	Ask the sub-teams to do large group report-outs on their followership type. Report-outs should begin by stating the common behaviors or characteristics for this type and asking the large group for additional comments. Then the sub-teams should report out their motivational strategies for their type and the large group should weigh in with additional ideas. Facilitators should then identify and discuss the underlying psychological issue team leaders will need to deal with for each type, and they are as follows: - *Self-Starters:* Impatience. Self-Starters have little tolerance for leaders who dither, fail to paint a clear direction, do not secure needed resources, or fail to clear obstacles. - *Brown-Nosers/Yes People:* Self-confidence. These team members often have the knowledge, skills, and experience needed to solve problems, but do not want to be responsible for making decisions. - *Slackers:* Work motivation. Most Slackers put considerable time and effort toward activities outside of work. They have plenty of motivation, they just aren't motivated to work on assigned tasks. - *Criticizers:* Recognition. Most Criticizers were Self-Starters in the past and got recognized for their work accomplishments. But they somehow came up short on a promotion or during a reorganization and now get their recognition through complaints and whining.	Flip Charts
Step 6 15 min.	Demonstrate how a Followership Scatterplot works. Team leaders should pick a team member, evaluate his or her Critical Thinking skills using the descriptors on the left, and then evaluate his or her level of Engagement using the descriptors at the bottom of the scatterplot. They should write the team member's name at the intersection of their Critical Thinking and Engagement scores. They should repeat this process for the remaining team members.	Followership PPT 5-6 Followership Scatterplot Handout
Step 7 20 min.	Ask team leaders to share their Followership Scatterplots with a partner. They should provide some context about the team, what they have done to develop different followers, what they need to do to create more Self-Starters, etc. Partners should provide guidance, advice, and coaching as needed.	Followership Scatterplots
Step 8 20 min.	Once the peer coaching is completed, ask team leaders to indicate their own followership journey on their Followership Scatterplots. They should note their followership type when they first started working, and then draw a line depicting how it has changed over the course of their careers. They should share their follower journey with their partners.	Followership PPT 7 Followership Scatterplots
Step 9 10 min.	Do a large group debrief on the Followership Scatterplots. Ask participants if their followership type changed over time. What does this say about their current scatterplot? People move. Why did they move? The number one reason has to do with how they were being led at the time. What does this have to do with their scatterplots?	

POST-EXERCISE ACTIVITIES

Team leaders should develop plans to move 1-3 team members to Self-Starters or to keep them as Self-Starters.

Team leaders should redo Followership Scatterplots every six months to gauge progress.

Example of a Completed Followership Type Flip Chart #1

Slacker

Key Behaviors:

- Can't be found.

- Always have excuses.

- Tasks are never done quite right or on time.

- Do just enough to stay out of trouble.

- Never volunteer.

- Watch the clock.

- No initiative or sense of urgency.

Motivational Strategies:

- Set clear expectations.

- Monitor closely.

- Provide feedback.

- Administer consequences.

- Transfer to another team.

- Put into a different role on the team.

Team Improvement Activity
18

Feedforward Exercise

PURPOSE

Improve Team Talent

Provide team members with feedback to improve team functioning and performance.

Build Trust

Share strengths and areas targeted for improvement.

PREPARATION

Review Data

Review Talent score and relevant comments on the Team Assessment Survey or Team Interview Summary. Were there any comments that conveyed frustration with team member behavior or skill gaps?

Time Needed

This activity takes 90-120 minutes, depending on the size of the team.

Room Requirements

The room should be conducive to private conversations, have an LCD projector for the slides, and flip charts and markers for individual team members.

Materials Needed

- 1 pack of Post-It notes per team member.
- 1 copy of Team Norms (if formally established).

FACILITATION

		Materials
Step 1 1 min.	Introduce the activity and its purpose, which is to provide team members with feedback in order to improve team functioning and performance.	Feedforward PPT 1
Step 2 30-40 min.	Pass out packs of Post-It notes, flip chart paper, markers, and Team Norms (if established) to team members. Tell team members they are to write down two behaviors each team member should keep doing and two behaviors they need to start, stop, or do differently in order to improve team performance. They should use one Post-It note for each behavior, so each member will get four Post-Its from each of his or her peers. If available, then team members can/should use Team Norms as a guideline for their Post-Its.	Post-It Notes Team Norms Feedforward PPT 2
Step 3 20 min.	Ask participants to create a Feedforward Flip Chart with their names and put them up around the room. They should then affix their four notes to the appropriate flip charts.	Feedforward PPT 3 Flip Chart #1
Step 4 20 min.	Once all the Post-Its have been affixed on flip charts, team members should privately review all of their comments. They should move the Post-Its around in order to identify common themes, and then identify two behaviors they intend to keep doing and two they intend to do differently to help the team improve, and write them down at the bottom of their flip charts.	Flip Chart #1

Materials

Step 5
20-30 min.

Prior to doing individual report-outs, state that everyone got a lot of feedback. In these situations, it is best to focus on a few things to keep doing or to do differently rather than trying to do everything. It is also more effective if people review their feedback and determine for themselves what they are willing to do. With this in mind, do individual report-outs of the two behaviors he or she intends to keep doing and two he or she intends to do differently. Solicit reactions and affirmations from the team after each report-out, and note the commitments on a flip chart.

Ask team members what they learned, and if there are any common themes across the flip charts.

POST-EXERCISE ACTIVITIES

- Create an electronic draft of the "keep doing" and "do differently" commitments and circulate it among team members for additional comments.
- Provide peer feedback on these commitments on a semi-annual basis. One way to do this is to have team members rate the two "keep doing" and two "do differently" behaviors for fellow team members on a 1 to 5 scale, where:

  - 1 = No Change
  - 2 = Little Change
  - 3 = Some Change
  - 4 = Definite Change
  - 5 = Big Change

- This could be done by creating a form that lists the four behaviors, the 1-5 rating scale, and any comments for each team member. These forms could be passed out to everyone on the team and the completed forms sent to a facilitator or project manager who would consolidate the results for each team member. The raw and consolidated results would be shared with individual members who would, in turn, be asked to tell the group what they've learned.

Example of a Feedforward Flip Chart #1

<Team Member Name>

Keep Doing	Do Differently
Affix Keep Doing Post-Its here	Affix Do Differently Post-Its here

I commit to doing the following behaviors to help the team:

1. Keep Doing:

2. Keep Doing:

3. Do Differently:

4. Do Differently:

Eavesdropping Exercise

PURPOSE

Gain Alignment

Understand team members' expectations of fellow team members.

Build Trust

Share personal strengths and areas targeted for improvement while working on the team.

PREPARATION

Review Data

Review Talent and Courage scores and relevant comments on the Team Assessment Survey or Team Interview Summary. Were there any comments that conveyed frustration with team member behavior?

Time Needed

This activity takes 60-90 minutes, depending on the size of the team.

Room Requirements

The room should be conducive to private conversations, have an LCD projector for the slides, and flip charts and markers for individual team members.

Materials Needed

None.

FACILITATION

		Materials
Step 1 1 min.	Introduce the activity and its purpose, which is to allow team members to share expectations of themselves and for each other.	Eavesdrop PPT 1
Step 2 15 min.	Pass out flip chart paper and markers to team members. Describe the Eavesdropping Exercise by telling everyone that they will need to flip chart answers to the following questions:	Eavesdrop PPT 2-3 Flip Chart #1 *See a sample of a completed Eavesdropping Exercise Flip Chart #1 on p. 281*
Step 3 15-20 min.	If we are going to work together effectively as a team, what three things do you expect from fellow team members? How do team members need to show up and behave? Six months from now, what three things do you want team members to say about you? Two of these should be strengths or contributions to the team, and one should be something you are working on that you hope not to hear.	
Step 4 20-60 min.	Once team members have completed their flip charts, ask each individual to do a large group report-out. Each report-out should take about five minutes, including commentary and Q&A.	Flip Chart
Step 5 20 min.	Ask the team if there are any common themes across the flip charts. Note the common themes on a separate flip chart. Ask the team what it could do to leverage these learnings.	Flip Chart

POST-EXERCISE ACTIVITIES

- Create an electronic copy of the completed Eavesdropping flip charts and circulate it among team members for additional comments.
- Share the information when onboarding new team members.
- Revisit and update the team's context at least once a year.

Example of a Completed Eavesdropping Exercise Flip Chart #1

Roberta Smith

What I expect from others on this team	What I hope people say about me six months from now
1. Do your job.	1. Strength: Leveraged her experience doing user interface work with other projects to help the team create a product customers find easy to use.
2. No surprises.	2. Strength: All of her assignments were high quality and done on time.
3. No hidden agendas.	3. Hope Not to Hear: Worried more about what others on the team were doing than her own work.

Wingfinder Assessment

PURPOSE

Increase Self-Awareness

Provide team members with insights into their interpersonal skills, capacity for thinking, creativity, and drive.

Optimize Team Talent

Place team members in roles or leading projects that leverage strengths.

Build Trust

Share personality trait results to improve team trust.

PREPARATION

Review Data

Review the Talent score and relevant comments on the Team Assessment Survey or Team Interview Summary. Were there any comments that conveyed frustration with team member behavior? Personality conflicts? Team members in the wrong roles?

Key Considerations

- The first part of this activity involves team members completing a Wingfinder Assessment as prework before a team meeting, off-site, or leadership development program. The second part of the activity is reviewing collective Wingfinder results and discussing the implications for the team.

- Team members receive two Wingfinder Feedback Reports upon completion of the assessment. One is a 20-page Wingfinder Full Report that contains sensitive information about personality traits and mental abilities. The second is a one-page Wingfinder Talent Passport that only lists an individual's top four strengths and does not contain any sensitive information. *This Team Improvement Activity only involves the Wingfinder Talent Passport.*

- Team members will need to send in their Wingfinder Talent Passports to the facilitator prior to the off-site. The facilitator will use the passports to create a report depicting the team's collective results that will be shared during the off-site.

- Facilitators should complete a Wingfinder and become thoroughly familiar with the four areas of success, 25 psychological strengths, Wingfinder Full Report, and Wingfinder Talent Passport.

- There is no fee for the Wingfinder Assessment. Team members receive their Wingfinder Full Reports and Wingfinder Talent Passports immediately after completing their assessments.

Prework

- Team members should be sent the Wingfinder infographic and *The Psychology of Teams* article to gain an understanding of the Wingfinder model.

- Team members can take the assessment by pasting the following link into their browsers: www.wingfinder.com. It will take team members about 45 minutes to complete the Wingfinder Assessment.

- Facilitators should use the Wingfinder Group Report Template to create a group report for the team. The numbers on the report refer to the rank ordering of the top four strengths from each person's Wingfinder Talent Passport.

Time Needed

- It takes 30-60 minutes for facilitators to create Wingfinder Group Reports.
- It takes 60-90 minutes to facilitate a Wingfinder Feedback Session with a team.

Room Requirements

The room should be conducive to private conversations and have an LCD projector for the slides.

Materials Needed

- 1 copy of the completed Wingfinder Group Report for each team member.
- Team members should bring their Wingfinder Talent Passports to the session.

FACILITATION

		Materials
Step 1 1 min.	Ensure everyone has their Wingfinder Talent Passports before starting the session.	Wingfinder Talent Passports
Step 2 1 min.	Introduce the session, which is to identify team members' top four strengths, how they could affect team dynamics and performance, and to get to know each other better.	Wingfinder PPT 1
Step 3 15-20 min.	Describe the employability concept and model, Wingfinder validity, press articles, four major scales and 25 subscales, and Talent Passport.	Wingfinder PPTs 2-8

		Materials
Step 4	Pass out and review the Wingfinder Group Report with the team.	Wingfinder Group Report
30-40 min.	Discuss the implications of the team's most prevalent strengths and areas where there are no strengths.	Wingfinder PPTs 9-11
	Review where team members have similar and differing strengths and discuss how these results help or hinder the team in overcoming challenges, achieving goals, getting things done, communicating, making decisions, or creating conflict.	
	Ask members if their roles allow them to leverage their strengths and if they are under pressure or stress whether overuse of their strengths might be happening on the team.	
	Discuss how the team can use the Wingfinder Group Report to improve team dynamics and performance.	

POST-EXERCISE ACTIVITIES

- Ask new team members to complete a Wingfinder.
- Share Wingfinder Group Results when onboarding new team members.

Example of a Completed Wingfinder Group Report

Person 7	Person 6	Person 5	Person 4	Person 3	Person 2	Person 1		
	3	1				2	Adaptable	**CREATIVITY** — Creativity measures how original and innovative people's thinking is, or how logical and analytical it is.
							Focused	
	4						Innovative	
							Pragmatic	
	1				1		Open to Experience	
1					1		Classical	
			2	2			Diplomatic	**CONNECTIONS** — Connections measure how well people manage relationships and work independently.
							Direct	
			4	1			Supportive	
							Autonomous	
							Sociable	
		2					Independent	
							Balanced	
			3				Emotive	
4					3		Disciplined	**DRIVE** — Drive measures the level of ambition
		4					Relaxed	
			4				Achiever	
2							Patient	
	3				3		Confident	
					4		Modest	
		1					Agile	**THINKING** — Thinking measures the abilities people draw upon when solving problems.
	2				2		Analytical	
3					4		Balanced Learner	
			3				Hands-On Learner	
							Intuitive	

21

Hogan Personality Inventory (HPI)

Increase Self-Awareness

Provide team members with insights into their personality traits, how they are likely to be perceived by others, and why the team may act in certain ways.

Optimize Team Talent

Place team members in roles or on projects that leverage strengths.

Build Trust

Share personality trait results to improve team trust.

Review Data

Review the Talent score and relevant comments on the Team Assessment Survey or Team Interview Summary. Were there any comments that conveyed frustration with team member behavior? Personality conflicts? Team members in the wrong roles?

Key Considerations

- The Hogan Personality Inventory (HPI) can only be administered and interpreted by certified personnel. This individual may be an external consultant or someone within the organization who has been Hogan certified.
- Team leaders will need to determine whether they want to have HPI Insight or Potential Feedback Reports. Both report types provide insightful information, with Potential Feedback Reports being more extensive and targeted for executive audiences. They should coordinate the report type with the Hogan-certified person setting up the HPI assessments.
- Option: HPI Group Reports can be ordered through Hogan-certified personnel.
- Option: Team leaders can arrange for team members to get one-on-one feedback on their HPI results from a certified Hogan coach prior to or after the team meeting, off-site, or leadership development program. There will be an additional fee for this service if delivered by external consultants.

Prework

This activity is done as prework a week or so before a team meeting, off-site, or leadership development program.

Time Needed

- It takes 15-20 minutes for team members to complete HPIs.
- It takes 60-90 minutes to facilitate an HPI Feedback Session with a team.

Room Requirements

The room should be conducive to private conversations and have an LCD projector for the slides.

Materials Needed

1 copy of the HPI Feedback Report for each team member.

FACILITATION

		Materials
Step 1 1 min.	Introduce the session, which is to provide insights about how team members are likely to be perceived by fellow team members and why the team may act in certain ways.	HPI PPT 1
Step 2 10 min.	Ask the team to identify its key challenges, goals, and plans, and write them on a flip chart. Tell the team that they will be reviewing where their collective personalities may help or hinder team dynamics and performance.	Flip Chart
Step 3 20-30 min.	Pass out HPI Feedback Reports and ask everyone to turn to the graphic summary page. Do a Human Histogram for each of the seven personality characteristics by asking people to stand up and arrange themselves in a semi-circle by ascending scores, with one end being made up of the lowest and the other end made up of the highest scores on Adjustment. Describe what Adjustment measures, and what team members are like with lower scores and what they are like with higher scores. Given this distribution of Adjustment scores, ask the team to identify the implications for team challenges, goals, plans, roles, functioning, and performance. Repeat this process for Ambition, Sociability, Interpersonal Sensitivity, Prudence, Inquisitive, and Learning Approach.	HPI PPT 2 HPI Feedback Reports
Step 4 20-30 min.	Give team members time to review their results, and then ask them to pair up and share what they learned from their HPI Insight or Potential Feedback Reports. They can share as little or as much of their reports as they want.	HPI PPT 3 HPI Feedback Reports
Step 5 15 min.	Do a large group report-out. What did team members learn from their HPIs? How can the team use this knowledge to improve team dynamics and performance? What will the team specifically commit to doing given these results? Who is responsible for making this happen? When will it start and how will progress be measured?	Option: HPI Group Report

POST-EXERCISE ACTIVITIES

- Ask new team members to complete an HPI.
- Share the HPI Group Report when onboarding new team members.

Example of Hogan Personality Inventory Group Report Types

HPI HPI Composite Profile

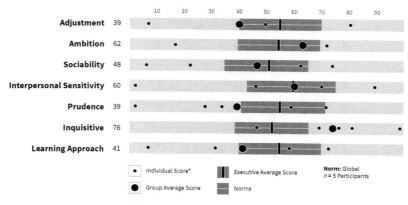

Adjustment	39	
Ambition	62	
Sociability	48	
Interpersonal Sensitivity	60	
Prudence	39	
Inquisitive	76	
Learning Approach	41	

Individual Score*   Executive Average Score   **Norm:** Global
Group Average Score   Norms   *n* = 5 Participants

* Individual score dots sometimes represent more than one participant

HPI HPI Average Scores

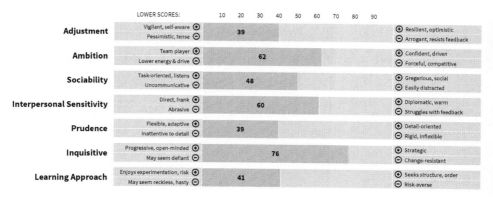

	LOWER SCORES:	10 20 30 40 50 60 70 80 90		
Adjustment	Vigilant, self-aware ⊕ / Pessimistic, tense ⊖	39	⊕ Resilient, optimistic / ⊖ Arrogant, resists feedback
Ambition	Team player ⊕ / Lower energy & drive ⊖	62	⊕ Confident, driven / ⊖ Forceful, competitive
Sociability	Task-oriented, listens ⊕ / Uncommunicative ⊖	48	⊕ Gregarious, social / ⊖ Easily distracted
Interpersonal Sensitivity	Direct, frank ⊕ / Abrasive ⊖	60	⊕ Diplomatic, warm / ⊖ Struggles with feedback
Prudence	Flexible, adaptive ⊕ / Inattentive to detail ⊖	39	⊕ Detail-oriented / ⊖ Rigid, inflexible
Inquisitive	Progressive, open-minded ⊕ / May seem defiant ⊖	76	⊕ Strategic / ⊖ Change-resistant
Learning Approach	Enjoys experimentation, risk ⊕ / May seem reckless, hasty ⊖	41	⊕ Seeks structure, order / ⊖ Risk-averse

Norm: Global

Hogan Development Survey (HDS)

Increase Self-Awareness

Provide team members with insights into how they are likely to behave when stressed and why the team may act in ways that impede performance.

Build Trust

Understand that the team's dark-side personality traits can improve team trust.

Review Data

Review the Talent score and relevant comments on the Team Assessment Survey or Team Interview Summary. Were there any comments that conveyed frustration with team member behavior? Personality conflicts? Team members in the wrong roles?

Key Considerations

- The Hogan Development Survey (HDS) can only be administered and interpreted by certified personnel. This individual may be an external consultant or someone within the organization who has been Hogan certified.
- Team leaders will need to determine whether they want to have HDS Insight or Challenge Feedback Reports. Both report types provide insightful information, with Challenge Feedback Reports being more extensive and targeted for executive audiences. They should coordinate the report type with the Hogan-certified person setting up the HDS assessments.
- Option: HDS Group Reports can be ordered through Hogan-certified personnel.
- Option: Team leaders can arrange for team members to get one-on-one feedback on their HDS results from a certified Hogan coach prior to or after the team meeting, off-site, or leadership development program. There will be an additional fee for this service if delivered by external consultants.

Prework

This activity is done as prework a week or so before a team meeting, off-site, or leadership development program.

Time Needed

- It takes 15-20 minutes for team members to complete the HDS.
- It takes 60-90 minutes to facilitate an HDS Feedback Session with a team.

Room Requirements

The room should be conducive to private conversations and have an LCD projector for the slides.

Materials Needed

1 copy of the HDS Feedback Report for each team member.

FACILITATION

		Materials
Step 1 1 min.	Introduce the session, which is to provide insight into how people behave when stressed and why the team may act in ways that impede performance.	HDS PPT 1
Step 2 10 min.	Ask the team to identify its key challenges and when it is the most stressed, and write them on a flip chart. Also, ask team members to identify and share the situations where they get most frustrated or stressed. Tell the team that they will be reviewing how they are apt to behave in a crisis or during highly stressful situations.	Flip Chart
Step 3 30-40 min.	Describe dark-side personality characteristics and when they are likely to happen. Pass out HDS Insight or Challenge Feedback Reports to team members and ask them to turn to the graphic summary page in their reports. Provide a high-level overview of each of the 11 HDS personality characteristics, percentile scores, and the interpretation of moderate and high HDS scores.	HDS PPT 2 HDS Feedback Report
Step 4 20-30 min.	Give team members time to review their results, identify the situations that cause their dark sides to emerge, and what they can do to navigate around them. Then ask them to pair up and share what they learned from their HDS Insight or Challenge Feedback Reports, situational triggers, and management strategies. They can share as little or as much of their reports as they want.	HDS PPT 3 HDS Feedback Report
Step 5 15 min.	Do a large group report-out. What did team members learn from their HDS? How can the team use this knowledge to improve team dynamics and performance? What will the team specifically commit to doing given these results? Who is responsible for making this happen? When will it start and how will progress be measured?	Option: HDS Group Report

POST-EXERCISE ACTIVITIES

- Ask new team members to complete an HDS.
- Share the HDS Group Report when onboarding new team members.

Example of a Hogan Development Survey Group Report Type

HDS HDS Composite Profile

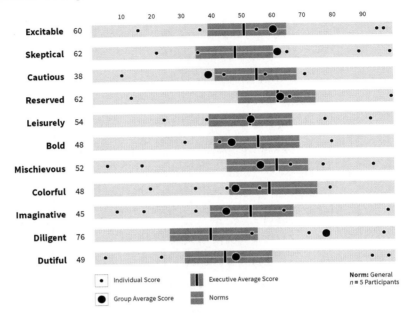

• Individual Score	▌ ▌ Executive Average Score
● Group Average Score	Norms

Norm: General
n = 5 Participants

Example of a Hogan Development Survey Group Report Type

HDS HDS Score Frequencies

	LOWER SCORES:	10 20 30 40 50 60 70 80 90	HIGHER SCORES:
Excitable	Steady, patient ⊕ / Lacks passion, urgency ⊖	40 / 20 / 40	⊕ Passionate / ⊖ Volatile, unpredictable
Skeptical	Positive, trusting ⊕ / Potentially Naïve ⊖	40 / 20 / 20 / 20	⊕ Perceptive / ⊖ Cynical, mistrusting
Cautious	Assertive, adventurous ⊕ / Unafraid of failure ⊖	40 / 40 / 20	⊕ Careful, measured / ⊖ Risk-averse, fears failure
Reserved	Supportive, engaging ⊕ / Lacks toughness ⊖	20 / 60 / 20	⊕ Ignores factors / ⊖ Volatile, unpredictable
Leisurely	Seeks feedback ⊕ / Critical, confrontational ⊖	60 / 20 / 20	⊕ Cooperative / ⊖ Passive aggressive
Bold	Modest, unassuming ⊕ / Lacks confidence ⊖	20 / 60 / 20	⊕ Highly confident / ⊖ Entitled, arrogant
Mischievous	Compliant, rule-following ⊕ / Risk-averse, unpersuasive ⊖	40 / 20 / 20 / 20	⊕ Charming, daring / ⊖ Risk-taking, untrustworthy
Colorful	Restrained, mature ⊕ / Low-impact communication ⊖	40 / 40 / 20	⊕ Interesting, dynamic / ⊖ Dramatic, attention-seeking
Imaginative	Pragmatic, grounded ⊕ / Unimaginative ⊖	60 / 20 / 20	⊕ Innovative, original / ⊖ Eccentric, impractical
Diligent	Relaxed standards ⊕ / Disorganized, hands-off ⊖	60 / 40	⊕ Hardworking, perfectionist / ⊖ Micromanages, overly tactical
Dutiful	Loyal, supportive ⊕ / Dependent on others ⊖	60 / 40	⊕ Independent, self-reliant / ⊖ May seem rebellious

No Risk (0-39%)   Low Risk (40-69%)   Moderate Risk (70-89%)   High Risk (90-100%)   **Norm:** General

New Team Member Onboarding Checklist

PURPOSE

Build Relationships

Help new team members build trust with peers.

Drive Execution

Help new team members accelerate contributions to team performance.

PREPARATION

Key Considerations

- This activity should be done whenever someone joins a team. It is most effective if checklist completion is done within the first two weeks and involves multiple team members.
- Having electronic copies of a team's Context Assessment, Scorecard, Roles and Responsibilities Matrix, Operating Rhythm, Norms, etc. makes this activity easier.

Time Needed

This activity usually takes 1-4 hours spread out over a few weeks.

Room Requirements

None.

Materials Needed

1 copy of the New Team Member Onboarding Checklist for new team members.

FACILITATION

		Materials
Step 1 60-120 min.	Option A: Go through the New Team Member Onboarding Checklist with the new team member within the first week of his or her arrival.	New Team Member Onboarding Checklist
120-240 min.	Option B: Review the New Team Member Onboarding Checklist with team members, and ask/assign them to review different Rocket Model components with members about to join the team. Note assignments and due dates and share the checklist with all relevant parties. Ensure the checklist is completed no later than two weeks after a new team member's arrival.	New Team Member PPTs 1-2 New Team Member Onboarding Checklist

POST-EXERCISE ACTIVITIES

None.

Example of a Completed New Team Member Onboarding Checklist

Component	Key Actions	Who	Due Date
Context	What does the team know about its key customers and competitors? Who are the key internal and external stakeholders? What are the team's political and economic realities? What are the team's top challenges?	Bob	June 1
Mission	What are the team's purpose and goals? How does it define success? What are the team's 30/60/90/120-day plans? When is progress against goals and plans reviewed?	Kumar	June 2
Talent	Who is responsible for what on this team? Who does the new team member need to work most closely with? How is the team rewarded for performance?	Julie	June 3
Norms	What processes or systems does the team use to get work done? When is the training for these processes and systems? What are the key work handoffs? What are the team's operating rhythm and meeting rules? What topics get discussed/decided in team meetings? How does the team make decisions? What are the team's rules about returning emails? What are the rules around ownership and accountability?	Ernesto and DeShawn	June 4-5
Buy-In	How does the team member contribute to team success?	Mary	June 8
Resources	What resources are available? What resources does the new team member need to succeed? How much authority and political capital does the team have?	Alfredo	June 9
Courage	What are the rules around team conflict? When is it appropriate to challenge others? Are there any topics that are taboo?	Moamar	June 10
Results	How has the team performed over the past year? How does the team win? What has the team learned from past successes and mistakes?	Jill	June 11

24

Team Norms

PURPOSE

Drive Accountability

Set clear expectations for team member behavior.

Build Trust

Help teams have candid conversations about acceptable and unacceptable team member behavior.

PREPARATION

Review Data

Review the Norms and Courage scores and relevant comments on the Team Assessment Survey or Team Interview Summary. Was there any frustration with team member behavior?

Key Consideration

Has the team completed the Motives, Values, Preferences Inventory; Hogan Personality Inventory; Hogan Development Survey; or Eavesdropping Exercise? These activities are not necessary but can provide helpful inputs when setting Team Norms.

Time Needed

This activity takes 60-90 minutes.

Room Requirements

The room should be conducive to private conversations, have an LCD projector for the slides, and flip charts and markers for sub-teams.

Materials Needed

1 copy of the Team Norm Form for each team member.

FACILITATION

		Materials
Step 1 1 min.	Introduce the session, which is to establish an agreed-upon set of rules governing team members' attitudes and behaviors. In other words, how should team members treat each other, how quickly should people respond to inquiries, how should the team handle disagreements, etc.	Team Norm PPT 1
Step 2 10-15 min.	Option A: If Motives, Values, Preferences Inventory; Hogan Personality Inventory; Hogan Development Survey Group Reports; or Eavesdropping Exercise results are available, then review them with the team and ask them to identify potential Team Norm topics. Topics might include dealing with conflict, conveying a sense of urgency, straight talk, following through with commitments, assuming positive intent, etc. Topics should be recorded on a flip chart. Option B: If these results are not available, then simply ask team members to identify where they need to set rules to govern team members' attitudes and behaviors. These might include dealing with conflict, conveying a sense of urgency, straight talk, following through with commitments, assuming positive intent, etc. Topics should be recorded on a flip chart.	Flip Chart
Step 3 15-30 min.	Pass out Team Norm Forms and review an example of a completed form. Divide the topics among sub-teams, and ask them to use flip charts to write the definition, three positive behaviors, and three negative behaviors for their assigned Norms. (15 minutes per assigned Norm.)	Team Norm PPT 2-3 Team Norm Form Flip Chart #1 *See a sample of a completed Team Norm Form #1 on p. 306*

		Materials
Step 4 60-90 min.	Ask sub-teams to do report-outs for their assigned Norm. The large group should ask questions, comment on, and make edits to Norm definitions and behaviors as needed. Make sure any edits are captured, and the definition and behaviors finalized on the flip chart before debriefing the next Norm. Repeat the process for the remaining Norms. (10 minutes per Norm.)	Flip Charts

POST-EXERCISE ACTIVITIES

- Create an electronic copy of the Team Norms and circulate it among team members for additional comments.
- Share the Team Norms when onboarding new team members.
- Periodically review the extent to which team members adhere to Team Norms, which can be done in several different ways:

  - Option 1: Ask team members to use fingers on one hand to indicate how well everyone is adhering to Team Norms, with one finger representing very little, three fingers representing to some extent, and five fingers representing to a great extent. Take one Norm at a time and ask team members to raise a hand with the number of fingers that represents their vote. Estimate the average score and discuss high and low votes and what the team needs to do differently to get a four or five on the Norm. Repeat for the remaining Norms. (30 minutes)
  - Option 2: Use the Team Norms as part of a Feedforward Exercise (page 275).
  - Option 3: Add a 1 = Very Little, 3 = To Some Extent, and 5 = To a Great Extent rating scale to the Team Norms. Add team members' names to the top of separate Team Norm Rating Forms. Make copies of each member's Team Norm Rating Form for every member of the team. Ask each team member to rate everyone else on the team using the Team Norm Rating Form. Collect the completed rating forms and organize them by team member. Give team members their peer Team Norm Rating Forms and ask them to share what they learned; what they intend to keep doing; and what they intend to start, stop, or do differently. Record key learnings; keep doing; and start, stop,

do differently commitments on a flip chart with names. Review progress on commitments as needed. (90 minutes to prepare, rate, collect, and consolidate peer Team Norm Rating Forms; 60-90 minutes to facilitate the Team Norms feedback discussion.)

Example of a Completed Team Norm Form Flip Chart #1

Norm: Fostering Healthy Conflict	**Definition:** Healthy conflict will enable team members to push back without repercussion, foster diverse points of view, and help the team make the best decisions. It is okay to agree to disagree.
Positive Behavior Examples: + Asking questions and not interrupting others when they are describing their point of view. + Freely sharing personal points of view pertaining to an issue. + Dude, I want to push back on that...	**Negative Behavior Examples:** − Dominating discussions and not letting others speak. − Failing to speak up, ask questions, or acknowledge others' perspectives. − Raising concerns after team meetings with team members or the team leader rather than sharing them in team meetings. − Failing to follow through on team decisions after they are debated but not agreed with.

Example of a Completed Peer Team Norm Rating Form
Bob Smith

How would you rate this team member on:	Rating Scale 1 = Very Little 3 = To Some Extent 5 = To a Great Extent
Fostering Healthy Conflict	4
Customer Focus	4
Sense of Urgency	2
Getting Things Done	2
Providing Mutual Support	4
Taking Ownership	2
No Surprises	4

25

Operating Rhythm

PURPOSE

Improve Efficiency

Make efficient and effective use of team members' time.

Drive Accountability

Set clear expectations for team member behavior during meetings.

PREPARATION

Review Data

Review the Norms score and relevant comments on the Team Assessment Survey or Team Interview Summary. Was there any frustration with team meetings?

Key Considerations

What is the team's current Operating Rhythm? When does it meet, how long are the meetings, who attends what meetings, what is the purpose of these meetings, etc.? How efficient and effective are these meetings?

Is this a top team or a virtual team? Board and investor meetings, preparation for these meetings, the geographic dispersion of team members, etc. need to be taken into account when establishing a team's Operating Rhythm and master calendar.

Time Needed

This activity takes 60-90 minutes.

Room Requirements

The room should be conducive to private conversations, have an LCD projector for the slides, and flip charts and markers for sub-teams.

Materials Needed

1 copy of the Operating Rhythm Handout for each team member.

FACILITATION

		Materials
Step 1 1 min.	Introduce the session, which is to establish an agreed-upon set of rules governing team meetings.	Operating Rhythm PPT 1
Step 2 10 min.	Pass out the Operating Rhythm Handout. Describe the three types of team meetings and the Meeting Mechanics and Rules of Engagement Forms in the handout.	Operating Rhythm PPTs 2-4 Operating Rhythm Handout
Step 3 20 min.	Assign Regular Updates, Scorecard Reviews, Special Topics, and Rules of Engagement to one of four sub-teams. The first three sub-teams will flip chart the Meetings Mechanics for their assigned meeting type, and the last sub-team will flip chart the Rules of Engagement that apply to all three types of meetings.	Operating Rhythm PPT 5 Flip Charts #1-2 *See sample of a completed Meeting Mechanics and Rules of Engagement Forms on pp. 309 and 310*

		Materials
Step 4 30-60 min.	Do a large group report-out on the Meeting Mechanics for Regular Updates. The large group should ask questions, comment on, and make edits to the Meeting Mechanics as needed. Make sure any edits are captured and Meeting Mechanics finalized on the flip chart before moving to the next meeting. Repeat the process for Scorecard Reviews, Special Topics, and Rules of Engagement. Consolidate and/or adjust meeting types and Rules of Engagement as needed.	Flip Charts
Step 5 10 min.	Review the GRPI Form in the Operating Rhythm Handout and ask meeting owners to create and send out GRPIs and any prework before their next and all subsequent meetings.	Operating Rhythm PPT 6

POST-EXERCISE ACTIVITIES

- Create an electronic draft of the Meeting Mechanics and Rules of Engagement. Add the meetings to an annual calendar, and circulate the Meeting Mechanics, Rules of Engagement, and annual calendar among team members for additional comment.
- To make efficient and effective use of everyone's time, ensure all meetings use GRPIs.
- Review the Meeting Mechanics, Rules of Engagement, and annual calendar on a semi-annual basis.

Example of a Completed Meeting Mechanics Form Flip Chart #1

Meeting Characteristics	Team Responses
Meeting Type/Purpose (Updates, Scorecard Reviews, Strategy Formulation, Budget Reviews, etc.)	Monthly Scorecard reviews
Dates (When should the meetings take place?)	The 5th of every month
Length (How long will the meetings be?)	8:00 – 11:50 AM CST

Meeting Characteristics	Team Responses
Location (Where will the meetings take place?)	St. Paul Board Room, others dial in
Participants (Who attends?)	All 12 members of the Business Unit Leadership Team
Goals, Agendas, and Owners (Who sets the meeting goals and agenda? How are topics added to the agenda and when do they get sent?)	Steve Smith, President of the Business Unit owns the meeting. Connie Olson will gather topics and send out the agenda and prework NLT the 3rd of every month.

Example of a Completed Rules of Engagement Flip Chart #2

Suggested Rules	Team Responses
Punctuality/Attendance (Okay to show up late/leave early/skip meetings?)	Everyone in place NLT 7:55; any exceptions cleared with Steve beforehand. Anyone arriving after 8:00 pays a $20 fine.
Meeting Management (Stick to agenda/okay to run late?)	Connie will review the agenda and ensure meetings run on time.
Do prework to prepare for meetings? (Yes/no? How much lead time?)	Agendas, Scorecards, and pre-reads will be sent no later than the 3rd of each month.
Meeting Behavior (Openness, engagement, respect, equal participation, etc.) Be specific.	Prework should be read before meetings. Straight talk presentations; no spin. Asking challenging questions is okay. Make suggestions and recommendations. Listen and understand before opining.
Use of laptops, tablets, phones, etc. (Okay or not okay? Or when is it okay?)	No devices are allowed in these meetings.
Take calls during meetings? (Okay or not okay? Or when is it okay?)	It is not permissible to take calls unless cleared with Steve beforehand. Calls will be handled outside the meeting room.
Send proxies or bring guests? (Okay or not okay? Or when is it okay?)	It is not okay to bring guests or send proxies unless approved by Steve.
Presentation Protocol (Bring hard copies of slides? Okay to ask questions during presentations or wait until the end?)	Presenters should bring hard copies of slides if they include small print. Questions should be held until the end of presentations.
Other ROEs	Team members are encouraged to call audibles when a topic should be dealt with by sub-teams, an individual on the team, or a level or two below the team.

Operating Level

PURPOSE

Improve Effectiveness

Ensure teams are dealing with the right issues.

Improve Empowerment

Help teams assign decisions to the appropriate parties.

PREPARATION

Review Data

Review the Norms score and relevant comments on the Team Assessment Survey or Team Interview Summary. Was there any frustration with the team not being strategic enough or not making decisions?

Key Consideration

Is this a top leadership team? If so, then the results of this exercise will have a profound effect on the rest of the organization. Top teams operating too high level disempower their staffs and cause widespread employee disengagement and turnover.

Time Needed

This activity takes 60-120 minutes.

Room Requirements

The room should be conducive to private conversations, have an LCD projector for the slides, and flip charts and markers for sub-teams.

Materials Needed

1 copy of the Operating Level Handout for each team member.

FACILITATION

		Materials
Step 1 1 min.	Introduce the session, which is to ensure the team is working on the right issues and operating at the right level.	Operating Level PPT 1
Step 2 10-15 min.	Pass out the Operating Level Handout. Describe the notion of team operating levels and the five types of issues teams deal with in meetings. Also state that high-performing teams maximize the amount of time working on legitimate issues and minimize time on the other types of issues identified in the handout.	Operating Level PPT 2 Operating Level Handout
Step 3 15 min.	Ask team members to individually identify the types of issues that fall into each topic and estimate the percentage of time the team spends working on these issues. The five percentages should add up to 100% when the handout is completed.	Operating Level Handout
Step 4 20-30 min.	Break into three to four sub-teams. Sub-teams should discuss the issues that fall into the Urgent but Trivial category and come to a consensus on the percentage of time spent working on these issues. These should be noted on a flip chart. They should then repeat the process for the other four topics, and revise the percentages so they total 100%.	Operating Level PPTs 3-4 Flip Chart #1 *See a sample of a completed Operating Level Analysis on p. 313*
Step 5 30-40 min.	Do large group report-outs on the five topics. Each group should report on the issues that fall into the Trivial but Urgent Issues; they should report the amount of time spent on each issue. They should come to a consensus on the time spent working on these issues and note if any changes are needed. They should repeat the process for the other four categories.	Flip Charts

		Materials
Step 6 15-20 min.	The group should build an action plan to reduce the amount of time spent on Urgent but Trivial Issues, Unresolved Issues, Delegable Issues, and Sub-Team Issues.	Operating Level PPT 5 Operating Level Handout Flip Chart #2 *See a sample of a completed Operating Level Action Plan on p. 314*

POST-EXERCISE ACTIVITIES

- Create an electronic draft of the final time spent on topics estimates and the action plan to spend more time working on legitimate issues, and circulate among team members for additional comments.
- Redo the Operating Level exercise six months later to determine if the percentage of time spent working on legitimate issues has improved.

Example of a Completed Operating Level Analysis Flip Chart #1

Topics	What are these issues?	Percent Time Spent
Urgent but Trivial Issues	Debates about seating for the next town hall meeting Employee parking spaces Lunchroom menus, etc.	10%
Unresolved Issues	Organic growth initiatives Keystone acquisition	15%
Delegable Issues	Travel policies for vendors SOW templates Initial research on CRM upgrade	25%
Team vs. Sub-Team Issues	European product pricing and sales Transportation cost reduction Social media campaign	30%
Legitimate Issues	Market and competitive analyses Organizational strategy Annual goals and budgets Business results Talent Board preparation and presentations	20%

Example of a Completed Operating Level Action Plan
Flip Chart #2

Issues	Actions	Owners
Urgent but Trivial Issues	The team calls an audible whenever a trivial but urgent topic is raised, and decides to ignore the topic or delegate the topic to an individual or sub-team.	Joanie
Unresolved Issues	Make final decisions on the top three organic growth opportunities no later than Jan 30th.	Team
	Make final decision on the Keystone acquisition no later than Jan 30th.	Team
Delegable Issues	Ask Ali in Finance to make a final recommendation on travel policies for vendors by Feb 15th.	Ali
	Ask Stephanie in Legal to make standard SOW templates for all products and service deliveries by Mar 15th.	Stephanie
	Ask Jose in Sales and Ashish in IT to develop a set of recommendations and costs for a CRM upgrade no later than Apr 1st.	Jose and Ashish
Team vs. Sub-Team Issues	All product pricing issues will only involve regional leaders, product leaders, Marketing, and Finance. Product leaders make final decisions.	Product Leaders
	Finance and Supply Chain will review transportation options and Supply Chain will make final decisions on cost reduction initiatives.	Supply Chain
	Social media strategy will be determined by Marketing, product leaders, regional leaders, and Sales. Marketing makes final decisions.	Marketing

Decision-Making

Improve Efficiency

Leverage team expertise and time when making decisions.

Improve Empowerment

Clarify decision-making rights for team members.

PREPARATION

Review Data

Review the Norms score and relevant comments on the Team Assessment Survey or Team Interview Summary. Was there any frustration with team decision-making?

Key Consideration

Is this a top leadership or matrixed team? If so, know that these teams often have difficulties determining who should be involved in what decisions, how decisions should be made, and agreeing upon final decision makers.

Time Needed

This activity takes 60-120 minutes.

Room Requirements

The room should be conducive to private conversations, have an LCD projector for the slides, and flip charts and markers for sub-teams.

Materials Needed

1 copy of the Decision-Making Handout for each team member.

FACILITATION

		Materials
Step 1 1 min.	Introduce the session, which is to clarify final decision makers and who should be involved in various team decisions.	Decision-Making PPT 1
Step 2 10 min.	Pass out the Decision-Making Handout. Describe the advantages and disadvantages of the three decision-making types and when they are appropriate to use.	Decision-Making PPT 2 Decision-Making Handout
Step 3 10-15 min.	Ask the team to identify six to eight key decisions the team made over the past three months. List these in the far-left column on the Past Decisions Flip Chart, and ask team members to do the same on their handouts. Then ask team members to individually identify who was involved, what decision type was used, and final decision makers.	Decision-Making PPTs 3-4 Flip Chart #1 *See a sample of a completed Past Decisions Flip Chart on p. 317*
Step 4 20-40 min.	Working one decision at a time, ask team members to share who was involved, what decision type was used, and final decision makers. Encourage discussions and gain consensus on these three factors for each decision. Flip chart consensus opinions on who was involved, what decision type was used, and final decision makers. Once all of the past decisions have been discussed, ask the team what it learned from this exercise that it needs to apply to upcoming decisions.	Decision-Making Handout Flip Chart

| **Step 5**
30-40 min. | Ask the team to identify six to eight important upcoming decisions the team will need to make over the next three to six months. Be sure to add any upcoming decisions where there may be confusion about how the decision should be made. List these in the far-left column on a flip chart for upcoming decisions and Future Decisions Form in the handout. Then work with the team to identify who should be involved, what decision type should be used, and final decision makers for each upcoming decision. | Decision-Making Handout

Flip Chart |

POST-EXERCISE ACTIVITIES

- Create an electronic draft of the Future Decision-Making Form for upcoming decisions and circulate it among team members for additional comments.
- Share the Future Decision-Making Form with new team members, and do the Decision-Making Exercise as needed to clarify decision-making types, owners, and involved parties.

Example of a Completed Past Decisions Flip Chart #1

What Topics?	Who Involved?	How Made? (A, IG, or C)	Final Decision Maker?
1. Dreeble acquisition	CFO, CEO, and Bus Development	IG	CEO
2. New CFO	Executive Leadership Team	IG	CEO
3. Shut down Bakken operations	Executive Leadership Team	IG	CEO
4. Medical benefits program	Executive Leadership Team	IG	CHRO
5. New branding	CEO	A	CEO
6. New CRM software package	CIO, CFO, and CEO	IG	CEO
7. IT outsourcing decision	CIO, CFO, and CEO	IG	CIO

Communication

Improve Efficiency

Clarify communication expectations for team members.

Build Trust

Share information and reduce the number of surprises experienced by team members.

Review Data

Review the Norms score and relevant comments on the Team Assessment Survey or Team Interview Summary. Was there any frustration with information not being shared, being surprised or kept out of the loop, or the team not being able to talk about certain topics?

Key Consideration

Is this a virtual team? Time zone and language differences can make it more difficult for team members to communicate with each other.

Time Needed

This activity takes 30-75 minutes.

Room Requirements

The room should be conducive to private conversations, have an LCD projector for the slides, and flip charts and markers.

Materials Needed

1 copy of the Communication Handout for each team member.

FACILITATION

		Materials
Step 1 1 min.	Introduce the session, which is to establish explicit rules for team communication.	Communication PPT 1
Step 2 5-10 min.	Pass out the Communication Handout. Ask team members to individually rate the seven communication factors using the 1-5 scale.	Communication PPT 2 Communication Handout
Step 3 20-30 min.	Have team members write their scores on a Communication Flip Chart. Working one factor at a time, ask team members to discuss the team's range of ratings, average rating, and what if anything the team can do to improve the rating on this factor. Note the improvements on a separate flip chart. Repeat the process for the remaining six communication factors.	Communication PPT 3 Flip Chart #1 *See a sample of a completed Communication Form on p. 321*
Step 4 20-30 min.	Once all seven communication factors have been discussed, ask the team to establish specific rules for improving communication. Note these on a flip chart.	Communication PPT 4 Communication Handout Flip Chart #2 *See a sample of a completed set of Communication Rules on p. 322*

POST-EXERCISE ACTIVITIES

- Create an electronic draft of the Communication Rules and circulate it among team members for additional comments.
- Share the Communication Rules with new team members.
- Periodically ask the team to evaluate the extent to which it is abiding by these rules using the following options:
  - Option 1: Ask team members to use fingers on one hand to indicate how well everyone is adhering to the team's communication rules, with one finger representing very little, three fingers representing to some extent, and five fingers representing to a great extent. Take one communication rule at a time and ask team members to raise a hand with the number of fingers that represents their vote. Estimate the average score, and discuss high and low votes and what the team needs to do differently to get a four or five on the rule. Repeat for the remaining rules. (30 minutes)
  - Option 2: Use the Communication Rules as part of a Feedforward Team Improvement Activity (page 275).

Example of a Completed Communication Form
Flip Chart #1

How would you rate:	Rating Scale 1 = Poor 3 = So-So 5 = Outstanding
The overall level of team communication?	3, 2, 3, 2, 2, 4, 3
The quality, quantity, and timeliness of the information you receive?	2, 1, 1, 2, 3, 4, 2
The effectiveness of the team's primary communication mode (be it e-mail, voicemail, texting, video, face-to-face interactions, etc.)?	3, 3, 4, 3, 4, 5, 4
The extent you trust team members not to share private conversations or confidential information?	4, 3, 5, 3, 4, 4, 5
The responsiveness of team members to others' requests?	1, 2, 1, 1, 1, 2, 2

How would you rate:	Rating Scale 1 = Poor 3 = So-So 5 = Outstanding
The level of participation of all members in team meetings?	4, 4, 3, 5, 3, 4, 3
The degree to which difficult topics are raised and successfully resolved in team meetings?	1, 5, 2, 3, 2, 1, 2

Example of a Completed Communication Rules Flip Chart #2

Topic	Communication Rules
Lack of Information	• Bi-weekly team meetings will include corporate and team member updates. • Any information relevant to the ERP implementation will be communicated to all team members within 24 hours.
Responsiveness	• All e-mail requests will be responded to within 24 hours. • More urgent requests will be sent via phone calls or texts, and require a three-hour response time unless otherwise stated.
Difficult Topics	• Team members will be asked to share their perspectives on problems and potential solutions. They should be respectful, but not sugarcoat their opinions. • Team members cannot complain about team decisions if they did not raise their concerns during meetings.

Accountability Mechanisms

PURPOSE

Improve Ownership

Clarify the consequences for noncompliance and underperformance.

Reduce Favoritism

Clarify performance and behavioral expectations for team members.

PREPARATION

Review Data

Review the Norms score and relevant comments on the Team Assessment Survey or Team Interview Summary. Were there any comments conveying frustration with favoritism, ownership, accountability, follow-through, failing to adhere to rules, or inadequate consequences for underperformance?

Key Considerations

- Ownership and accountability are common problems for teams. Team leaders need to get everyone to commit to the team's deliverables and rules and be comfortable ensuring team members abide by these agreements. This means they need to be comfortable playing the role of team sheriff. More often than not, favoritism and the lack of consequences are bigger problems than a lack of accountability for teams. Many team leaders would rather be popular than confront problematic team member behavior.
- Team leaders complaining about a lack of ownership and accountability on their teams need to take a hard look in the mirror. Many leaders want team members to take ownership but prefer making all the decisions; they want accountability but are unwilling to administer consequences for noncompliance or underperformance.

Time Needed

This activity takes 30-75 minutes.

Room Requirements

The room should be conducive to private conversations, have an LCD projector for the slides, and flip charts and markers.

Materials Needed

1 copy of the Accountability Mechanisms Handout for each team member.

FACILITATION

		Materials
Step 1 1 min.	Introduce the session, which is to establish explicit rules for ownership and expectations for performance.	Accountability Mechanisms PPT 1

		Materials
Step 2 5-10 min.	Pass out the Accountability Mechanisms Handout. Ask team members to individually rate the eight accountability factors using the 1-5 scale.	Accountability Mechanisms PPT 2 Accountability Mechanisms Handout
Step 3 20-30 min.	Have team members write their scores on an Accountability Mechanisms Flip Chart. Working one factor at a time, ask team members to discuss the team's range of ratings, average rating, and what if anything the team can do to improve the rating on this factor. Note the improvements on a separate flip chart. Repeat the process for the remaining seven accountability factors.	Accountability Mechanisms PPT 3 Flip Chart #1 *See a sample of a completed Accountability Form on p. 326*
Step 4 20-30 min.	Once all eight accountability factors have been discussed, ask the team to establish specific rules for improving ownership and accountability. Note these on a flip chart.	Accountability Mechanisms PPT 4 Accountability Mechanisms Handout Flip Chart #2 *See a sample of a completed set of Accountability Rules on p. 327*

POST-EXERCISE ACTIVITIES

- Create an electronic draft of the Accountability Rules and circulate it among team members for additional comments.
- Share the Accountability Rules with new team members.
- Periodically ask the team to evaluate the extent to which it is abiding by these rules using the following options:
  - Option 1: Ask team members to use fingers on one hand to indicate how well everyone is adhering to the team's Accountability Rules, with one finger representing very little, three fingers representing to some extent, and five fingers representing to a great extent. Take

one Accountability Rule at a time and ask team members to raise a
hand with the number of fingers that represents their vote. Estimate
the average score, and discuss high and low votes and what the
team needs to do differently to get a four or five on the rule. Repeat
for the remaining rules. (30 minutes)

- Option 2: Use the Accountability Rules as part of a Feedforward
Exercise (page 275).

Example of a Completed Accountability Form
Flip Chart #1

How would you rate:	Rating Scale 1 = Poor 3 = So-So 5 = Outstanding
The clarity of team member roles?	2, 2, 3, 4, 1, 3, 2
The clarity of assigned tasks and performance expectations?	1, 2, 2, 3, 1, 3, 3
The clarity of Team Norms?	2, 3, 3, 2, 2, 1, 4
The extent to which everyone on the team completes assigned tasks on time and with high quality?	4, 2, 3, 3, 4, 4, 5
The extent to which team members take responsibility for their own mistakes?	3, 4, 3, 4, 4, 3, 5
The extent to which team members are treated fairly and equitably?	3, 4, 4, 3, 5, 3, 4
The extent to which all team members are equally held accountable for their behavior and performance?	5, 3, 4, 1, 1, 1, 2
The extent to which there are consequences for not adhering to team rules or substandard performance?	2, 3, 3, 2, 2, 2, 1

Example of a Completed Accountability Rules
Flip Chart #2

Topic	Accountability Rules
Clarify Team Members' Roles and Assigned Tasks	The team will create a Roles and Responsibilities Matrix to clarify team members' roles. Team members are expected to accomplish assigned tasks with high quality and on time.
	If there are any questions about assignments, then team members are responsible for checking in with the team leader to clarify expectations. If team members do not check in, then it means that they had no questions about the deliverable.
Clarify Team Norms	The team will establish an explicit set of rules for working together.
	Team members will provide peer feedback once a quarter to assess the extent to which everyone is abiding by team rules.
Favoritism	All team members need to abide by the Team Norms and will be held to the same standards for performance.
	Team members will provide the team leader with anonymous feedback once a quarter on the extent to which she is holding everyone to the same standards. She will share the results of this feedback in team meetings.
Consequences	The team leader will hold team members accountable for team rule violations or instances of substandard performance. This begins with one-on-one discussions to understand why the violations occurred and how to prevent them in the future. Team leaders should follow an escalation path if necessary.

30

Self-Adjustment

PURPOSE

Improve Teamwork

Gather feedback about team strengths and areas of improvement.

Build Trust

Initiate conversations on how to improve team functioning and performance.

PREPARATION

Review Data

Are there any concerns about a lack of teamwork, poor team dynamics, or team underperformance?

Key Consideration

There are several ways to evaluate team functioning and performance. Two of the best are reviewing Team Assessment Survey Feedback Reports and Team Interview Summaries. Having team members evaluate the extent to which the team is living up to its Norms can also be helpful. This activity provides another option for gathering real-time feedback on team dynamics.

Time Needed

This activity takes 30-75 minutes.

Room Requirements

The room should be conducive to private conversations, have an LCD projector for the slides, and flip charts and markers.

Materials Needed

1 copy of the Self-Adjustment Handout for each team member.

FACILITATION

		Materials
Step 1 1 min.	Introduce the session, which is to gather feedback about current team dynamics.	Self-Adjustment PPT 1
Step 2 5-10 min.	Pass out the Self-Adjustment Handout. Ask team members to individually rate the 10 Self-Adjustment Factors using the 1-5 scale.	Self-Adjustment PPT 2 Self-Adjustment Handout
Step 3 20-30 min.	Have team members write their scores on a Self-Adjustment Flip Chart. Working one factor at a time, ask team members to discuss the team's range of ratings, average rating, and what if anything the team can do to improve the rating on this factor. Note the improvements on a separate flip chart. Repeat the process for the remaining nine Self-Adjustment Factors.	Self-Adjustment PPT 3 Flip Chart #1 *See a sample of a completed Self-Adjustment Form on p. 331*

		Materials
Step 4 20-30 min.	Once all 10 Self-Adjustment Factors have been discussed, ask the team to identify which team improvement activities could be used to address areas of improvement, who will be responsible for facilitating the activity, and when this will happen. Note these on a flip chart.	Self-Adjustment PPT 4 Self-Adjustment Handout Flip Chart #2 *See a sample of a completed Team Improvement Plan on p. 332*

POST-EXERCISE ACTIVITIES

- Create an electronic draft of the Team Improvement Plan and circulate it among team members for additional comments.
- Share the Team Improvement Plan with new team members.
- Execute the Team Improvement Plan.

Example of a Completed Self-Adjustment Form
Flip Chart #1

How would you rate:	**Rating Scale** 1 = Poor 3 = So-So 5 = Outstanding
The level of agreement about the situation and challenges facing the team?	3, 4, 4, 3, 2, 4
The clarity of the team's purpose and the extent to which the team has meaningful and measurable goals?	2, 3, 2, 3, 3, 2
The clarity of team members' roles, their ability to fill these roles, and the extent to which everyone is a team player?	2, 3, 1, 2, 3, 2
The efficiency and effectiveness of team meetings?	4, 3, 4, 4, 4, 3
How the team makes decisions?	4, 3, 4, 3, 5, 4
The extent to which team members are held accountable for abiding to team rules and delivering work?	3, 2, 2, 2, 2, 1
The level of commitment to team goals, roles, and rules?	2, 3, 4, 3, 4, 2

How would you rate:	Rating Scale 1 = Poor 3 = So-So 5 = Outstanding
The extent to which the team has the resources needed to accomplish its goals?	4, 5, 5, 5, 4, 4
How the team manages conflict?	3, 4, 3, 3, 4, 4
How the team is performing against its goals? The competition?	2, 3, 1, 3, 1, 2

Example of a Completed Team Improvement Plan
Flip Chart #2

Team Improvement Areas	Team Improvement Activities	Owners	Dates
Purpose	Team Purpose	Juan	June 25
Goals	Team Scorecard	DeWayne	July 15
Plans	Team Action Plans	Ming	August 15
Roles	Roles and Responsibilities Matrix	Rastislav	August 31
Accountability	Accountability	Staffan	September 15

31

Journey Lines

PURPOSE

Improve Talent

Understanding team members' past experiences can help the team better deploy its talent.

Build Trust

Demonstrating vulnerability and sharing personal experiences with fellow team members builds trust.

PREPARATION

Review Data

Review the Buy-In and Courage scores and relevant comments on the Team Assessment Survey or Team Interview Summary. Were there any comments about a lack of trust or low familiarity with others on the team?

Key Considerations

- This activity is a very powerful way for team members to get to know each other at a deeper level. Team size matters, as time constraints and tedium make it difficult to do this exercise with teams consisting of 12 or more people. Teams should consider doing the Motives, Values, Preferences Inventory or Hogan Personality Inventory activity if they consist of more than 12 people and want to get to know everyone better.

- Team leaders should prepare their Journey Lines prior to the team session. If an external facilitator is running the session, then team leaders should review their Journey Lines and what they plan to share with the facilitator before running the session.
- Team leaders play a critical role in the success of this exercise. They will be the first ones to share their Journey Lines, and the degree to which they come across as vulnerable or guarded will set the tone for the rest of the team.
- This is a good activity to do right before a team does a social hour or goes to dinner.

Time Needed

This activity takes 90-150 minutes.

Room Requirements

The room should be conducive to private conversations, have an LCD projector for the slides, flip charts, markers, and wall space and masking tape to post Journey Line Flip Charts.

Materials Needed

1 copy of the Journey Line Handout for each team member.

FACILITATION

		Materials
Step 1 1 min.	Introduce the session, which is to learn how team members' past experiences shape current behavior.	Journey Lines PPT 1

		Materials
Step 2 5-10 min.	Pass out the Journey Line Handout and explain the Emotional Energy and Time dimensions. Emotional Energy represents how an individual was doing overall at any point in time, with the horizontal line in the middle of the graph indicating that the individual was doing fine. Portions of the line above the midpoint indicate periods when an individual was doing really well, and parts of the line below the midpoint indicate periods when things could have been better. The farther a line is from the midpoint, the more extreme the feeling. The Emotional Energy line can include personal and professional or just professional highs and lows—it is up to team members to decide what he or she will include in their Journey Lines. The Time dimension should be broken up into significant life segments, such as growing up, attending college, segments to represent different jobs, etc. Team members can start their lines whenever they want.	Journey Lines PPT 2 Journey Line Handout
Step 3 5 min.	Team leaders or facilitators should share their Journey Lines in order to model the way. They should not share their entire Journey Lines, but rather go through their first one or two life segments so team members know how to do their own.	Flip Chart #1 *See a sample of a completed Journey Line on p. 336*
Step 4 15 min.	Ask team members to sketch their Journey Lines on the handout. If possible, they should use pencils to draw their Journey Lines, as they will likely make changes as they do the exercise. They should begin by identifying their life segments on the Time dimension. They should then draw a line that represents their emotional energy during the first segment, and then repeat the process as they transition to and live out their other life segments.	Journey Line Handout
Step 5 15 min.	Team members should draw their Journey Lines on a flip chart in landscape mode once they have been finalized. They should put their names on their Journey Lines and tape them up around the room.	Flip Charts
Step 6 60-120 min.	Do large group report-outs on each team member's Journey Line, with the team leader going first. Report-outs should be limited to 5-8 minutes with 2-5 minutes of Q&A. Team members should be encouraged to ask questions about each other's Journey Lines, what caused their emotional energy levels to change, what they learned from these experiences, how their experiences shape who they are today, etc. Facilitators will need to monitor time so that each Journey Line takes no more than 10 minutes.	
Step 7 10 min.	Once all the large groups are finished, ask team members to comment on common observations and themes.	

POST-EXERCISE ACTIVITIES

None. This is largely a one and done activity, as it probably should not be done again unless there has been significant turnover on a team.

Example of a Completed Journey Line
Flip Chart #1

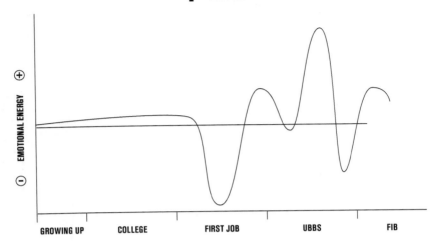

32

Motives, Values, Preferences Inventory (MVPI)

PURPOSE

Increase Self-Awareness

Provide team members with insights into their work values, what they believe to be important at work, and where they will focus their energy and attention.

Shape Team Norms

Work values often play a key role in Team Norms.

Build Trust

Sharing work values can improve team trust.

PREPARATION

Review Data

Review the Buy-In and Courage scores and relevant comments on the Team Assessment Survey or Team Interview Summary. Were there any comments that conveyed frustration with team members' commitment levels? Team priorities? Lack of follow-through?

Key Considerations

- Motives, Values, Preferences Inventories (MVPIs) can only be administered and interpreted by certified personnel. This individual may be an external consultant or someone within the organization who has been Hogan certified.
- Team leaders will need to determine whether they want to have MVPI Insight or Values Feedback Reports. Both report types provide insightful information, with Potential Feedback Reports being more extensive and targeted for executive audiences. They should coordinate the report type with the Hogan-certified person setting up the MVPI assessments.
- Option: MVPI Group Reports can be ordered through Hogan-certified personnel.
- Option: Team leaders can arrange for team members to get one-on-one feedback on their MVPI results from a certified Hogan coach prior to or after the team meeting, off-site, or leadership development program. There will be an additional fee for this service if delivered by external consultants.

Prework

This activity is done as prework a week or so before a team meeting, off-site, or leadership development program.

Time Needed

- It takes 15-20 minutes for team members to complete an MVPI.
- It takes 60-90 minutes to facilitate an MVPI Feedback Session with a team.

Room Requirements

The room should be conducive to private conversations and have an LCD projector for the slides.

Materials Needed

1 copy of the MVPI Feedback Report for each team member.

FACILITATION

		Materials
Step 1 1 min.	Introduce the session, which is to provide insights about individual and teamwork values.	MVPI PPT 1
Step 2 30-40 min.	Pass out the MVPI and ask everyone to turn to the graphic summary page. Do a Human Histogram for each of the 10 work values by asking people to stand up and arrange themselves in a semicircle by ascending scores, with one end being made up of the lowest and the other end made up of the highest scores on Recognition. Describe what Recognition measures, and what team members are like with lower scores and what they are like with higher scores. Given this distribution of Recognition scores, ask the team to identify the implications for team challenges, goals, roles, norms, conflict, and performance.	MVPI PPT 2 MVPI Feedback Reports
Step 3 20-30 min.	Repeat this process for the nine other work values on the MVPI. Note the highest scoring MVPI work values on a flip chart.	Flip Chart
Step 4 20-30 min.	Give team members time to review their results, and then ask them to pair up and share what they learned from their MVPI Insight or Values Feedback Reports. They can share as little or as much of their reports as they want.	MVPI PPT 3 MVPI Feedback Reports
Step 5 15 min.	Do a large group report-out. What did team members learn from their MVPIs? How can the team use this knowledge to improve team dynamics and performance? What will the team specifically commit to doing given these results? Who is responsible for making this happen? When will it start, and how will progress be measured?	Option: MVPI Group Report

- Ask new team members to complete an MVPI.
- Share the MVPI Group Report when onboarding new team members.

Example of Motives, Values, Preference Inventory Group Report Types

MVPI MVPI Composite Profile

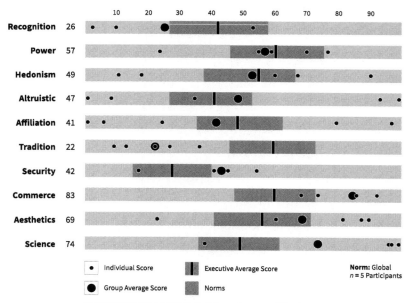

		Individual Score		Executive Average Score		**Norm:** Global

Individual Score   Executive Average Score   **Norm:** Global *n* = 5 Participants

Group Average Score   Norms

* Individual score dots sometimes represent more than one participant

Example of Motives, Values, Preference Inventory Group Report Types

MVPI Average Scores

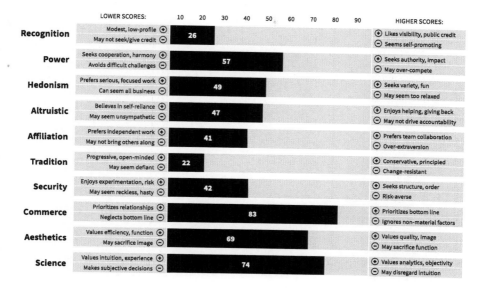

	LOWER SCORES:	Score	HIGHER SCORES:
Recognition	Modest, low-profile ⊕ / May not seek/give credit ⊖	26	⊕ Likes visibility, public credit / ⊖ Seems self-promoting
Power	Seeks cooperation, harmony ⊕ / Avoids difficult challenges ⊖	57	⊕ Seeks authority, impact / ⊖ May over-compete
Hedonism	Prefers serious, focused work ⊕ / Can seem all business ⊖	49	⊕ Seeks variety, fun / ⊖ May seem too relaxed
Altruistic	Believes in self-reliance ⊕ / May seem unsympathetic ⊖	47	⊕ Enjoys helping, giving back / ⊖ May not drive accountability
Affiliation	Prefers independent work ⊕ / May not bring others along ⊖	41	⊕ Prefers team collaboration / ⊖ Over-extraversion
Tradition	Progressive, open-minded ⊕ / May seem defiant ⊖	22	⊕ Conservative, principled / ⊖ Change-resistant
Security	Enjoys experimentation, risk ⊕ / May seem reckless, hasty ⊖	42	⊕ Seeks structure, order / ⊖ Risk-averse
Commerce	Prioritizes relationships ⊕ / Neglects bottom line ⊖	83	⊕ Prioritizes bottom line / ⊖ Ignores non-material factors
Aesthetics	Values efficiency, function ⊕ / May sacrifice image ⊖	69	⊕ Values quality, image / ⊖ May sacrifice function
Science	Values intuition, experience ⊕ / Makes subjective decisions ⊖	74	⊕ Values analytics, objectivity / ⊖ May disregard intuition

Norm: General

Expectancy Theory

Improve Motivation

Clarify the links between team members' actions, assigned tasks, and rewards.

Review Data

Review the Buy-In score and relevant comments on the Team Assessment Survey or Team Interview Summary. Were there any comments conveying frustration with a lack of commitment to team goals? Do team members lack confidence about whether they can accomplish team goals?

Key Considerations

- Team members have choices about where they spend their time and effort. Are team members spending their time accomplishing the tasks needed to achieve team goals or pursuing other endeavors? Whereas goal-setting and feedback are important motivational tools, Expectancy Theory can help clarify the choices team members make about where they spend their time and effort. Expectancy Theory consists of three components:

- Expectancy (E): The link between effort and performance. If they put forth effort, then do team members feel they can get the job done? Are they optimistic or pessimistic about the odds of completing assigned tasks? Do they have the skills, resources, motivation, time, data, etc. needed to complete assigned tasks?
- Instrumentality (I): The link between task accomplishment and rewards. If team members do their assigned tasks, will they receive any rewards for getting the job done? What's in it for them if they complete their assigned tasks?
- Valence (V): The importance of rewards. Do team members value or care about the rewards?

- Expectancy Theory is a multiplicative model, where E x I x V = Motivational Force, or the level and duration of effort team members exert toward assigned tasks. If E, I, or V are low, then Motivational Force will also be low and team members will exert little effort toward task accomplishment. To maximize Buy-In for a task, team leaders must maximize EIV for the team member.
- **This exercise is typically not done in team settings.** Team leaders should do Expectancy Theory analyses on their own or as part of a leadership development program.

Time Needed

This activity takes 10-15 minutes for each activity being analyzed. Team leaders do not do the analysis for all assigned tasks, but rather for those where motivation appears lacking.

Room Requirements

A private room or setting to do an EIV analysis.

Materials Needed

1 copy of the Expectancy Theory Handout for each team leader.

FACILITATION

		Materials
Step 1 1 min.	Introduce the session, which is to clarify the links between team members' actions and rewards.	Expectancy Theory PPT 1
Step 2 5-10 min.	Pass out the Expectancy Theory Handout. Ask team leaders to identify any team tasks where difficulties are being encountered or are in danger of not being accomplished and write them down in the left column of the handout.	Expectancy Theory PPT 2 Expectancy Theory Handout
Step 3 10 min.	Explain the Expectancy, Instrumentality, and Valence components of Expectancy Theory. Provide practical examples of the three components for different tasks and explain the rating scales in the handout. Explain what Motivational Force is, how it is calculated, and what happens if E, I, or V are 0.	Expectancy Theory PPT 3
Step 4 15-30 min.	Ask team leaders to rate the Expectancy, Instrumentality, and Valence of the tasks listed on their handouts. They should then calculate the Motivational Force for each task and write down the specific actions they can take to improve the Motivational Force scores in their action plans.	Expectancy Theory PPT 4 Expectancy Theory Handout *See a sample of a completed Expectancy Theory Analysis and Action Plan on p. 346*
Step 5 15 min.	Ask team leaders to pair up and share the results of their Expectancy Theory analyses and action plans. They should discuss what they learned by doing this exercise.	Expectancy Theory Handout
Step 6 10 min.	Do a large group report-out. What did team leaders learn from this exercise? What do they plan on doing to improve the Motivational Force of team members?	

POST-EXERCISE ACTIVITIES

Team leaders should take action on their Expectancy Theory analysis. They should redo the exercise whenever team tasks are encountering difficulties or are in danger of not being accomplished.

Example of a Completed Expectancy Theory Analysis

Tasks	Owners	Expectancy *Can they complete the task?* (Skills, time, motivation, resources, data, etc.) 0 = No 1 = Probably not 2 = Maybe 3 = Absolutely	Instrumentality *If they complete the task, will they get rewarded?* (Links between tasks, goals, and rewards) 0 = No 1 = Probably not 2 = Maybe 3 = Absolutely	Valence *Do the rewards matter?* (Recognition, time off, money, flexibility, etc.) 0 = No 1 = Not really 2 = Modest value 3 = High value	Motivational Force $MF = E \times I \times V$ Scores range from 3 to 27
Manage the lead generation project	Becky	0	2	3	0
Update the website	Ron	3	3	1	9
Manage Client X	Rajiv	2	1	2	4

Example of a Completed Expectancy Theory Action Plan

Tasks	Owners	Actions	Dates
Lead generation project	Becky	• Take Becky off the social media campaign so she has time to work on the lead generation project.	Mar 15
		• Send Becky to Kevin Smith at Company D and Josie Curry at Company E to get ideas on how they do lead generation.	Mar 30
		• Check in with Becky to see what else she needs for the project.	Mar 30
Website update	Ron	• Tell Ron how adamant the CEO feels about updating the website, and its role in lead generation and the team's year-end revenue goals.	Mar 7
		• Tell Ron this is a high-visibility project, and that he will likely get to present the final product and its data capture capabilities to the ELT.	Mar 7
		• Ask Ron if he wants flex time, the ability to work from home, or if there is something else he wants for seeing this project through to completion.	Mar 7
Client X	Rajiv	• Point out the connection between Client X's net promoter score, client referrals, sales opportunities, and revenues.	Mar 12
		• Coach Rajiv on how to best interact with Client X, and how these actions can affect net promoter scores.	Mar 12
		• Ask Rajiv why he volunteered to take on Client X, what he hoped to learn by taking on the team's toughest client, and what he wants if he is successful.	Mar 12

Personal Commitments

PURPOSE

Gain Buy-In

Get team members to commit to the team's purpose, goals, roles, and rules.

Build Trust

Share Personal Commitments while working on the team.

PREPARATION

Review Data

Review Buy-In scores and relevant comments on the Team Assessment Survey or Team Interview Summary. Were there any comments that conveyed frustration with members' commitment to the team?

Time Needed

This activity takes 45-60 minutes, depending on the size of the team.

Room Requirements

The room should be conducive to private conversations, have an LCD projector for the slides, and flip charts and markers for individual team members.

Materials Needed

1 copy of the Personal Commitments Handout for each team member.

FACILITATION

		Materials
Step 1 1 min.	Introduce the activity, which is to get everyone to make Personal Commitments to the team's success.	Personal Commitments PPT 1
Step 2 10 min.	Pass out Personal Commitments Handouts to team members. Ask people to jot down their answers to three questions: • What is one thing you will continue to do to help the team operate more effectively? • What is the one thing you are going to start, stop, or do differently to help the team operate more effectively? • How should you be held accountable for these behaviors?	Personal Commitments PPTs 2-3 Personal Commitments Handout Flip Chart #1 *See a sample of a completed Personal Commitments Flip Chart #1 on p. 349*
Step 3 10 min.	Once team members have noted their Personal Commitments on the handouts, they should transfer them to flip charts. They should put their names at the top of the flip chart.	Flip Charts
Step 4 20-40 min.	Ask individuals to do large group report-outs on their commitments. The large group should comment on common themes, and create a common accountability mechanism by agreeing to provide peer feedback on the commitments.	Flip Charts
Step 5 10 min.	Ask the team if there are any common themes across the flip charts. What does this mean for Team Norms, team functioning, etc.?	

POST-EXERCISE ACTIVITIES

- Create an electronic draft of Personal Commitments and circulate it among team members for additional comments.
- Share the Personal Commitments when onboarding new team members.
- Collect peer feedback on the Personal Commitments three to six months later. This can be done by creating customized Personal Commitments Rating Forms for each team member that includes their Personal Commitments. Send out copies of everyone's Personal Commitments Rating Forms to each member on the team and ask them to do the ratings. Collect the completed Personal Commitments Rating Forms and forward the collated forms to the appropriate team members. Ask team members to review their feedback and debrief the results at a team meeting. An example of a completed Personal Commitments Rating Form can be found on page 350.

Example of a Completed Personal Commitments Flip Chart #1

Name: Bob Hanson

What is one thing you are going to continue doing to help the team operate more effectively?	I will keep working on the lead generation project and make sure it gets done on time and under budget.
What is one thing you are going to stop, start, or do differently in order to help the team operate more effectively?	I will do a better job of listening before speaking and not cutting people off mid-sentence.
How should you be held accountable for these behaviors?	I plan on asking peers for feedback after team meetings.

Example of a Completed Peer Feedback Form

Name of the person being rated: Bob Hanson

Commitments	Rating 1 = Did not stick to commitments 3 = Varying commitment 5 = Stuck to all commitments	Comments
Keep Doing: I will keep working on the lead generation project and make sure it gets done on time and under budget.	4	Bob did a nice job managing the lead generation project, although it finished six weeks late.
Start, Stop, Do Differently: I will do a better job of listening before speaking and not cutting people off mid-sentence.	3	There were times when Bob had problems speaking over people and dominating airtime in meetings.

35

Resource Analysis

PURPOSE

Improve Execution

Make effective use of resources currently available to the team.

Improve Efficiency

Clarify the resources needed to achieve team goals.

PREPARATION

Review Data

Review the Resources score and relevant comments on the Team Assessment Survey or Team Interview Summary. Were there any comments conveying frustration with a lack of systems, data, hardware or software, budgets, authority, etc.?

Key Consideration

This is a good exercise to do when launching a new team or when teams are being combined or reconfigured. It should also be done whenever team goals change.

Time Needed

This activity takes 30-60 minutes.

Room Requirements

The room should be conducive to private conversations, have an LCD projector for the slides, and flip charts and markers.

Materials Needed

1 copy of the Resource Analysis Handout for each team member.

FACILITATION

		Materials
Step 1 1 min.	Introduce the session, which is to clarify what resources the team needs to be successful.	Resource Analysis PPT 1
Step 2 20 min.	Pass out the Resource Analysis Handout and remind the team of its purpose and goals. Ask team members to report out what resources they currently have to achieve the team's goals in each row of the handout. Team members should note the available resources in the handouts and on the flip chart.	Resource Analysis PPT 2 Resource Analysis Handout Flip Chart #1 *See a sample of a completed Resource Analysis Flip Chart on p. 353*
Step 3 30 min.	Once all of the available resources to achieve the team's goals have been identified, team members need to identify what resources they still need to succeed. They should do this by first identifying any equipment needs. They should note any needs on their handouts and the flip chart, and then do the same for hardware and software, etc.	Resource Analysis Handout Flip Chart #1
Step 4 10-20 min.	The team should prioritize its resource needs. It can do this by having a large group discussion or by voting. If voting, then give team members 3-6 votes and ask them to put check marks by the greatest needs. They can place multiple votes on a need, and team leaders should vote last. Tally the votes and get sign-off from the team leader on the prioritized needs.	Flip Chart #1

		Materials
Step 5 20-30 mins	Work with the team to build a Resource Acquisition Action Plan for securing high-priority resources. Note: Teams may opt to do Stakeholder Mapping (p. 355) before building action plans to acquire needed resources, particularly if the resources will be difficult to obtain.	Resource Analysis PPT 3 Resource Analysis Handout Flip Chart #2 *See a sample of a completed Resource Acquisition Action Plan Flip Chart on p. 354*

POST-EXERCISE ACTIVITIES

- Create an electronic draft of the Resource Acquisition Action Plan and circulate it among team members for additional comments.
- Review progress against the plan on a regular basis.

Example of a Completed Resource Analysis Flip Chart #1

Resources for Team Goals	Have	Need
Equipment: Specialized gear, tools, machines, vehicles, etc.	Account execs drive company cars.	No other needs.
Hardware and Software: Computers, servers, apps, programs, video, printers, phones, etc.	Everyone has updated company laptops with Zoom and cell phones.	Latest version of Salesforce.
Budget: total dollars, personnel budgets, discretionary and travel budgets, etc.	$2.6M. We can allocate these funds any way we want. Finance is looking for a 5% underspend, however.	Need an additional $130K for new account exec hire and sales training.
Data: Customer, market, supplier, operations, financial, people, quality, etc.	Have good access to sales pipeline, Net Promoter Scores, and financial data.	Need competitor and business intelligence data and analysis.
Service Support: IT, Finance, HR, Legal, Business Intelligence, Quality, R&D, etc.	IT, HR, Finance, and Legal support as needed.	Legal has been taking too long to review proposals and contracts. Need more help.

Resources for Team Goals	Have	Need
Facilities: Offices, cubicles, meeting rooms, storage, etc.	Everyone works out of their homes. We secure meeting space as needed at the regional office.	No other needs.
Authority: Signing, resource allocation, hiring, firing, decision-making, etc.	Have authority to sign $50,000 deals without approval. Have a robust hiring and onboarding process.	Need authority to sign $200,000 deals without approval. Need to shorten hiring process.
Other:	None.	No other needs.

Example of a Completed Resource Acquisition Action Plan
Flip Chart #2

Resource Needs	Action Steps	Owners	Due Dates
Upgrade to latest version of Salesforce	• Do a needs assessment and present results to the chief commercial officer.	Jorge	Oct 20
	• Work with chief commercial officer to secure approval and funding for CRM upgrade.	Jorge	Nov 1
	• Get CRM funding included in next year's sales budget.	Jorge	Dec 15
Secure $130K in additional funding for next year	• Do a cost-benefit and revenue generation analysis for hiring additional account executive and sales training program..	Karishma	Oct 15
	• Present results to chief commercial officer and chief financial officer	Brian	Nov 1
	• Get additional 130k in funding included in next year's sales budget.	Brian	Dec 15
Get authority for approving deals up to $200k	• Do a review of deal sizes and approval times from the beginning of the year.	Alfred	Oct 25
	• Present results and a risk/reward analysis to chief commercial officer, chief financial officer, and general counsel.	Alfred and Jorge	Nov 10
	• Get final approval to sign off on deals up to $200k by YE.	Alfred and Jorge	Dec 31

Stakeholder Mapping

Improve Execution

Devise strategies to increase political support or acquire additional resources.

Influence Others

Leverage relationships to influence without authority.

Review Data

Review the Resources score and relevant comments on the Team Assessment Survey or Team Interview Summary. Were there any comments conveying frustration with a lack of political support, budget, authority, etc.?

Key Consideration

This is a good exercise to do whenever teams face a resource shortfall.

Time Needed

This activity takes 60-90 minutes.

Room Requirements

The room should be conducive to private conversations, have an LCD projector for the slides, and flip charts and markers.

Materials Needed

1 copy of the Stakeholder Mapping Handout for each team member.

FACILITATION

		Materials
Step 1 1 min.	Introduce the session, which is to help the team devise strategies to increase political support or acquire additional resources.	Stakeholder Mapping PPT 1
Step 2 10 min.	Pass out the Stakeholder Mapping Handout and work with the team to identify key resource gaps. Does the team not have access to the right data, lack authority, need more budget or better software, etc.? Write the key resource shortfalls in the left column of the flip chart.	Stakeholder Mapping PPT 2 Stakeholder Mapping Handout Flip Chart #1 *See a sample of a completed Stakeholder Mapping Flip Chart on p. 358*
Step 3 10 min.	Ask team members to identify the key stakeholders for each key gap—these might include other internal teams, certain leaders or functions, headquarters, the board of directors, employees, etc. Write the stakeholders next to each key gap listed on the flip chart.	Stakeholder Mapping Handout Flip Chart #1

Materials

Step 4 20-30 min.	Ask team members to write down the stakeholders on their Stakeholder Analysis. Review the Attitude and Power rating scales and ask team members to independently rate each stakeholder on the two dimensions. Once everyone is finished, they should place their ratings for each stakeholder on a flip chart and then do a facilitated discussion to gain consensus on the ratings. Note the final Attitude and Power ratings for each stakeholder on the flip chart.	Stakeholder Mapping PPT 3 Stakeholder Mapping Handout Flip Chart #2 *See a sample of a completed Attitude and Power Rating Flip Chart on p. 358*
Step 5 20 min.	Use the final ratings to map stakeholders into the appropriate quadrant on the Attitude and Power grid. Review the suggested strategies for stakeholders in each of the four quadrants.	Stakeholder Mapping PPT 4 Flip Chart #3 *See a sample of a completed Attitude and Power Mapping Flip Chart on p. 359*
Step 6 20-30 min.	Build a Stakeholder Action Plan to close resource gaps using the suggested strategies for the four stakeholder types. This can either be done in the large group, or the stakeholders can be assigned to sub-teams who will draft plans and review them with the large group.	Stakeholder Mapping PPT 5 Flip Chart #4 *See a sample of a completed Stakeholder Action Plan Flip Chart on p. 359*

POST-EXERCISE ACTIVITIES

- Create an electronic draft of the Stakeholder Action Plan and circulate it among team members for additional comments.
- Review progress against the plan on a regular basis.

Example of a Completed Stakeholder Mapping
Flip Chart #1

Resource Gaps	Key Stakeholders
CRM Upgrade	Chief Commercial Officer Chief Information Officer Chief Financial Officer
Advanced Sales Training	Chief Commercial Officer Chief Learning Officer Chief Financial Officer
Lead Generation Process	Chief Commercial Officer Chief Marketing Officer Chief Finance Officer

Example of a Completed Attitude and Power Rating
Flip Chart #2

Stakeholders	Attitude 1 = Very Unsupportive 2 = Unsupportive 3 = Neutral 4 = Supportive 5 = Very Supportive	Power 1 = Very Low Power 2 = Low Power 3 = Modest Power 4 = High Power 5 = Very High Power
Chief Commercial Officer-CRM Upgrade	5, 5, 5, 5, 5, 5, 5 Average = 5.0	4, 5, 4, 3, 3, 5, 4 Average = 4.0
Chief Information Officer-CRM Upgrade	4, 3, 2, 2, 3, 4, 3 Average = 3.0	4, 3, 3, 4, 3, 4, 4 Average = 3.6
Chief Financial Officer-CRM Upgrade	2, 1, 3, 2, 1, 3, 2 Average = 2.0	4, 5, 4, 5, 4, 5, 4 Average = 4.4
Chief Commercial Officer-Sales Training	5, 4, 5, 5, 4, 4, 5 Average = 4.6	3, 4, 3, 3, 4, 4, 3 Average = 3.4
Chief Learning Officer-Sales Training	2, 1, 2, 2, 1, 1, 3 Average = 1.7	3, 2, 4, 3, 4, 2, 3 Average = 3.0
Chief Financial Officer-Sales Training	1, 2, 1, 1, 3, 1, 2 Average = 1.6	4, 5, 4, 3, 4, 4, 4 Average = 4.0

Example of a Completed Attitude and Power Mapping
Flip Chart #3

	Potential Allies	Powerful Friends
Supportive	CIO-CRM Upgrade CCO-Sales Training	CCO-CRM Upgrade
	Potential Foes	**Powerful Enemies**
Unsupportive	CIO-CRM Upgrade CLO-Sales Training	CFO-CRM Upgrade CFO-Sales Training
Power	Low	High

Example of a Completed Stakeholder Action Plan
Flip Chart #4

Stakeholder	Action Steps	Owner	Due Date
CCO-CRM Upgrade	Do a cost-benefit analysis for the CRM upgrade. Equip the CCO to influence the CIO and CFO for the upgrade. Ask the CCO for ideas on how to influence the CIO and CFO.	Luis	Jun 30
CIO-CRM Upgrade	Ask CCO to meet with the CIO to discuss the CRM upgrade.	Luis	Jul 15
	Do a presentation to the IT leadership team on the need for a CRM.	Steve	Aug 1
	Enlist the IT leadership team's help in choosing the right features and timing for the CRM upgrade.	Steve	Aug 15
	Get the CCO and CIO to add the CRM upgrade to next year's strategic plan and budget.	Steve	Sep 15
CFO-CRM Upgrade	Ask the CCO and CIO to meet with the CFO to discuss the CRM upgrade and why it is important.	Steve	Sep 1
	Do a presentation on the cost-benefit of the CRM upgrade with Sales and IT staff.	Luis	Sep 15

After-Action Reviews

PURPOSE

Improve Capacity

Practice having challenging conversations about team projects.

Productive Dialogues

Share key learnings and foster growth mindsets in team members.

PREPARATION

Review Data

Review the Courage score and relevant comments on the Team Assessment Survey or Team Interview Summary. Were there any comments conveying artificial harmony, unresolved conflict, an unwillingness to challenge team members, or low trust?

Key Considerations

- This is a good exercise to start doing at the end of a successful project or important team milestone. It should then be repeated after every project and major milestone.

- Team leaders are critical to the success of this exercise. If he or she is unwilling to provide an unvarnished view of what they did well or could have done better, then team members will not provide honest input. If using a team facilitator, then team leaders and facilitators should jointly review the After-Action Review instructions, determine which option to use, and discuss their roles prior to running the activity.

Time Needed

This activity takes 45-120 minutes.

Room Requirements

The room should be conducive to private conversations, have an LCD projector for the slides, and flip charts and markers. Seating should be arranged so that team members are sitting in a circle facing each other. There should not be any tables in the middle of the circle.

Materials Needed

1 copy of the After-Action Review Handout for each team member.

FACILITATION

		Materials
Step 1 1 min.	Introduce the session, which is to foster growth mindsets and productive dialogues among team members.	After-Action Review PPT 1
Step 2 5 min.	Pass out the After-Action Review Handout. Tell the team that professional sports teams are constantly reviewing videotapes of past games to improve team performance, and this exercise is a way for other teams to learn from experience.	After-Action Review PPT 2 After-Action Review Handout

		Materials
Step 3 10 min.	Identify a project that everyone on the team was recently involved with, and then ask team members to jot down what they did well and could have done differently or better on their After-Action Review Handout.	After-Action Review Handout *See a sample of a completed After-Action Review Form on p. 364*
Step 4 20-60 min.	Option 1: Go over the rules for an After-Action Review, and then have team members note what they did well and could have done differently or better on the project on a flip chart. The large group should discuss and identify common themes for what it did well and needs to keep doing on upcoming projects. People should be encouraged to challenge or comment on what the team did well or could have done better. Key lessons learned should be noted on a separate flip chart.	After-Action Review PPT 3 After-Action Review Handout
	Option 2: Go over the rules for an After-Action Review, and then ask the team leader to share what he or she did well and what they could have done differently or better to make the project even more successful. Facilitate a large group discussion on what the leader did well or could have done differently or better. Ask the leader to summarize his or her lessons learned after the large group discussion and note it on a flip chart. Repeat the process for all team members, reminding everyone this process is to encourage a growth mindset and foster productive dialogues.	After-Action Review PPT 3 After-Action Review Handout
Step 5 10-20 min.	Review the lessons learned flip chart, and do a large group discussion on how the team can deploy these lessons into day-to-day actions or the next big project.	After-Action Review PPT 4 Flip Chart #1 *See a sample of a completed Team Lessons Learned Flip Chart on p. 364*

POST-EXERCISE ACTIVITIES

- Create an electronic draft of the Team Lessons Learned and circulate it among team members for additional comments.
- Do After-Action Reviews after all major projects. Discuss whether the lessons learned from past projects are being implemented in new projects. If not, then work with the team to devise ways to make it happen.

Example of a Completed After-Action Review Form

Project: _____

What I did well on this project	What I could have done better or differently on the project
By establishing a close relationship with the client, we were able to structure a proposal that closely matched their needs.	I should have brought Sheryl and Zhang in to meet the client before we put the proposal together. This would have given them better insight into how the deal needed to be structured.
My insights into the client helped scope and price the proposal correctly.	Sometimes it seemed like touching base with the client was interfering with what the client management team was trying to do.
My regular check-ins with the client after we won the proposal helped the team to correct issues before they became major problems.	There were times when the client management team and I were not on the same page and were sending conflicting messages to the content creation team.

Example of a Completed Team Lessons Learned Flip Chart #1

Lessons Learned
Get client management teams involved early in the sales process. They should be notified as soon as clients begin to hint that an RFP may be forthcoming. Clarify who owns the primary relationship with a client early on. In most cases, this should be the client management team. However, clients may want the primary relationship to reside with one of the owners. All messages from Sales and Client Management to Creative need to be coordinated beforehand.

38

Team Journey Lines

Build Capacity

Sharing reactions to different events encourages dialogue and builds trust.

Build Trust

Review how reactions to and things learned from past experiences can be applied to future events.

Review Data

Review the Courage scores and relevant comments on the Team Assessment Survey or Team Interview Summary. Were there any comments about a lack of trust or an inability to learn from past mistakes?

Key Considerations

This activity can help teams learn how to have productive dialogues.

Team leaders play a critical role in the success of this exercise. They will be the first ones to share their Team Journey Lines, and the degree to which they come across as vulnerable or guarded will set the tone for the rest of the team.

Time Needed

This activity takes 40-60 minutes.

Room Requirements

The room should be conducive to private conversations, have an LCD projector for the slides, and flip charts and markers.

Materials Needed

1 copy of the Team Journey Lines Handout for each team member.

FACILITATION

		Materials
Step 1 1 min.	Introduce the session, which is to promote team trust by systematically reviewing past team experiences.	Team Journey Lines PPT 1
Step 2 5-10 min.	Pass out the Team Journey Lines Handout and explain the Emotional Energy and Time dimensions. Emotional Energy represents how an individual was doing overall at any point in time, with the horizontal line in the middle of the graph indicating that the individual was doing fine. Portions of the line above the midpoint indicate periods when an individual was doing really well, and parts of the line below the midpoint indicate periods when things could have been better. The farther a line is from the midpoint, the more extreme the feeling. The Emotional Energy line can include personal and professional or just professional highs and lows—it is up to team members to decide what they will include in their Journey Lines. The Time dimension should be broken up into significant project or team segments, such as by project milestones or monthly increments. Time segments should be noted on a flip chart. Team members should all use the same time segments, and this should be noted in their handouts.	Team Journey Lines PPT 2 Team Journey Lines Handout . Flip Chart

		Materials
Step 3 5-10 min.	Team leaders or facilitators should share an example of a Team Journey Line in order to model the way. They should flip chart and share a Team Journey Line for a project they have been on in the past so team members can see how to do their own.	Flip Chart #1 *See a sample of a Team Journey Line for an Individual on p. 368*
Step 4 15 min.	Ask team members to sketch their Team Journey Lines in the Team Journey Lines Handout. If possible, they should use pencils to draw their Team Journey Lines, as they will likely make changes as they do the exercise. They should then draw a line that represents their emotional energy during the first time segment, and then repeat the process as they transitioned to and lived out the other time segments.	Team Journey Lines Handout
Step 5 15 min.	Team members should draw their Team Journey Lines on one flip chart in landscape mode once they have been finalized. They should use different colors and put their names on their Team Journey Lines as they annotate the flip chart.	Flip Chart #2 *See a sample of a completed Team Journey Line on p. 368*
Step 6 40-80 min.	Do large group report-outs on each team member's Team Journey Line, with the team leader going first. Report-outs should be limited to 5-8 minutes with 2-5 minutes of Q&A. Team members should be encouraged to ask questions about each other's Team Journey Lines—what caused their emotional energy levels to change, what they learned from these experiences, etc. Facilitators will need to note lessons learned on a separate flip chart and monitor time.	Flip Chart #2
Step 7 10 min.	Once all the large groups are finished, ask team members to comment on common themes and the lessons learned.	

POST-EXERCISE ACTIVITIES

This activity can be done with teams at the conclusion of additional projects or the achievement of major milestones.

Example of a Completed
Team Journey Line for an Individual
Flip Chart #1

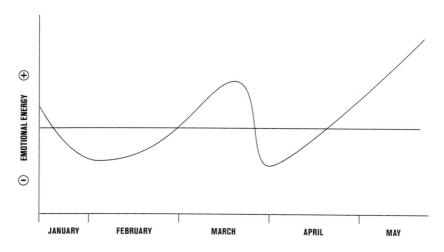

Example of a Completed Team Journey Line
Flip Chart #2

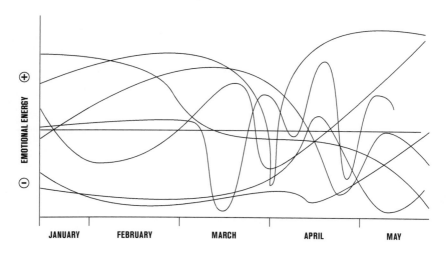

Team Improvement Activity

39

Conflict Management Styles

Increase Self-Awareness

Provide team members with insight into how they are likely to manage conflict.

Build Trust

Share Conflict Management Styles to improve team trust.

Review Data

Review the Courage score and relevant comments on the Team Assessment Survey or Team Interview Summary. Were there any comments that conveyed frustration with the team's inability to manage conflict?

Key Considerations

- The Thomas-Kilmann Conflict Mode Instrument (TKI) does not require any type of certification. However, the person leading the activity should take the TKI and be familiar with the five conflict-handling modes, the pros and cons of each mode, implications for over- or underusing modes, the types of situations best suited for different modes, instrument scoring, etc.
- Team leaders or facilitators can order paper and pencil or online versions of the Thomas-Kilmann Conflict Mode Instrument using the following link: https://www.themyersbriggs.com/en-US/Products-and-Services/TKI

Prework

The paper and pencil and online versions of the TKI can be completed as prework a week or so before a team meeting, off-site, or leadership development program. The paper and pencil version can also be completed during a team off-site or meeting.

Time Needed

- It takes 15 minutes for team members to complete a TKI.
- It takes 45-75 minutes to facilitate a TKI Feedback Session with a team.

Room Requirements

The room should be conducive to private conversations, have an LCD projector for the slides, and a flip chart and set of markers.

Materials Needed

1 copy of the paper and pencil version of the TKI for each team member if completing the inventory during a session. If the paper and pencil or online versions were administered as prework, then team members should be reminded to bring their reports to the session.

FACILITATION

		Materials
Step 1	Ensure everyone has their TKI reports if the instrument was administered as prework.	TKI Reports
Step 2 1 min.	Introduce the session, which is to provide insights about how team members are likely to manage conflict.	Conflict Management Styles PPT 1
Step 3 5 min.	Ask the team to identify where it experiences the most conflict. Note these areas on a flip chart.	Flip Chart
Step 4 15-20 min.	If completing a paper and pencil version of the TKI, then pass out and ask team members to complete a Thomas-Kilmann Conflict Mode Instrument.	Thomas-Kilmann Conflict Mode Instrument
Step 5 20-30 min.	Ask team members to go to the TKI page that lists their percentile scores, and then do a Human Histogram for each of the five conflict management modes. Begin by asking people to stand up and arrange themselves from the lowest to highest scores on Collaborating. Describe what Collaboration means, when to use it, how it works, potential watch-outs, etc. Given this distribution of Collaboration scores, ask the team to identify the implications for team conflict. Where is this mode over- or underused? Write down raw and average scores and implications on a flip chart. Repeat this process for the Competing, Accommodating, Avoiding, and Compromising conflict management modes.	Conflict Management Styles PPT 2 Thomas-Kilmann Conflict Mode Instrument Flip Chart #1 See a sample of a TKI Group Results flip chart on p. 372
Step 6 20 min.	Give team members time to review their results, and then ask them to pair up and share what they learned from their TKI reports. They can share as little or as much of their reports as they want.	Conflict Management Styles PPT 3 Thomas-Kilmann Conflict Mode Instrument
Step 7 15 min.	Do a large group report-out. What did team members learn from their TKIs? How can the team use this knowledge to improve how they handle conflict? What will the team specifically commit to doing to make this happen? Who is responsible for making this happen? When will it start, and how will progress be measured?	

POST-EXERCISE ACTIVITIES

- Create an electronic copy of the TKI Group Results and circulate it among team members for additional comments.

- Ask new team members to complete a Thomas-Kilmann Conflict Mode Instrument.
- Share TKI Group Results when onboarding new team members.

Example of Thomas-Kilmann Conflict Mode Instrument Group Report Flip Chart #1

Conflict Modes	Team Scores	Average Score	Implications
Collaborating	62, 62, 72, 72, 85, 90	74	This team likes collaboration! But we waste too much time seeking win-win solutions for relatively unimportant tasks.
Competing	28, 42, 50, 62, 70, 95	58	Half of us like to compete, the other half do not. We yield too often to Ben's ideas, and he has a high Compete score.
Accommodating	4, 24, 34, 50, 50, 84	41	Big differences in scores on this one.
Avoiding	2, 6, 6, 18, 30, 60	20	This team does not avoid conflict. Maybe there are times it should.
Compromising	33, 44, 50, 55, 62, 74	53	This is our fall-back position if collaborating doesn't work.

40

Personal and Team Learning

PURPOSE

Improve Performance

Get team members to reflect on Personal and Team Learnings.

Build Trust

Share Personal and Team Learnings with the team.

PREPARATION

Review Data

Review Results scores and relevant comments on the Team Assessment Survey or Team Interview Summary. Were there any comments about not learning from experience, repeating the same mistakes, etc.?

Time Needed

This activity takes 60-90 minutes, depending on the size of the team.

Room Requirements

The room should be conducive to private conversations, have an LCD projector for the slides, and flip charts and markers for individual team members.

Materials Needed

1 copy of the Personal and Team Learning Handout for each team member.

FACILITATION

		Materials
Step 1 1 min.	Introduce the activity, which is to help improve team performance by reflecting on key learnings.	Personal and Team Learning PPT 1
Step 2 10 min.	Pass out Personal and Team Learning Handouts to team members. Ask people to jot down their answers to the following questions: - How has the team improved over time? What can it do now that it could not do three to six months ago? - What have been your biggest personal learnings over the past three to six months?	Personal and Team Learning PPT 2 Personal and Team Learning Handouts
Step 3 10 min.	Once team members have noted their learnings on the handouts, they should transfer them to flip charts. They should put their names at the top of the flip chart.	Flip Chart #1 *See a sample of a completed Personal and Team Learning Flip Chart #1 on p. 375*
Step 4 20-60 min.	Ask individuals to do large group report-outs on their learnings. Each report-out should take about five minutes, including commentary, questions and answers, etc. Once all the report-outs have been completed, the large group should comment on common themes.	Flip Charts
Step 5 10 min.	Ask the team if there are any common themes across the flip charts. Ask the team what it will do to leverage these learnings.	

POST-EXERCISE ACTIVITIES

- Create an electronic draft of the common learnings and circulate it among team members for additional comments.
- Share common learnings when onboarding new team members.
- Repeat the exercise every six months.

Example of a Completed Personal and Team Learning Flip Chart #1

Beverly Wong

How has the team improved over the past 3-6 months?	What are my key learnings over the past 3-6 months?
1. We are getting much better at qualifying leads and only pursue those with good chances of winning.	1. Not to respond to RFPs unless we had some influence in shaping the RFP.
2. We are putting together much stronger proposals and sales pitches than we were six months ago.	2. Learning how to get meetings with people who can say yes to proposals rather than wasting time building relationships with people who can only say no.
3. We have greatly improved our close rates, based on our success on #1 and #2.	3. How to write compelling proposals. I still need to get better at sales presentations, however.

Printed in Poland
by Amazon Fulfillment
Poland Sp. z o.o., Wrocław

54437116R00219